The Complete Book of
Stumpwork Embroidery

Jane Nicholas

SALLYMILNER
PUBLISHING

First published in 2005 by
Sally Milner Publishing Pty Ltd
734 Woodville Rd
BINDA NSW AUSTRALIA

© Jane Nicholas, 2005
Reprinted 2005, 2006, 2011

Design by Anna Warren, Warren Ventures and Ingrid Carlstrom
Photography by Andrew Elton
Printed in China

National Library of Australia Cataloguing-in-Publication data:

Nicholas, Jane.

  The complete book of stumpwork embroidery.

Bibliography.

Includes index.

ISBN 1 86351 341 8.

1. Stump work. 2. Embroidery. I. Title. (Series : Milner

craft series).

746.44

Disclaimer
The information in this instruction book is presented in good faith. However, no warranty is given, nor results guaranteed, nor
is freedom from any patent to be inferred. Since we have no control over the use of the information contained in this book, the
publisher and the author disclaim liability for untoward results.

10 9 8 7 6 5 4

The Complete Book of
Stumpwork Embroidery

Contents

Foreword

The seventeenth century in England, despite its political upheaval and turmoils, was a most interesting era, and to fully appreciate the style of embroidery dating from the last half of that century it is important to picture the aesthetic tastes of that time. It was the age of oak – the panelled rooms had heavy beams and were furnished with deeply carved oak joined chairs, court cupboards and tester bedsteads. Fabrics were an important ingredient and inventories are full of references to cushions, screens, wall hangings and bed coverings. Against this background it is not at all strange that a heavy form of embroidery was popular at this time.

Many examples of this heavy, padded, raised embroidery, now known as stumpwork, have survived, most in surprisingly good condition. These embroideries have faded over the centuries and it is only when examining an unfinished example that has been kept away from the light that one becomes aware of the vibrant colours used. The unfinished examples also show us the black outline of the pattern on the white satin, and it is thought that stumpwork was sold 'as a kit' exactly as we buy twentieth-century embroidery.

Over ten years ago Jane Nicholas and I first discussed our passion for stumpwork. We debated about the intricacies of this form of embroidery, speculated about the carved wood or ivory used as padding for hands and faces, and admired the use of mica for castle windows. Verbally, I followed the progress of Jane's sampler 'Homage to the Seventeenth Century', but I did not see it until it was exhibited in 1992 at the Festival of Embroidery organised by the Embroiderers' Guild of NSW. In this embroidery I saw Jane's rare exacting ability as an embroiderer combined with her deep knowledge of the techniques of seventeenth-century embroidery, and, as expected, her work was overwhelmingly voted the winner of the Viewers' Choice award.

Since then Jane has added another dimension to her passion for stumpwork. She has the ability, with great patience, to pass on her knowledge, and she now teaches to fully booked classes all around Australia and has been invited by the Embroiderers' Guild of America to teach at their National Seminar in 1996.

There has long been a need for a comprehensive instruction book on the art of stumpwork. This was the next task that Jane undertook and we now see the result. As with everything Jane undertakes, it more than fulfils the requirement. The Introduction is very important, as in it Jane not only graphically describes stumpwork, but also recalls her steps when embroidering 'Homage to the Seventeenth Century'. This alone would entice any keen embroiderer to undertake one of the projects so clearly outlined.

Every requirement for undertaking stumpwork is discussed. Step-by-step instructions for working every shape are clearly set out with detailed sketches. Full instructions for every individual element (flowers, fruits and insects) have been fully described with diagrams for every stage of the work in progress. Especially enchanting are the quotations included with the individual elements. The projects are presented with comprehensive instructions and many an embroiderer will experience great joy and satisfaction when they have completed one of these works of art. In this book, Jane Nicholas has not tried to duplicate seventeenth-century stumpwork. She has created a style that is distinctively her own, that will live on and give lasting pleasure.

Nerylla Taunton

Introduction

'Stumpwork' is a term used to refer to a particular form of domestic raised embroidery practised in England between 1650 and 1700. The term is a contemporary one, being in use only from the end of the nineteenth century. In the seventeenth century, the technique was known as raised or embossed work, a more accurate description of the three-dimensional effects achieved by padding and applying detached motifs. It was probably first inspired by the high-relief ecclesiastical embroideries of Europe, and declined when the interest in Chinoiserie swept England at the beginning of the eighteenth century.

Embroidery was an essential part of the education of young girls from affluent Stuart households. They would progress from samplers in whitework and coloured silks (learning their alphabet at the same time), to canvas and beadwork, and would complete their embroidery education by working a piece in raised work – the culmination of all acquired needlework skills. The final product would usually be sent to a cabinetmaker to be mounted onto a casket, which could be used for toilet articles, writing materials or as a work box. Other stumpwork items included mirror frames, book covers, cushions, gloves, pincushions and small purses.

It is likely that many of these pieces were worked from kits containing most of the required materials. The design, often biblical or allegorical in origin, may have been already printed or painted on the ivory satin background, and further motifs could have been copied from the numerous pattern books of 'birds, beasts, flowers, fruits, flies and fishes' that were available at the time. Small carved pieces of boxwood, ivory or wax, often used for faces and hands, were probably included in the kit, also moulded fruits, such as pears and apples, to be covered in detached buttonhole stitches. A tantalising assortment of materials was available to the embroiderer including gold threads and gimp cord imported from Italy, dyed silk and chenille threads, metal purl, spangles and beads.

A typical example of stumpwork would include several figures (perhaps under a canopy), a castle, a stag, a lion, birds, butterflies, fruit and flowers, all set in a stylised rural setting. Other motifs could include a unicorn, griffin, camel and elephant, parrots, peacocks, turkeys, dogs and rabbits, with snails, caterpillars, bugs, beetles and flies filling any open spaces! All motifs were disproportionate to each other and no attention was paid to size, distance or perspective.

The embroidered figures often represented the Stuart kings and queens, and were a way of showing loyalty to the Crown during a period of great political turmoil. The reigning King Charles I clashed with Parliament and was tried and executed in 1649. England was under Puritan rule, led by Oliver Cromwell and Parliament, until the restoration of Charles II as king in 1660. The Great Plague ravaged London during his reign (1665), followed a year later by the Great Fire.

My fascination with stumpwork began in 1982. I was enchanted by the subjects depicted and the extremely fine nature of the work, and decided that the best way to learn about stumpwork was to work a sampler. As I wanted to follow the original pieces in design, technique, materials and colour, this started an engrossing journey that took me through countless history and embroidery reference books.

My sampler was worked on ivory satin, backed with strong canvas and mounted on a rectangular frame. I began with the two figures in the middle who stand on the required 'mound' worked in burden stitch. As the figures were frequently dressed in perfect period costume, this made a fascinating study in itself. I embroidered the woman's underskirt on silk mesh in tent stitch, worked fine silk stockings in Ceylon stitch, then applied small pieces of silk, velvet, suede and lace, beads and a feather to complete the figures.

An arbour of flowers, fruits and insects was common in raised work, indicating the fascination at the time with gardens, topiary and exotic flowers. I learned to cover beads with detached buttonhole stitch, to embroider wired petals and leaves on fine linen, to cut them out and apply them, and even how a spider constructs its web.

I ventured on to the border, starting with the fish pond in Florentine stitch on canvas and surrounding it with padded rocks covered in various detached buttonhole stitches, hollie point and trellis stitch. A fish, silk-wrapped wire seaweed and tiny shells were stitched on – no glue was used.

Stumpwork pictures traditionally contained a castle and several animals. I chose to do the lion and the stag, which I embroidered in split stitch on fine linen and then applied to the main background with stuffing inserted to give them shape. I wrapped fine wire for the stag's antlers, and used rococo stitch for his mound. The castle was done on needlepoint canvas, with mica windows and detached buttonhole stitch doors. The forest at the base was worked in French knots in wool. Then followed a pear tree in raised stem band with pears in trellis stitch, a squirrel with a velvety tail, a beehive and tiny bees.

The tent was made of satin, silk-wrapped vellum and tassels, with flaps in detached buttonhole stitch, and houses a wrapped wire basket full of bead apples. I made acorns for the oak tree, and a peacock, whose tail of embroidered eyelets filled with beads was applied over a real peacock feather. Other motifs include a thistle, in couched and laid work with Turkey-work tops, and a rose, with freestanding wired petals filled with detached buttonhole stitch. A bee, dragonfly, beetles, ladybird, butterfly, caterpillar, snail and tiny peas in peapods were all worked with the typical disregard for scale – a charming characteristic of stumpwork!

Many embroideries had the sun, clouds and stars all visible at the same time, so mine was to be no exception. I worked the sun in couched gold thread and lined my silk trellis-stitched clouds with silver (of course). Metal spangles were very common on these embroideries, but none was to be had until I was given a real treasure, an old silk fan embellished with metal spangles in all shapes and sizes. I sanded the stars with emery paper, sealed them to prevent tarnishing, then applied them with transparent thread to finish my work. This sampler, which took five years to work, is titled 'Homage to the Seventeenth Century', and forms the endpapers of this book.

That was nearly four years ago and proved to be but a starting point! Although it is important to move forward, we should never lose sight of the past. As Candace Bahouth, in her book *Medieval Needlepoint*, writes, 'If one is alive and open to everything, one has the privilege of moving forward without ever having to leave anything behind'. This book was written to share some new ideas and designs for raised embroidery. It draws on traditional techniques –

surface stitchery, appliqué, goldwork, quilting, needlelace and canvaswork –
and uses them in different ways. The materials that can be used are only limited
by your imagination. Whet your appetite with this inventory from the past!

> Silver and gold threads, fine gimp cords, lightly twisted silks, chenille
> threads, wools, satin ribbons, tiny brocade tassels, silk-covered wire coils
> or 'purls', painted bullion, spangles, seed pearls, semi-precious stones, beads
> (floral glass, amber, turquoise), coral, tiny sea shells, slivers of mother-of-
> pearl, fine kid leather, peacock plumules, wrapped and looped vellum,
> sheets of mica and talc and scraps of treasured fabrics.

It is easy to see why stumpwork is so addictive!

As a self-taught embroiderer, I am indebted to the writings of Mrs Grace
Christie, and subscribe to a statement made by her husband, A. H. Christie, in
1909: 'Let us not forget that the main object of all embroidery is to give pleasure
in some way, to charm the eye or delight the mind, and that is the principal
reason for its existence'. It has certainly achieved that for me. The study of
stumpwork has enabled me to expand my knowledge of embroidery, and provided
me with opportunities to share my passion with many wonderful people.

*If you have never worked stumpwork before or are just beginning, it is important that you read the
'Materials and Equipment' and 'General Instructions' chapters before undertaking any of the
projects. You might also like to work some of the individual elements (in Chapter 3) separately or
on a sampler before combining them in the designs provided.*

*Those of you who are familiar with stumpwork embroidery may have your own preferred
methods of working, and will be able to substitute these as well as varying the colours and materials
suggested in the projects if desired.*

*If you decide that you would like to know more about this form of embroidery (and I know
many of you will!), some of the books available are listed in the Bibliography and Further Reading
section at the end of the book.*

How to Use This Book

Before you begin, it will be helpful if you read the following information:

*   If you are new to stumpwork, it is important that you read the *Materials and Equipment* and *General Instructions* chapters before undertaking any of the projects. You might also like to work some of the individual elements in Chapter 3 separately or on a sampler before combining them in the designs provided.

*   The diagrams accompanying the instructions for the projects are accurate in size unless otherwise specified. However, the explanatory drawings accompanying the individual motifs may not be true to scale.

*   The transferring of designs is done with tracing paper (baking parchment) and lead pencil (see page 40) unless otherwise specified. When tracing on to a light coloured background, use a minimum amount of lead.

*   DMC threads are used throughout the book unless otherwise indicated.

*   The majority of stitching is done with one strand of thread in a fine (size 10) crewel/embroidery needle. Select the needle size according to the number (or thickness) of threads being used.

*   Many of the designs can be used for surface embroidery without the raised components.

The stumpwork embroiderer's workbox should contain the following equipment:

- Good quality embroidery hoops — 7 cm, 10 cm, 15 cm, 23 cm (3″, 4″, 6″, 9″)

- Needles: Crewel/Embroidery (sizes 3—10)
  Straw/Milliners (sizes 1—10)
  Sharps (sizes 10—12)
  Tapestry (sizes 24—26)
  Chenille (sizes 18—24)
  Yarn Darners (size 14)

- Scissors — small, with sharp points

- Thimble

- Pins — fine glass-headed pins

- Wire cutters

- Screwdriver (for tightening the embroidery hoop)

- Tweezers (fine — from medical suppliers)

- Eyebrow comb (for Turkey knots)

- Ideas diary and pencil

GLOSSARY OF PRODUCT NAMES

This list gives equivalent names for products used throughout this book and which may not be available under the same name in every country.

PRODUCT	EQUIVALENT
Vilene	non-woven interfacing
GLAD Bake	baking parchment
Drawing pins	thumb tacks
Calico	muslin
Clutch pencil	mechanical pencil
Biro	ballpoint pen

Chapter 1

Materials and Equipment

F ABRIC

Almost any fabric can be used for stumpwork, as long as it has an appropriate backing. The fabric 'sandwich' needs to be sturdy enough to support the characteristic padded and wired elements.

In the seventeenth century, raised embroidery was worked on a thick, white silk satin imported from Italy, who dominated the silk trade at the time. Following this tradition, I like to use a good-quality, ivory duchess satin, usually polyester, as it seems to be more resilient than its silk counterpart, although the silk does have a superb lustre!

The satin is backed with one or two layers of 'quilter's muslin', a fine, smooth, closely woven form of calico. (A good-quality calico can be used in its place.) I also use quilter's muslin for embroidering detached elements such as leaves and petals. Detached shapes, such as ladybird wings, can also be worked on a coloured cotton fabric matching the thread, but I find it a little harder to see the stitches.

T HREADS

One of the most fascinating aspects of stumpwork is the variety of threads that can be used – cotton, silk, wool, synthetic and metallic – in various weights and forms. Following are some of the threads that I use and examples of their application.

COTTON

- *Stranded cotton (DMC Stranded Cotton)* Most of my embroidery is worked with one strand of thread, although occasionally I 'lash out' and use two or even three strands!

- *Stranded variegated cotton (Needle Necessities Overdyed Stranded and Minnamurra Stranded Cotton)* When it is difficult to change threads and shading is desired (e.g. when working needle-lace petals), variegated threads are invaluable. I also like to

use these threads for currants, pansies and snails, where
they provide beautiful colour gradation.

- *Cotton pearl thread (DMC Coton Perlé)* This shiny, twisted
  thread is ideal for 'whipping' (e.g. for whipped spider web
  centres and aubergine bud).

- *Soft cotton thread (DMC Tapestry Cotton)* This is the ideal thread
  for wrapping and padding, the amount of padding being
  determined by the number of strands used. It's excellent for
  rose stems and insect bodies.

SILK

- *Stranded silk (Au Ver à Soie Soie d'Alger and Madeira Silk)* For
  superb lustre and delicious colours, nothing can beat silk.
  I have a few favourites, which I use constantly for pansies
  and black currants.

- *Silk buttonhole twist (Kanagawa Silk 1000 denier and Au Ver à Soie
  Soie Perlée)* These twisted silk threads are beautiful to use
  for detached buttonhole stitches (e.g. strawberries), and
  needleweaving (e.g. sepals).

- *Fine silk thread (Cifonda Silk)* Use for highlights and when
  fine, shiny silk embroidery is required. Perfect for spiders
  and hedgehog spines!

SYNTHETIC

- *Chenille thread* This is a furry (*chenille* is French for 'caterpillar') velvet thread, either plain or variegated, which can
  be couched or stitched with a large needle. Use for a
  butterfly's thorax.

- *Machine embroidery thread (Madeira Rayon No. 40)* This very fine,
  shiny thread is ideal for stitching bee's wings and spider's
  legs, for embroidering initials and for tacking, as it does not
  leave any lint behind when it is removed.

- *Nylon clear thread* Use this for invisible stitching of detached pieces, sequins, beads and snakeskin!

- *Strong thread (Gütermann)* This strong polyester thread is used for lacing and securing finished work.

METALLIC

- *Metallic (machine) embroidery thread (Madeira Metallic No. 40 and Gütermann Metallic)* The Madeira is available in many varie-gated and plain colours. It is a very fine metallic thread that can be stitched, without damaging the fibre, into spider webs and veins on insect wings. The Gütermann Metallic threads have visible polyester fibres and are better (easier) for wrapping uncovered wire for insect antennae.

- *Blending filaments* These are very shiny, 1 ply metallic threads, which I use for decorating wings and insect bodies, and embroidering veins.

- *Metallic cord (Kreinik Metallic Cord)* A 1 ply gimp that can be used for couching and stitching, this is my favourite 'insect leg' thread.

Needles

The era of raised embroidery coincided with the emergence of Britain as a major producer of the steel needle, a vast improve-ment on the less refined bronze needle made by individual 'needlers' in various parts of the country. Although it remained a costly and rare item, the steel needle became more readily available than it had been in the past, when it had to be imported from Spain.

In the range of needles available to us today, there is a size, gauge and type to suit every purpose. When selecting a needle, make sure that it is the appropriate type to suit the purpose. The thread should pass easily through the eye, and the needle should make a hole in the fabric large enough for the double thickness of the thread to pass through easily (without damaging the thread).

The following are the needles that I use:

- *Crewel/Embroidery (Milward) sizes 3–10* Crewel needles can be used for nearly all embroidery stitches. They have a sharp point and long eye to take one or more strands of thread. I usually work with one strand of thread in a size 10 needle.

- *Straw/Millinery (Milward) sizes 5–10* Straw needles have a round eye and a long shaft that does not vary in diameter from the eye until it tapers at the point. The fact that there is no bulge at the eye makes these needles ideal for stitching French and bullion knots, and I also use them when working with metallic embroidery threads.

- *Tapestry (Bohin) size 26* Tapestry needles have an elongated eye and a blunt point, which slips easily between the threads in needlepoint, needlelace, raised stem band and whipped spider webs.

- *Sharps (Piecemakers Hand Appliqué and Mill Hill) size 12* These tiny, sharp needles with a round eye are ideal for stitching fine machine threads and nylon clear thread, and for applying petite beads and snakeskin!

- *Chenille (Milward) sizes 18–22* Chenille needles are thick and sharp and have an elongated eye. Use for stitching chenille and thick thread (e.g. soft cotton), and for applying small wired shapes (e.g. dragonfly antennae).

- *Yarn darners (Milward) size 14* Yarn darners are sharp and thick with a long eye, perfect for applying detached wired shapes (e.g. bee wings) and very thick threads.

HOOPS AND FRAMES

As it is worked with two or more layers of fabric and with such a diversity of materials, and because it cannot be washed or 'blocked', stumpwork has to be worked and kept taut in a frame until the completion of the embroidery.

The choice of frame depends on the size of the embroidery and personal preference. As the fabric will not be removed until the end and the edges are likely to become a little marked, the frame has to be larger than the finished design and border. I like to work with the smallest frame possible, as I find it makes it easier to manipulate the threads and detached elements.

HOOPS

Buy the best quality hoop you can find, preferably a birchwood frame, which has a screw that you can tighten with a screw-driver. (I have used my Bernina hoop for more than twenty years!) Bind the inside ring with cotton tape to prevent the fabric from slipping. When mounting the satin and calico into a hoop, make sure that each layer is 'drum' tight at all times.

If a piece of fabric is too small to fit in a hoop (e.g. organza ribbon), mount it onto a larger backing of calico by stitching around the edges. Carefully cut the calico away from behind the ribbon, then mount into a hoop.

SQUARE FRAMES

If a hoop larger than 23 cm (9") is required, use a silk-screen frame (or artists' stretcher frame) or a slate frame as used in goldwork. Attach the satin and calico to a square frame using the following method:

1. Staple the main fabric and backing fabric together along one long side of the frame *back*.

2. Stretch and staple the backing fabric *then* the main fabric along the other long side of the frame *back*.

3. Staple the main fabric and backing fabric together along one short side of the frame *back*.

4. Stretch and staple the backing fabric *then* the main fabric along the remaining short side of the frame *back*.

BEADS AND OTHER TREASURES

If you become 'hooked' on stumpwork, you can justify collecting every treasure that catches your eye, from beads to fish scales! In the seventeenth century, beads, pearls and semiprecious stones were used extensively in embroidered items and garments for both men and women. Some embroideries were executed entirely in beads, either sewn onto a fabric backing and made, for example, into purses and caskets, or threaded onto a frame of iron wire and wrought into a basket, often given as a christening gift. The beads were imported from Venice and the surviving examples of beadwork indicate that the popular colours were emerald and lime green, royal blue, turquoise, yellow and brown.

BEADS

*   *Glass beads* Mill Hill glass beads come in a beautiful range of colours and are available in the following varieties and sizes: Glass Seed Beads (2 mm), Petite Glass Beads (1 mm – the ideal size for insect eyes), Frosted Glass Beads (2 mm – the purple are perfect for grapes), Antique Glass Beads (1.5 mm), Pebble Beads (5 mm – suitable for covering with thread as they have a large hole) and three sizes of Bugle Beads (6 mm, 9 mm and 15 mm – which make ideal segments for hoverfly bodies!). There are many other types of glass beads to collect, for example, cut-glass, crystal, and unusual sizes and shapes.

*   *Wooden beads* Collect unusual shapes to cover with thread or fabric, or to use on their own.

- Metal beads

- Seed pearls and coral

SEQUINS AND SPANGLES

Sequins are available in all shapes, sizes and colours – my favourites are tiny (3 mm) laser sequins, which are perfect for Christmas embroideries.

Metal spangles are more difficult to find, but occasionally damaged old evening bags and garments yield treasures.

MISCELLANEOUS TREASURES TO COLLECT

- Broken jewellery, thin metal chains, charms, rings and jewellery findings

- Metal threads and wires as used in goldwork

- Feathers, shells, fish scales, beetle wings

- Slivers of mica, 'shisha' mirror disks

- Scraps of kid leather

- Exotic (often old) threads, braids, ribbons, cords and fabrics.

WIRE

For the detached, wired shapes, I use a good-quality cake decorators' wire, either covered or uncovered.

- *Covered wire* Use a 30 gauge covered wire. This has a very tightly wrapped, thin paper covering and is available in several colours, including green, white and orange. It is easier to stitch over than the uncovered wire and is used for most detached shapes, such as butterfly wings, petals and leaves.

· *Uncovered wire* Use a 28 gauge wire as the 30 gauge is a little too thin to retain its shape when stitched. This wire is silver in colour and is used when a finer effect is required, such as for bee wings, antennae and tendrils.

· *Cake and flower-decorating wire* This wire, available in several different weights, is covered with a double layer of artificial silk that will not deteriorate in moist conditions and can be readily dyed. Use the fine gauge on the edges of small embroidered petals.

· *Brass wire* Use uncovered 34 gauge brass wire, or stretched coils of purl wire to make very pretty antennae (e.g. for the cricket).

OTHER EQUIPMENT

· Scissors – small, sharp-pointed scissors (FISKARS embroidery scissors)

· Thimble

· Pins – fine glass-headed pins

· Wire cutters (FISKARS diagonal craft cutter)

· Screwdriver (for tightening the embroidery hoop)

· Tweezers (eyebrow – for shaping wire)

· Eyebrow brush/comb (for Turkey knots)

Chapter 2

General Instructions

RAISED PADDED SHAPES

Raised padded shapes can be achieved in many different ways.

PADDED APPLIED FABRIC SHAPES

1. Cut out the embroidered fabric shape with a small seam allowance and apply it with stab stitches to the main background, leaving a small opening for inserting polyester stuffing. See, for example, the aubergine.

2. Embroider the fabric with a 'split' in the shape, then cut out the shape with a small seam allowance and apply it with stab stitches to the main background. Stitch beads through the split until the shape is filled. See the split fig.

3. Embroider the fabric shape with French knots and apply it to the main background without stuffing, relying on the seam allowance and the French knots for the raised effect. See the blackberries.

PADDED APPLIED NEEDLEPOINT SHAPES

1. Work a slightly enlarged shape in needlepoint (also called a 'slip') and cut it out with a small seam allowance. Cut a thin cardboard template the actual size of the shape and gather the needlepoint slip around this, inserting a small amount of stuffing. Apply the padded shape to the main background with invisible stab stitches. See, for example, the orange.

2. Needlepoint slips can also be applied without any padding.

PADDED NEEDLELACE SHAPES

1. Apply the felt padding to the main fabric. Cover the shape with detached needlelace stitch of choice. See the strawberry (in trellis stitch).

2. Detached needlelace stitches can be worked directly onto the fabric, without padding, if required.

3. Work the needlelace over other forms of padding. See the acorn (trellis stitch worked over an embroidered shape) and the blueberry (raised cup stitch worked over a wooden bead).

PADDED EMBROIDERED SHAPES

1. Work satin stitch over a padded felt shape (e.g. the gooseberry).

2. Work satin stitch and trellis couching over a padded felt shape (e.g. the thistle base).

3. Work raised stem band over a padding of soft cotton thread (e.g. the dragonfly abdomen).

4. Wrap soft cotton thread padding with embroidery thread, and couch in place with metallic thread (e.g. the tiny snail and the rose stem).

5. Couch rows of gold thread, chenille thread or wrapped thread to give a raised effect (e.g. a mound).

6. Cover a pebble bead with satin stitches and attach to the main background (e.g. the cotoneaster).

7. Work a raised mound in French knots and petite beads (e.g. the anemone centre).

RAISED DETACHED SHAPES

Raised detached shapes can be wrought in fabric, needlelace or wire.

DETACHED FABRIC SHAPES

Using one of the following techniques, petals, leaves and wings can be worked on fabric (in a hoop), cut out and applied to the main background as freestanding shapes.

Soft detached fabric shape (e.g. butterfly wing)

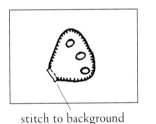

stitch to background

Outline the wing on calico in chain stitch or split backstitch. Cover the outline with buttonhole stitch or overcast stitch. Embroider the wing as desired. Cut out the wing close to the buttonholed edge and, using invisible stitches, apply it as a freestanding shape to the main background.

Soft detached fabric shape with wire support (e.g. leaf)

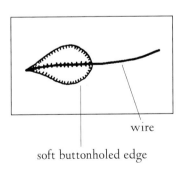

wire

soft buttonholed edge

A wire can be inserted into a soft fabric shape to enable it to be curved.

Couch, then overcast green covered wire along the central vein of a leaf shape. Work the outside edge in buttonhole stitch over a split backstitch outline. Embroider the leaf as desired. Cut out the leaf close to the buttonholed edge, avoiding the wire. Use the tail of the wire to attach the shape to the main background.

Wired detached fabric shape

Attaching wire around the outside edge of detached petals, leaves and wings allows plenty of scope for shaping. There are two methods that can be used:

✦ *Method 1: embroidered surface and edge (e.g. leaf)*

(a) Mount the calico into a hoop and trace the leaf outline and vein.

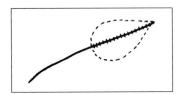

(b) Using green covered wire and one strand of thread, couch, then overcast the wire down the central vein, starting the wire at the tip of the leaf.

(c) Using tweezers or fingers, bend, then couch the wire around the outline of the leaf, leaving a tail of wire.

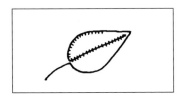

(d) Stitch the wire to the calico, around the leaf outline, with close buttonhole or overcast stitch, incorporating the couching stitches and leaving the tail free.

(e) Embroider the leaf surface as desired.

(f) Using small sharp scissors, cut out the leaf close to the worked edge and attach to the main background with the wire tail.

✦ *Method 2: embroidered edge only (e.g. wing)*

Wings are worked by stitching uncovered wire to organza or any sheer decorative fabric with fine rayon machine embroidery thread. It is easier to stitch if two layers of 'wing' fabric are fused together using paper-backed fusible web (see p. 38).

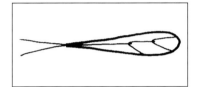

(a) Mount the prepared fabric into a small hoop.

(b) Bend the uncovered wire into a wing shape, with two tails.

(c) Overcast the wire to the wing fabric using one strand of rayon machine embroidery thread – do not couch first as the couching stitches may show through the sheer fabric. Leave the wire tails free.

(d) Embroider the veins, if required, in feather stitch with metallic thread in a straw needle.

(e) Using small sharp scissors, cut out the wing close to the worked edge and attach to the main background using the wire tails.

DETACHED NEEDLELACE SHAPES

Detached petals, leaves and wings can be worked in many needlelace stitches, most of which are variations on the basic detached buttonhole stitch.

The method used in this book consists of transferring the outline of the shape to a 'buttonhole pad', then couching wire or a firm thread along the outline. This wire or thread becomes the framework, or skeleton of the shape, onto which is worked a foundation row of detached buttonhole stitch. Fill the shape with detached buttonhole stitch (or needlelace stitch of choice), remove the couching stitches – and the lace motif becomes free of its fabric backing.

To make a buttonhole pad, sandwich one layer of Pellon and two layers of medium-weight vilene between two layers of closely woven poplin, and stitch around the edges (a 15 cm, or 6", circle is ideal). The outline of the shape to be worked can be either drawn directly onto the pad, or traced onto paper, which is secured to the pad with clear self-adhesive plastic.

Soft detached needlelace shape (e.g. petal)

Using machine thread in a crewel needle, couch a firm thread along the shape outline on a buttonhole pad. With one strand of embroidery thread in a size 26 tapestry needle, fill the shape with rows of detached buttonhole stitch. Cut the couching stitches and remove the soft needlelace shape. Apply one edge to the main background with tiny stitches.

Soft detached needlelace shape with wire support (e.g. oak leaf)

Detached buttonhole stitches are worked around a central wire support, which has been couched onto the buttonhole pad.

   To work the oak leaf:

1. Bend a 12 cm (4 3/4") length of green covered wire in half and couch to a buttonhole pad, leaving a 2 mm ($^1/_{16}$") gap between the wires.

2. Using a size 26 tapestry needle, knot a long strand of green thread to the wire (leaving a tail), and work detached button-hole stitch around both sides, with one or two needle widths between each stitch. Make the number of buttonhole stitches slightly 'longer' than the required finished length of the leaf.

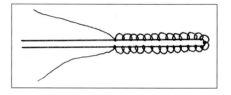

3. Work rows of detached buttonhole stitch around the wire, increasing at the curves by working two stitches into one space, until the leaf is wide enough. In the final row, work three stitches into one space, at regular intervals, to form 'knobs' at the edge of the leaf. Leave a tail of thread.

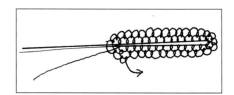

4. Overcast the two central wires together to form the vein, then cut the couching stitches and remove the leaf from the pad. The leaf can be 'ruffled', if desired, by gently pushing the needlelace shape along the wires.

5. Attach the leaf to the main background by inserting the wire and thread tails through to the back of the work.

Wired detached needlelace shape

This is the ideal technique for working detached flowers and butterflies, as the wired outside edge can be easily shaped and 'cupped' for petals and wings.

Wire, either wrapped or unwrapped, is couched along an outline on a buttonhole pad, with machine thread in a crewel needle. Using one of the following methods, and a long strand of embroidery thread in a size 26 tapestry needle, the shape is then filled with rows of detached buttonhole stitch. Colours can be graded if required, by joining in a new thread, or by using a variegated silk or cotton. Attach the petals to the main background by inserting the wire and thread tails through to the back of the work.

Method 1 (e.g. rose)

(a) Knot the thread to the wire (leaving a tail), then work a row of detached buttonhole stitch around the inside of the wire. Take the thread across the base of the petal to the first stitch and secure.

(b) Continue working rows of buttonhole stitch in the same direction (decreasing where necessary by missing a space in the previous row), until the shape is nearly filled, stopping with the thread at the centre of the petal. Work this thread to the base of the petal, closing any gap in the needlelace as you go. Leave a thread tail.

· Method 2 (e.g. poppy)

(a) Knot the thread to the wire (leaving a tail), then work
a row of detached buttonhole stitch around the inside of
the wire. Take the thread to the top inside edge of the
petal and stitch a thread from one corner to the other.

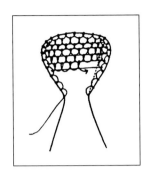

(b) Work a row of detached buttonhole stitch over this
thread and into the row above (corded detached buttonhole stitch). Continue laying threads and buttonholing
over them until the base of the petal is reached, decreasing, if necessary, by missing a space at each side edge of
the row.

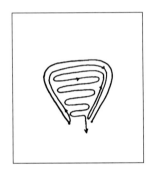

· Method 3 (e.g. hellebore)

This method produces a pointed petal with a row of
decorative 'holes' down the centre.

(a) Knot the thread to the wire (leaving a tail), then
work a row of detached buttonhole stitch around the
inside of the wire. Take the thread to the top inside edge
of the petal and stitch a thread from one corner, through
the middle buttonhole and then to the other corner.

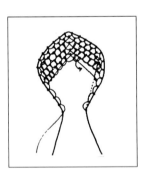

(b) Work a row of detached buttonhole stitch over this
thread and into the row above (corded detached buttonhole stitch). Continue laying threads and buttonholing
over them until the base of the petal is reached, decreasing one stitch in the middle of every row.

DETACHED WIRE SHAPES

Wrapped wire

Wire can be wrapped and manipulated into many different
shapes (e.g. tendrils, stamen and antennae), and attached to the

main background. Wrap covered or uncovered wire with stranded or metallic thread using one of the following methods:

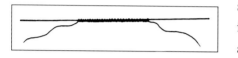

1. *Wire wrapped in the middle (e.g. petals, wings, vines)* Knot one strand of thread to the covered wire, wrap the middle section for the required length, then knot again, leaving a tail of thread at each end.

For the vine, twist the wrapped wire into the desired shape and insert the unwrapped ends (and tails of thread) through to the back of the work and secure.

For a petal, couch the wrapped wire to the outline on a buttonhole pad, and proceed with detached buttonhole stitch.

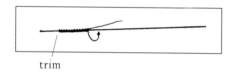

trim

2. *Wire wrapped from the end (e.g. tendrils, antennae)* Knot one strand of thread 1 cm (3/8") from the end of the uncovered wire. Wrap over the wire (enclosing the thread tail) to the required length. Knot again, leaving a tail of thread. Insert the wire and tail of thread through to the back of the work and secure. Cut the unwrapped 1 cm of wire close to the knot. The wrapped wire can be coiled around a darning needle to form tendrils before it is attached to the work.

Metallic thread looks very effective when wrapped for antennae. The ends can be dipped in glue (or nail polish) if desired.

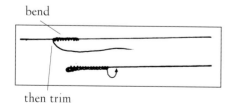

bend

then trim

3. *Wire bent then wrapped from end (e.g. stamen)* To form a 'knob' at the end, wrap a small section of uncovered wire, bend this in half, then wrap both wires together for 2–3 mm (1/8"). Trim the short end of the wire, then continue wrapping over the single wire to the required length. Knot the thread, leaving a tail.

Unwrapped and uncovered wire

1. Unwrapped wire can be used for butterfly wings and petals. Couch the wire to the outline on a buttonhole pad and fill with preferred needlelace stitch. Work a row of detached buttonhole stitch around the outside edge (in a decorative thread if desired), filling the spaces left between the previous stitches.

2. Purl wire (as used in goldwork) and uncovered brass wire (34 gauge) can be used for antennae.

METHODS FOR WORKING LEAVES AND STEMS

EMBROIDERING WIRED DETACHED LEAVES

Detached leaves are worked on calico mounted in a hoop, using green covered wire (30 gauge) and one strand of thread in a size 10 crewel needle. The surface can be embroidered in many different ways.

Leaves with a wired central vein

Couch, then overcast the wire down the central vein, starting at the tip of the leaf. Bend and couch the wire around the outline, leaving the tail of wire free. Buttonhole or overcast the wire to the calico, then embroider the leaf surface using one of the following methods:

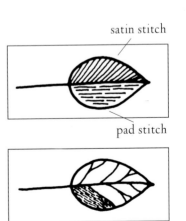

satin stitch

pad stitch

1. *Padded satin stitch* Pad the leaf with straight or chain stitches, then cover with satin stitch, inserting the needle as close to the inside edge of the wire as possible. Work the veins, if required, in straight stitches.

2. *Long and short stitch* Embroider the leaf surface inside the wired edge with long and short stitch. Either work the veins first or on top of the embroidered leaf.

3. *Stem stitch filling*   Work rows of stem stitch, following the outline of the shape, until the surface is filled. Veins can be embroidered over the surface.

Leaves without a wired central vein

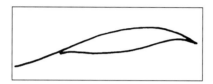

This method is used for thin, long leaves (e.g. tulip leaves). Couch the wire around the outline of the leaf, leaving a tail of wire free. Overcast the wire to the calico, then embroider the leaf surface with rows of stem stitch filling.

EMBROIDERING LEAVES ON THE MAIN FABRIC

The leaves are embroidered with one strand of green thread in a size 10 crewel needle. The edges of the leaf are usually worked first, in a darker green, using one of the following stitches:

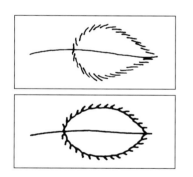

- split backstitch or stem stitch (smooth edge)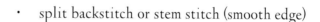

- slanted stem stitch (serrated edge)

- single feather stitch (spiked edge)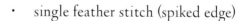

Using a lighter green (or colour), work the central vein in stem stitch, split backstitch or chain stitch, then embroider the leaf surface using one of the following methods:

1. *Padded satin stitch*   Pad the leaf with straight or chain stitches, then cover with satin stitch, inserting the needle close to the central vein. Work the veins, if required, in straight stitches.

2. *Long and short stitch*   Embroider the leaf surface inside the wired edge with long and short stitch. Either work the veins first or on top of the embroidered leaf.

3. *Stem stitch filling*   Work rows of stem stitch, following the outline of the shape, until the surface is filled. Veins can be embroidered over the surface.

4. *Buttonhole stitch*   With this method, the edge and the surface of the leaf are worked at the same time.

   Embroider the central vein, then pad the leaf surface with straight stitches. Working from the base to the point, embroider one side of the leaf in buttonhole stitch, inserting the needle close to the central vein. Repeat for the other side of the leaf. The buttonhole stitches have to be worked at an angle, close together and following the outline of the leaf. If required, the veins can be worked in straight stitches.

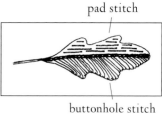

pad stitch

buttonhole stitch

WORKING STEMS

The following methods are all worked in stranded thread. The required thickness of the stem will determine the number of strands used and consequently the size of the needle. A detached chain stitch in stranded thread can be worked at the end of the stems to give a neat finish.

1. *Stem stitch*

2. *Chain stitch*

3. *Whipped chain stitch*   This can be whipped with the same stranded thread or with a metallic thread for a more exotic effect.

4. *Overcast stitch*   This is worked over a row of chain stitch or over a length of laid thread (soft cotton or pearl).

5. *Raised stem band*   This is worked over a padding of soft cotton thread. The number of threads used determines the result – from a thin branch to a tree trunk!

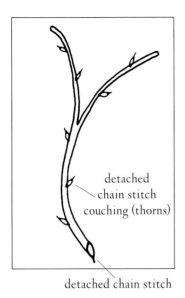

detached
chain stitch
couching (thorns)

detached chain stitch

6. *Wrapped wire*

7. *Wrapped thread*   This is an ideal method for working stems that need to overlap another section of embroidery.

Bring the required number of strands of soft cotton thread through to the front of the work. Using a long length of stranded thread in a size 26 tapestry needle, wrap the soft cotton closely for the required distance, then insert all through to the back of the work and secure. If required, the soft cotton threads can be separated and wrapped individually to form thinner stems. Attach the wrapped stems to the main background with invisible stitches, or couch in place with detached chain stitches (in metallic thread if desired) to form 'thorns'.

GENERAL TECHNIQUES

ATTACHING WIRE TO MAIN BACKGROUND

All wire tails are attached to the main background by inserting them through a 'tunnel' formed by the eye of a large needle. Use a size 14–16 sharp yarn darner or a large chenille needle.

fabric

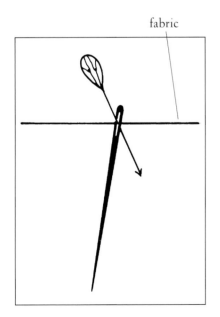

1. Pierce the background with the needle so that the eye is halfway through the fabric.

2. Slide the wire and thread tails through the tunnel formed by the eye of the needle to the back of the work.

3. Gently pull the needle all the way through, leaving the wire in the 'hole'.

4. Stitch the wire to the back of the work, then trim with wire cutters.

5. Use tweezers or fingers to shape the wired element as required.

PADDING WITH FELT

By applying one or more layers of felt to the main fabric, a smooth, domed shape can be achieved. This can be covered with satin stitch, needlelace, fine fabric or thin kid leather.

1. Cut one piece of felt the exact size of the shape, and one or more successively smaller pieces, depending on the amount of padding required.

2. Using small stab stitches (coming out of the background fabric and into the felt), apply the felt pieces to the main fabric, starting with the smallest shape and finishing with the largest piece on top.

3. Work buttonhole stitch (several needle widths apart) around the edge of the top layer of felt to give a smooth outline.

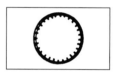

Felt can also be manipulated for detached padded shapes; for example, a piece of felt rolled into a cylinder is used for making the acorn.

USING PAPER-BACKED FUSIBLE WEB

Paper-backed fusible web has many different uses in embroidery and is much easier to use than its counterpart in the past, which was fine tissue paper, glued to fabrics with a paste made from wheat starch! Use GLAD Bake to protect your iron and the main fabric, and test the temperature of the iron – too hot and the fabric can bubble, too cool and the fabrics will not fuse.

Fusing fabric to main background
(e.g. appliqué wings to main fabric)

Iron paper-backed fusible web to the wing fabric and trace the wing outline onto the paper side. Carefully cut out the wings and remove the paper backing. With the glue side down, iron the wings to the main fabric. Couch metallic thread around the outline to cover the raw edges. See, for example, the hoverfly.

Fusing wing fabrics together

Detached wings are worked by overcasting uncovered wire to organza, organza ribbon, metal organdie, lamé or any sheer decorative fabric. As wing fabrics are delicate, they are much easier to stitch if two layers are fused together, and they can be fused together in many different combinations to achieve the desired effect.

Iron paper-backed fusible web to one layer, remove the paper backing, then fuse the two layers of wing fabric together. See the bee wings.

Fusing a pattern outline to felt

It is very difficult to trace a small shape onto felt and to cut it out accurately.

Trace the shape onto the paper side of paper-backed fusible web, iron it onto the felt, then cut out the accurate shape. Remove the paper before stitching the felt to the main fabric. See the thistle base.

Fusing a pattern outline to organza

When working embroidery stitches over felt, you will find that the fibres often work their way through, giving a 'furry' effect. To avoid this and to give an accurate embroidery outline, cover the felt with organza.

Iron paper-backed fusible web to the organza, then trace the design onto the organza side. Remove the paper, then fuse the organza to the felt. Cut out the felt shape and stitch to the main fabric, organza side up. See the beehive.

Save the paper after using paper-backed fusible web as it makes great tracing paper!

TRANSFERRING A DESIGN TO MAIN FABRIC

I use several different methods to transfer a design to the main fabric. To prevent distortion of the design, always stretch your main fabric and backing into the hoop or frame before you commence.

Using tracing paper and lead pencil

You will need:

- Tracing paper (I use GLAD Bake)

- Clutch pencil with fine (0.5 mm) HB lead

- Sticky tape

- Empty biro (optional)

1. Trace the design onto the tracing paper with the pencil, then turn the paper over and draw over the back of the tracing lines – this leaves a thin line of lead underneath your tracing.

2. Position the tracing (right side up) over the main fabric, securing at the edges with a little sticky tape, if necessary.

3. With a hard surface underneath your fabric (e.g. a paperweight or tin lid), draw firmly over the outline with your pencil or an empty biro. This should leave a very fine line of lead on your fabric, which is easily covered.

Using carbon paper

You will need:

- Dressmaker's carbon paper: white or orange

- Equipment as above

For a dark background, use dressmaker's carbon paper between the tracing paper and the fabric and proceed as above, using a pencil or an empty biro to draw over the outlines.

Using tacking (basting)

You will need:

- Tracing paper (I use thin greaseproof paper)

- Fine (0.4 mm) waterproof marking pen (not pencil)

- Sticky tape or drawing pins

- Fine rayon machine embroidery thread (e.g. Madeira Rayon No. 40)

- Crewel needle size 10

This method offers greater flexibility as does not permanently mark the fabric; however, it is difficult to reproduce fine details of design accurately.

1. Draw the design onto the tracing paper with the marking pen.

2. Attach the tracing to the edges of your frame or hoop with the sticky tape or drawing pins.

3. Tack the outlines with machine thread, using small stitches to retain as much detail as possible.

4. Run the point of the needle gently along the tacked lines to score the paper, then carefully tear the paper away.

5. Remove the tacking threads as you embroider.

FINISHING TECHNIQUES

The great majority of seventeenth-century raised needlework pictures have survived because they were mounted in a frame behind glass. Although not a very practical form of embroidery, stumpwork was used to decorate gloves, pincushions, purses and bookbindings, and to cover boxes, caskets and mirror frames. Today, you can frame your finished embroidery, or display it in a box, brooch or paperweight.

TO MOUNT INSIDE THE LID OF A BOX

You will need:

·   Small cardboard box

·   Acrylic paint and paintbrush (if required), and gold paint and sponge (optional)

·   Strong thread

·   Cardboard: 1.5 mm thick, cut in a circle to fit inside lid of box

·   PVA glue

1. If necessary, paint the box with acrylic paint. Gold paint can also be sponged on the top.

2. Using the strong thread, gather the embroidery evenly over the cardboard circle and secure it well. Make sure the design is centred.

3. Glue the embroidery inside the lid of the box with PVA glue.

Stumpwork embroidery can also be mounted into the lids of porcelain and wooden boxes, and gilded brooch frames, all of which are readily available (made by Framecraft).

TO MOUNT INTO A PAPERWEIGHT

You will need:

·   Strong thread

·   Cardboard: acid-free, 1.5 mm thick, cut in a circle to fit inside recess of wooden base

·   PVA glue

·   Recessed wooden base (available from Chelsea Fabrics)

·   Glass paperweight (Framecraft 2 5/8", or 6.5 mm; or 3 1/2", or 9 mm)

·   Clear silicone sealant (Selleys Window and Glass Sealant)

·   Self-adhesive suede or felt

1. Using the strong thread, gather the embroidery firmly over the cardboard circle, then lace, using the strong thread. Gather the calico backing and the satin separately for a smoother finish.

2. Using the PVA glue, glue the embroidery-covered cardboard into the recessed wooden base, pressing gently until it is secure.

3. Gently brush or vacuum the surface to remove any dust or stray threads, then arrange the detached elements (e.g. wings) as desired, using tweezers.

> To vacuum, cover the nozzle of the vacuum cleaner with organza. With the cleaner set on the minimum power, hold the nozzle just above the embroidery.

4. Attach the glass paperweight to the wooden base with the clear silicone sealant. Leave under a weight until the sealant has cured.

5. Stick a circle of the self-adhesive suede or felt to the base of the paperweight.

TO MAKE A STUMPWORK BROOCH

You will need:

- Strong thread

- Cardboard: 2 mm thick, cut into two circles, each the size of brooch

- Brooch pin

- Glass seed beads for edging

1. Using the strong thread, gather the embroidery over one cardboard circle and secure it well. Make sure the design is centred.

2. Cut a circle of fabric and gather over the remaining cardboard for the brooch back. Attach a brooch pin to the back by stitching through the fabric and the cardboard.

3. Stitch the front circle to the back circle with invisible slip stitches, making sure that the brooch pin is in the correct position.

4. To make a bead edging, thread onto one strand of strong thread enough seed beads to fit snugly around the circumference of the brooch. Tie the thread into a circle around the edge of the brooch, allowing the beads to rest in the groove formed between the two circles of cardboard.

5. Slip stitch the strong thread in place between every three or four beads.

TO LACE STUMPWORK TO BOARD BEFORE FRAMING

Many embroiderers take their unlaced work to the framer, but if you want to do your own lacing, here is one method.

You will need:

·   Cardboard: acid-free, thick, white (or foam-core board)

·   Flannelette or Pellon

·   PVA glue

·   Glass-headed pins

·   Strong thread

·   Needle

1. Pad the cardboard with a layer of flannelette or Pellon, cut 5 cm (2") larger on each side than the cardboard. Glue the 5 cm surround to the back of the board with PVA glue, trimming the corners. (Never put glue on the front of the board.)

2. Lay the embroidery face down on a padded surface with a layer of white tissue paper in between to prevent the raised elements from catching.

3. Pin the calico backing to the edge of the board, checking that the embroidery is positioned correctly. Using strong thread, lace the two longer sides of calico first, then the two shorter sides, trimming the corners for a neat finish.

4. Pin the satin to the edge of the board. Using strong thread, lace the two longer sides of satin first, then the two shorter sides, mitring the corners.

5. Gently brush or vacuum the surface to remove any dust or stray threads, then arrange the detached elements (e.g. wings) as desired, using tweezers.

6. Take your laced embroidery to your framer. (I could not survive without Charles Hewitt!)

Acorn

Chapter 3

Individual Elements

The mighty oak is intertwined with the history of Britain, going back to the ancient Druids, who were said to have held their religious rites in oak groves at a time when vast areas of Britain were covered by oak forests. Acorns and oak leaves became traditional Stuart emblems after Charles II spent one day hiding in an oak tree during his flight through England in 1651. Royal Oak Day was decreed by Parliament in 1664 to commemorate Charles II's restoration to the throne in 1660.

Carry an acorn in your pocket to protect yourself from storms, from losing your bearings and from evil intent.

Put a handful of oak leaves in your bath, and you will be cleansed both in body and spirit.

Carry three acorns about your person and you will have a charm for youthfulness, beauty and attainment in life.

CLAIRE NAHMAD, GARDEN SPELLS, 1994

MATERIALS REQUIRED

- Beige felt, 0.9 cm x 2.25 cm (3/8" x 7/8")

- Mill Hill Glass Seed Beads 221 (bronze)

- Needles: Crewel 10
  Large sharp yarn darner
  Tapestry 26

- Threads: Light brown stranded thread – DMC 3045
  Green/brown twisted silk thread – Au Ver à Soie Soie
  Perlée 580 or 455 or 274

Acorn kernel

The acorn kernel is basically a padded tassel head that can be applied either flat on the surface or quite raised.

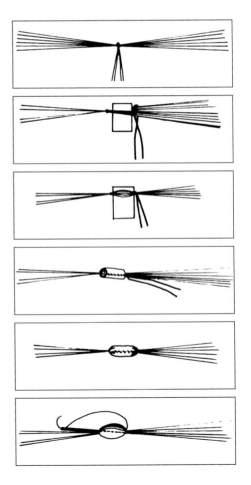

1. Cut five 40 cm (16") lengths of the stranded thread and set aside one length (6 strands) to be used as working threads. Separate the remaining four lengths (24 strands) and gather them into a bundle. Tie a knot in the middle of the bundle with two working threads.

2. Insert the felt, for padding, into the middle of the bundle and secure with two more working threads.

3. Roll the felt into a cylinder around the bundle of threads, and stitch to secure with one of the working threads.

4. Work several stitches at each end of the cylinder to taper (round) the ends.

5. Cover the felt cylinder with long satin stitches, using five or six strands from the bundle (one at a time in a crewel needle).

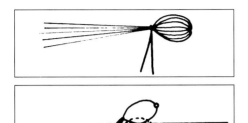

6. Smooth the remaining threads over the satin-stitched shape (as in a tassel) and secure with the one remaining working thread.

7. Using the yarn darner, sink the remaining threads through to the back of the work and secure. (Trim the ends after working the acorn base.) Stitch the acorn kernel in place with invisible stitches. The bronze bead or a French knot can be stitched at the end of the kernel if desired.

Acorn base

1. Using one strand of twisted silk in a tapestry needle, make one long stitch, halfway down and across the acorn kernel, and secure at the back of the work.

2. Cover the acorn base with trellis stitch, working the first row over the long stitch. Work each row from left to right, decreasing at the edges where necessary.

PARTS OF A FLOWER

Most flowers have four main parts:

1. The *calyx* consists of small leaf-like sepals, which protect the flower bud.

2. The *corolla* usually consists of a group of colourful petals.

3. The *stamens* bear the pollen and may vary in number from one to more than a thousand.

4. The *pistil* is the seed-bearing part of the plant.

The shape, colour and number of these parts vary from one kind of plant to another. A typical flower grows on a 'receptacle', an enlarged part of the flower stalk.

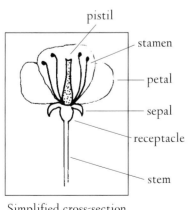

Simplified cross-section
of a typical flower

ANEMONE (WINDFLOWER)

Anemone hath the name because the floure never openeth it self, but when the wind bloweth.

WILLIAM TURNER, A NEW HERBALL, 1551–62

In the seventeenth and eighteenth centuries, brilliant and showy anemones were developed by plant enthusiasts. The colours included bright red, purple and magenta, with these shades being intensified by the complementary green of the ruff and the striking indigo and violet of the centre and stamens.

MATERIALS REQUIRED

- Pad for working detached buttonhole stitch (see General Instructions)

- Wire: 30 gauge red or orange covered, cut in 12 cm (4 3/4") lengths

- Mill Hill Petite Glass Beads 40374 (blue/black)

- Needles: Crewel 10
  Tapestry 26
  Large chenille or sharp yarn darner

- Threads: Red stranded thread in 3 shades – DMC 349 (dark), 350 (medium), 351 (light)
  Green stranded thread – DMC 936
  Black stranded thread – DMC 310

1. *To embroider anemone petals on background:* Trace the anemone onto the main fabric. With one strand of the darkest red thread, outline the petals in long and short buttonhole stitch. Work the stitches close together in random lengths, keeping the stitch direction towards the centre of the anemone.

Fill in the petal with long and short stitches, grading the colours to palest red at the centre. Leave a small gap (1 mm) between the embroidery and centre outline, in which to insert the detached petals.

2. *To embroider sepals:* With one strand of the green thread, work three detached chain stitches inside each other, at the junction of the petals. The sepals look better if the largest chain stitch has a long securing stitch.

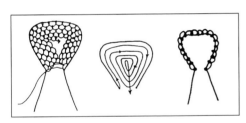

3. *To work detached anemone petals:* Tack a piece of wire to the pad around the petal outline. With one strand of the medium red thread in a tapestry needle, work the petal in detached buttonhole stitch (using method 1, p. 19), changing to the paler shade towards the centre of the petal.

Finish the petal (ruffled edge) by working detached buttonhole stitch around the outside edge (working into the spaces left between the inside buttonhole stitches), with the darkest red thread. Work five petals.

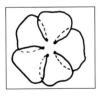

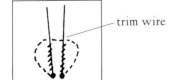

trim wire

4. *To apply detached petals:* Use the yarn darner to make five holes around the centre outline, then insert the petals. The wires for each petal are separate but *do* share a common hole with neighbouring petals.

To secure the detached petals, bend the wires underneath each petal at the back of the work and stitch with tiny stitches. Trim the wires. (It is easier if each petal is secured before proceeding to the next.)

5. Work the centre of the anemone with beads and French knots (1 wrap), using two strands of the black thread.

6. Bend the petals with tweezers or fingers into the desired shapes.

AUBERGINE

Native to the tropics, the aubergine (also known as the eggplant) was imported to Europe in the fifteenth century, where it was known as the 'madde apple' and grown chiefly for decorative purposes. Beautiful to look at, the aubergine is oval with a shiny skin. The colours vary from white and white mottled with pink, to all shades of violet, the most exotic being a rich black/purple.

MATERIALS REQUIRED

- Calico (or quilter's muslin), 20 cm x 20 cm (8" x 8")

- 10 cm (4") embroidery hoop

- Felt, paper-backed fusible web and organza, 5 cm x 8 cm (2" x 3")

- Small amount of stuffing and saté stick

- Needles: Crewel 10 and 6

- Threads: Plum/purple stranded thread in 3 shades – Au Ver à Soie Soie d'Alger 4636 (dark), 4635 (medium), 4634 (light)
  Green Pearl (5) cotton thread – DMC 731
  Olive-green stranded thread – DMC 731, 732

Aubergine fruit

1. Mount the calico into the hoop and trace the slightly enlarged shape. Using one strand of the dark purple thread, outline the shape in split backstitch and embroider in long and short stitches, introducing the medium purple thread near the centre of the fruit for shading.

2. Cut out the shape, leaving a small turning. Trace the fruit outline onto the main fabric. Apply the embroidered shape with small stab stitches, turning in the raw edges as you go and easing the shape to fit the outline. Leave a small opening at the top of the fruit, use the saté stick to insert the stuffing, then stitch the opening closed. If necessary, cover the stab stitches with straight stitches using one strand of the dark purple thread.

3. To form the calyx, make three stitches into the top of the fruit with the Pearl cotton, and work whipped spider web stitch with one strand of the olive-green thread. Wrap the end of each rib with the olive-green thread to form peaks.

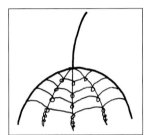

Aubergine bud

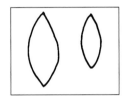

1. Using the paper-backed fusible web and organza, cut two pieces of felt to pad the bud, one the actual shape of the bud and one slightly smaller.

2. Using one strand of the olive-green thread, stab stitch the smaller shape in place. Apply the larger shape on top with buttonhole stitch, keeping the organza side uppermost (to prevent the felt fibres working their way through when embroidering).
   Using the Pearl thread, work three stitches over the felt shape (in and out of the same two points) to form the ribs of the bud.

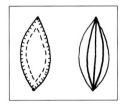
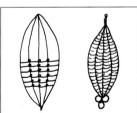

3. With one strand of the olive-green thread, cover the bud with whipped spider web stitch, starting in the middle and working to each end in turn. To complete, whip the top of the bud with the same thread, then work three French knots (3 strands, 1 wrap) at the base.

Aubergine flower bud

1. Embroider the bud in straight stitches with one strand of the light purple thread.

2. Work the sepals in detached chain stitches with one strand of the olive-green thread.

PARTS OF AN INSECT

It is difficult to generalise about insects as the variety is so great; however, it is useful to know that an insect's body is divided into three parts: the head, the thorax and the abdomen.

1. The head carries the sensory organs (mouthparts, antennae, palps and eyes).

2. The thorax consists of three segments, each bearing a pair of legs. It has two pairs of wings (growing from the second and third segments), one pair or none at all.

3. The abdomen is the largest part, and actually has 11 segments, which are often fused and not discernible.

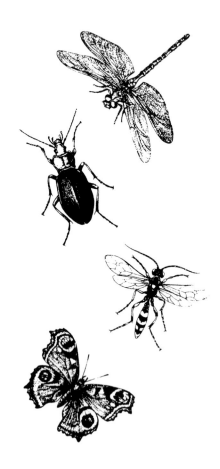

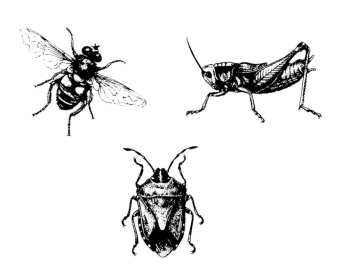

Bee

A sweet scented path of thyme, most beloved of bee flowers, may lead to the hives set in the midst of a garden or grassy orchard, and round about it, both for the bee's happiness and to increase the yield of honey, grow those plants which bees particularly delight in. For early flowering; crocus, butter-bur, hepatica and black-helebor. Those of sweetest savour: savory, smallage, sage, violets, lavender, sweet marjoram, saffron, poppies, balm, beans, mustard-seed, melilot, forget-me-not, roses, clovers, hollyhock, honeysuckle, mignonette, catmint, sunflower, arabis, borage, vetch, marshmallow, bell-flowers, heather, broom, and 'bee flower', the old name for the wallflower, as it is especially sweet to bees. Of fruit trees and fruiting plants they most delight in are: the apple, cherry, almond, peach, pear, raspberries, strawberries, and gooseberries which are valuable as they flower early. Pine, willow, lime and fir are the trees they prefer. Holly and gorse would provide a shelter from strong winds. If the hives are rubbed with balm or sweet cicely, this would please the bees even more. But — perchance you should be caught unawares in the bee-garden, then a leaf of either dock, mallow, rue, hollyhock or ivy, which may be growing close at hand, should be rubbed on the sting in the hope it will help bring relief.

SAMUEL BAGSTER, THE MANAGEMENT OF BEES, 1838

Chosen as a personal emblem by Napoleon III, the bee was a symbol of industry and order.

The bee was considered to be of great virtue, providing both honey for pleasure and wax for thrift and was hence used as a symbol of industriousness.

SARAH DON, TRADITIONAL EMBROIDERED ANIMALS, 1990

What living creature can you keep about you that yields more pleasure, delight and profit, than these that possess so little room as a small part of your garden?

JOHN WORLIDGE, SYSTEMA HORTI-CULTURAE, 1677

MATERIALS REQUIRED

- Eyebrow brush/comb

- Wing fabric (pearl metal organdie), 15 cm x 15 cm (6" x 6")

- Paper-backed fusible web and organza, 15 cm x 15 cm

- 10 cm (4") embroidery hoop

- Wire: 28 gauge uncovered, cut in 12 cm (4 3/4") lengths

- Mill Hill Glass Seed Beads 374 (blue/black)

- Needles: Straw 9
  Crewel 10
  Large chenille or sharp yarn darner

- Threads: Black stranded thread – DMC 310
  Yellow stranded thread – DMC 783
  White rayon machine embroidery thread – Madeira Rayon
  No. 40 col. 1001
  Gold/black metallic thread – Kreinik Cord 205c

Thorax and abdomen

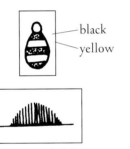

thorax
abdomen

black
yellow

Cross-section of abdomen

1. Trace the bee thorax and abdomen onto the main fabric and outline with small backstitches with one strand of the black thread.

2. Work the abdomen in Turkey knots using two strands of thread in a straw needle. Stitch two rows of Turkey knots in each colour, starting with black at the thorax end of the abdomen. The aim is to work five stripes, but often the tail has only one row of black – it depends on the size of your stitches. The Turkey knots should pierce the backstitches but not protrude outside them.

3. Cut the loops between the knots and comb the threads upwards. Cut the threads in a curved shape, to form a velvety mound.

Wings

1. Iron the wing fabric to the organza, using paper-backed fusible web, and mount in the hoop. Either side of the fabric 'sandwich' can be used.

2. Bend the wire into a wing shape – do not cross the wires at *.

3. Using one strand of the rayon thread in a crewel needle, overcast the wire to the fabric, starting and ending at * with a few stitches over both wires.

4. With sharp scissors, carefully cut around the wings. If they vary in size (they nearly always do!), select the two larger ones for the front wings.

To apply wings and finish bee

1. Using the yarn darner, insert two wings on each side of the thorax (they will be very close together), and bend the wires under the abdomen. Hold the wires in place with a pin at the edge of the work until the bee is finished. Fill the thorax (and secure the wings) with satin stitches (or Turkey knots – difficult but possible!) with two strands of the black thread, working towards the abdomen.

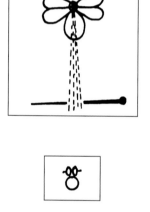

2. To form the head/eyes, stitch two beads together (from side to side) close to the thorax. Finish with one stitch between the beads towards the thorax – this makes the beads sit evenly to form the head.

3. With two strands of the metallic thread in a straw needle, work three backstitches for each leg, stitching in the order and direction as shown for best results.

Complete by working a fly stitch for the feelers with one strand of metallic thread. Cut the wires off at the tail end of the abdomen.

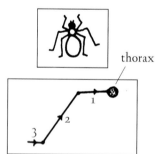

thorax

Beehive

European beekeepers developed the skep, a woven straw hive resembling an inverted basket, to provide shelter for honeybees and their honeycombs.

MATERIALS REQUIRED

- Felt, paper-backed fusible web and organza, 5 cm x 8 cm (2" x 3")

- Threads: Straw-yellow stranded thread in 2 shades – DMC 680 (medium), 729 (light)
  Brown stranded thread – DMC 3371

- Needles: Crewel 10

1. Iron the fusible web to the organza (protect the iron with GLAD Bake). On the organza side, trace the beehive outline (and all internal lines) and two smaller shapes for padding. Remove the paper and fuse the organza to the felt. Cut the shapes out carefully.

2. With one strand of the light yellow thread, stab stitch the padding layers in place, starting with the smallest layer and keeping the organza side uppermost. Stitch the upper layer of beehive in place with stab stitches at the end of each 'round' as shown.

3. Embroider the hive entrance in satin stitch with one strand of the brown thread.

4. Using pencil lines on the organza as a guide, embroider each round of the beehive as follows:

(a) Work 10 long satin stitches in 729.

(b) Work two long satin stitches on either side in 680.

(c) Couch all in place with 680 (keep within the pencil lines).

Repeat for each round, staggering the couching stitches to form a 'brick' pattern.

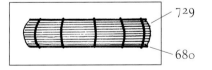

729

680

TINY BEES

MATERIALS REQUIRED

- Threads: Black stranded thread – DMC 310
  Yellow stranded thread – DMC 783
  Silver/black metallic thread – Kreinik Cord 105c

- Needles: Crewel 10

1. With one strand of the black thread, work seven small satin stitches into the same two holes to pad the body.

2. Using one strand of thread, work satin stitches over the padded body, in black and yellow (two stitches in each colour – three black stripes and two yellow).

3. With one strand of the black thread, work a French knot (2 wraps) for the head.

4. Using the metallic thread, work two detached chain stitches for the wings.

BLACKBERRIES

October 10 is the day in folklore on which you are not supposed to pick any more blackberries, as it was once thought that the Devil spits on them on this day, making them poisonous. The custom arose because October 10 used to be St Michael's Day before the calendar change in 1752, and there is a legend that when St Michael threw the Devil out of heaven, the latter landed in a blackberry bush.

FRUIT CHEESE

This apple and blackberry puree is delicious as a spread.

1 kg (2 ¼ lb) apples, washed
1 kg blackberries, cleaned
450 g (16 oz) sugar for each 450 g of pulp

Cut up and core the apples, then place them in a large saucepan. Add the blackberries and enough water to just cover the fruit. Simmer, stirring occasionally, until the apples are soft. Sieve the pulp and weigh it, then add the correct amount of sugar. Put the pulp back in the saucepan and boil, stirring continuously, until the mixture thickens. Allow to cool, then bottle like jam or set in a mould.

MATERIALS REQUIRED

- Red cotton (homespun), 20 cm x 20 cm (8" x 8")

- 10 cm (4") embroidery hoops (2)

- Calico (or quilter's muslin), 20 cm x 20 cm

- Beads: Mill Hill Glass Seed Beads 367 (garnet), 2012 (plum)
  Mill Hill Frosted Glass Beads 62013 (red/black), 62032 (cranberry)

- Needles: Straw 1 or 3
  Crewel 10
  Tapestry 26

- Threads: Range of stranded threads from reds to pinks to 'unripe' green – DMC 902, 815, 304, 347, 3328, 3712, 760, 754, 3013
  Green twisted silk thread – Kanagawa Silk 1000 denier col. 113

Ripe blackberries

1. Mount the red cotton into the hoop and draw the
blackberry outlines.

2. Using six strands of thread in a straw needle, embroider
the blackberries in French knots (1 wrap), grading the colours
from dark red to light. Beads can also be stitched in, with one
strand of matching thread, to provide a sparkle:
Ripe berry Threads 902, 815, 304; beads 367, 2012
Almost ripe berry Threads 304, 347, 3328, 3712; beads 62032,
62013

Unripe blackberries

1. Mount the calico into the hoop and draw the blackberry
outlines.

2. Using six strands of thread in a straw needle, embroider
the blackberries in French knots (1 wrap), grading the colours
from mid-pink to pale green:
Unripe berry Threads 3712, 760, 754, 3013

To apply blackberries

1. Cut out the embroidered blackberry shapes, allowing small
turnings. Turn the raw edges in and tack the blackberries in
place.

2. With one strand of thread, stitch each blackberry into
position with tiny stab stitches around the edge. Cover the
edge with French knots (6 strands, 1 wrap) in colours to blend
with the blackberry. Press gently around the edges with your
fingernails to shape the berries.

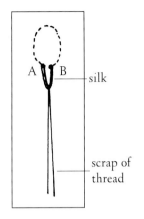

Sepals

Using the green twisted silk in a tapestry needle, work three sepals at the base of each blackberry.

1. Bring the silk out at A and insert at B to form a loop. Hold the loop at the required length of sepal with a scrap of thread.

2. Bring the needle out again at A and work the loop with needleweaving, inserting the needle through the centre of the loop, alternately from the left then the right.

3. When the loop is filled, remove the scrap thread, insert the needle through to the back of the work and secure. Allow the sepal to curve slightly. Work two more sepals, one on each side of the first.

BLUEBERRIES

Blueberries belong to the heath family and count azaleas, rhododendrons and huckleberries among their cousins. They are beautiful 'frosted' and served with thick cream. To frost blueberries, dip them in a dish of beaten eggwhite, roll in caster sugar, then leave to dry on a sieve in a warm spot.

MATERIALS REQUIRED

·   Beads: 6 mm (¹/₄") wooden beads
    Mill Hill Antique Glass Beads 3004 (purple)

·   Threads: Dark blue/purple twisted silk thread – Au Ver à Soie Soie Perlée 636 or Kanagawa Silk 1000 denier col. 818

·   Needles: Tapestry 26

Blueberries are worked in raised cup stitch. They can be worked with or without a central wooden bead, using the same technique.

1. With the silk thread in a tapestry needle, make a triangle of three backstitches onto the main fabric where the blueberry is to be worked.

2. Make three detached buttonhole stitches into each leg of the triangle to form the first row. Work three rows of detached buttonhole stitch, increasing by three stitches in the third row and in the fourth row if necessary. Work one or two more rows, then insert a wooden bead into the 'cup'.

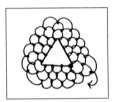

3. Continue working rows of detached buttonhole stitch, decreasing where necessary, until the bead is covered. Insert the thread down the centre of the bead, pulling firmly, and secure at the back of work.

4. Stitch an antique bead through the hole of each blueberry to complete.

Butterfly – FABRIC

The butterfly is a much-loved motif, and has been used to decorate all manner of items, from the borders of illuminated manuscripts to the gloriously embroidered gowns of the sixteenth and seventeenth centuries.

   Because of the various stages of its life cycle, the butterfly symbolised immortality and resurrection. During the period of the Restoration, the butterfly symbolised the rebirth of the monarchy and was a means by which an embroiderer could covertly show loyalty to the Crown.

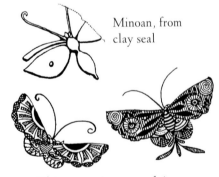

Minoan, from clay seal

Chinese, antique porcelain

MATERIALS REQUIRED

·   Calico (or quilter's muslin), 20 cm x 20 cm (8" x 8")

·   10 cm (4") embroidery hoop

·   Wire: 30 gauge blue or green covered, cut in 12 cm
    (4 3/4") lengths
    28 gauge uncovered

·   Mill Hill Petite Glass Beads 40374 (blue/black)

·   Needles: Crewel 10
    Straw 9
    Large chenille or sharp yarn darner

·   Threads: Blue/green stranded thread in 2 shades – DMC
    924 (dark), 3768 (medium)
    Bronze/black metallic thread – Kreinik Cord 215c
    Red/orange stranded thread – DMC 900
    Ecru stranded thread – DMC ecru
    Brown soft cotton thread – DMC Tapestry Cotton 2609
    Brown stranded thread – DMC 3790
    Tan chenille thread

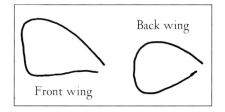

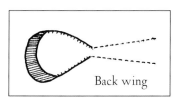

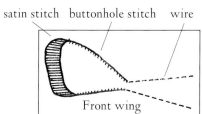

To embroider detached wings

1. Mount the calico into the hoop, and trace one front and
one back wing.

2. With one strand of the dark blue/green thread, couch the
covered wire to the calico around the outlines, then buttonhole over the wire, incorporating the couching stitches. Leave
the tails of wire free at each end.
    Work a row of split backstitch around the inside edge of
the wire. Embroider the ends of the wings with a 3 mm (1/8")
border of satin stitch.

3. Embroider the wings with rows of buttonhole couching, working 'short rows' as required to fill the shape. Buttonhole couching is worked as follows:

(a) Stitch six long stitches, close together, in the medium blue/green stranded thread.

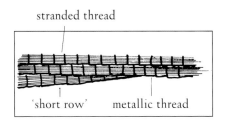

stranded thread

'short row'   metallic thread

(b) Couch these stitches in place with buttonhole stitch, worked through the fabric with one strand of the metallic thread in a straw needle.

When working the back wing, embroider a teardrop shape in the red/orange stranded thread, then work buttonhole couching over this in the metallic thread.

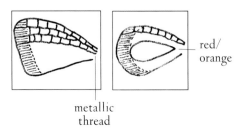

red/ orange

metallic thread

4. Decorate the wings with satin stitch spots (red/orange and ecru) worked with one strand of thread.

To embroider wings on main fabric

1. Trace the wing outlines onto the main fabric. With one strand of the dark blue/green thread, embroider the end of the wings with a border of buttonhole stitches (3 mm, or 1/8", wide and close together – to mirror the detached wings) and the side edges in stem stitch.

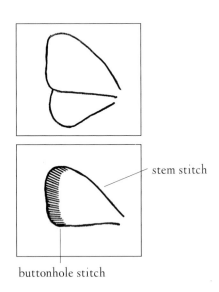

stem stitch

buttonhole stitch

2. Embroider the wings with rows of buttonhole couching to match the detached wings. Decorate the wings as before with satin stitch spots.

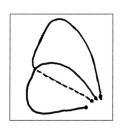

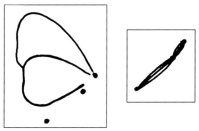

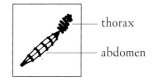

thorax

abdomen

To assemble and complete butterfly

1.   Cut out the detached wings. Using a chenille needle, apply the front wing by inserting the wires to correspond with the wing on the ground. Apply the back wing, overlapping the front wing as shown. Secure the wires to the back of the work and trim.

2.   Mark three dots for the thorax and abdomen, below the applied wings, on the main fabric. Pad the thorax and abdomen by stitching three strands of the soft cotton thread between each dot using a chenille needle.

3.   Using one strand of the brown thread in a tapestry needle, work couching stitches over the padding of the abdomen, then cover the abdomen in raised stem band, entering and leaving through the same two holes.

4.   Embroider the thorax with the chenille thread (in a large chenille needle) by working straight stitches over the padding stitches (stitching towards the wings). Take care not to twist the chenille thread and keep the stitches fairly loose.

5.   Work the head in satin stitch, with one strand of the brown thread. Stitch in a bead for the eye.

6.   With one strand of the metallic thread in a straw needle, work three backstitches for each leg. Embroider three (or six) legs.

7.   Wrap the uncovered wire with metallic thread to form two antennae. The ends can be dipped in nail polish to make a little knob if desired. Using a chenille needle, insert the antennae at the top of the head and secure to the back of the work. Trim the wires.

SMALL BUTTERFLY – FABRIC

MATERIALS REQUIRED

- Calico (or quilter's muslin), 20 cm x 20 cm (8" x 8")

- 10 cm (4") embroidery hoop

- Wire: 30 gauge white covered, cut in 12 cm (4 3/4") lengths

- Needles: Crewel 10
  Chenille 18
  Straw 1 or 3

- Threads: Yellow stranded thread in 2 shades – DMC 743 (medium), 744 (light)
  Variegated metallic machine embroidery thread – Madeira No. 40 astro-3
  Teal stranded thread – DMC 3808
  Chenille thread
  Dark brown stranded thread – DMC 3371

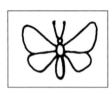

1. Mount the calico into the hoop and trace two front and two back wings.

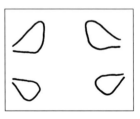

2. Using one strand of the medium yellow thread, couch the wire around the wing outline, leaving the tails of wire free at each end. With the same thread, buttonhole stitch the wire to the calico, incorporating the couching stitches.

3. Pad stitch, then satin stitch the wings with one strand of the pale yellow thread. Work the veins in fly stitches with the metallic thread. Embroider the spots in satin stitch with one strand of the teal thread.

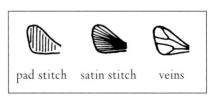

pad stitch   satin stitch   veins

4. Mark dots for the wings and abdomen on the main fabric. Carefully cut out the wings and apply by inserting wires through the dots as shown, using a chenille needle. Secure the wires to the back of the work with tiny stitches. Trim the wires.

5. To form the thorax, cover where the wings join with one stitch of the chenille thread.

6. Work one bullion knot for the abdomen, using eight strands of the brown thread in a straw (or crewel) needle, with as many wraps as necessary. Using the same thread, work a French knot (1 wrap) for the head.

7. Use the metallic thread to embroider the antennae – straight stitches with a French knot at the ends.

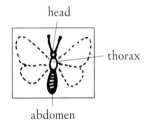

head

thorax

abdomen

BUTTERFLY – NEEDLELACE

MATERIALS REQUIRED

· Pad for working detached buttonhole stitch (see General Instructions)

· Wire: 30 gauge blue or green covered, cut in 12 cm (4 3/4") lengths
28 gauge uncovered

· Mill Hill Petite Glass Beads 40374 (blue/black)

· Needles: Crewel 9
Tapestry 26
Chenille 18

- Threads: Twisted silk thread in 2 colours for the wings –
  Au Ver à Soie Soie Perlée
  Metallic thread or sequins to decorate wings
  Brown soft cotton thread – DMC Tapestry Cotton 2609
  Brown stranded thread – DMC 3709
  Chenille thread
  Bronze/black metallic thread – Kreinik Cord 215c

To embroider detached wings

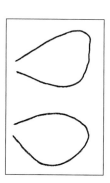

1. Tack a piece of the covered wire to the pad around each wing shape, leaving the ends free.

2. With the twisted silk thread in a tapestry needle, work a row of detached buttonhole stitches inside the wire, leaving a needle-width space between each stitch. Fill the wing shape with rows of detached buttonhole stitch, decreasing when necessary by missing a stitch from the previous row.

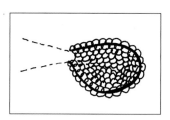

3. To finish the edge of the wing, work a row of detached buttonhole stitches around the outside of the wire between the previous stitches.

4. Remove the wing from the pad and decorate as desired by embroidering over the needlelace with the metallic or stranded thread.

To embroider wings on main fabric

1. Trace the wings onto the main fabric. Work the outline in small backstitches using the twisted silk in a crewel needle.

2. Embroider the wings as for the detached wings, working the first row of detached buttonhole stitch into the backstitches instead of over the wire.

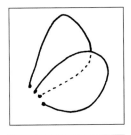

To assemble and complete butterfly

1. Apply the detached wings by inserting wires through the points as shown, using a chenille needle. Make sure the back wing is overlapping the front wing. Secure the wires to the back of the work and trim.

2. Work the head, thorax, abdomen and antennae as for the Fabric Butterfly.

Turkish,
16th century

CARNATION

In the Dianthus genus of plants are found Sweet Williams, cottage pinks and carnations (also known as 'gillyflowers' in the seventeenth century when there were at least 360 named varieties!). The emblem of love and affection, 'carnation' was the name of a colour (pale red or deep blush) in the sixteenth century, as well as a flower. It was originally spelled 'coronation', which reflects the flower's early use in garlands, wreaths and crowns. Carnations added a spicy flavour to ales and wines and were popularly called 'sops in wine' by Elizabethan *bon vivants*.

Rhodian dish
with carnations

Bring hether the Pincke and purple Cullambine,
With Gelliflowers;
Bring Coronations, and Sops-in-wine
Worne of Paramoures:
Strowe me the ground with Daffadowndillies,
And Cowslips, and Kingcups, and loved Lillies:

FROM EDMUND SPENSER, 'A DITTY', 1552–1599

The carnation has been a favourite with designers and needleworkers alike, appearing in many guises, from the stylised motifs found on ceramics and textiles from Turkey and Persia, to the wonderfully ornamental flowers decorating seventeenth- and eighteenth-century embroideries.

MATERIALS REQUIRED

- Mill Hill Petite Glass Beads 42028 (ginger)

- Needles: Crewel 10 and 3
  Tapestry 26
  Sharps 12

- Threads: Yellow stranded thread – Madeira Silk 2307
  Medium green stranded thread – DMC 470
  Green soft cotton thread – DMC Tapestry Cotton 2470

Flower

The carnation is worked in whipped spider web stitch.

1. Trace the carnation base onto the main fabric, then mark 17 dots evenly around the top, as shown.

   With one long strand of the yellow thread in a size 10 crewel needle, work 17 single chain stitches from the top of the base to each dot, thus forming a grid of spokes over which the whipped stitches will be worked. (It is easier to embroider the first five chain stitches in the order as marked, then evenly distribute the remaining 12.)

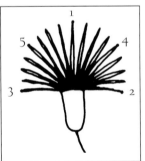

2. To achieve the required dome shape, work the first row of whipped spider web stitch over the three centre spokes, then the centre five, seven, nine and so on, until all 17 spokes have been whipped, working from right to left, and piercing the fabric at the beginning and end of each row.

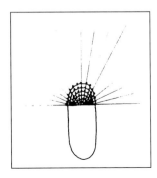

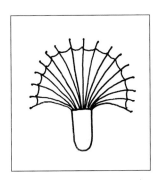

3. Change to a tapestry needle and a long strand of the yellow thread, and work the remainder of the carnation top in whipped spider web stitch, working from right to left, but now sliding the needle between the fabric and the flower to return to the right-hand side to commence the next row. Working the flower in this detached way allows the edges of the petals to be pulled into a gentle curve. Whip the spokes until 3–4 mm (1/8–3/16") from the dots.

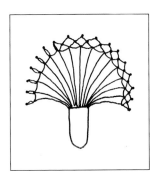

4. The remaining ends of the chain stitches are pulled together to form a diamond pattern at the top of the carnation. Bring the needle up at a point halfway between the two chain stitch ends. Slide the needle under one side of one chain stitch end, then over one side of the other chain stitch end. Insert the needle back through the same point and pull the thread, drawing the two sides of the chain stitch ends together. Continue all around the carnation top, forming a diamond pattern.

   If desired, a French knot can be worked at the top of each chain stitch, over the dot. Stitch a bead into the centre of each diamond.

Carnation base

1. With one strand of the green thread, outline the base in backstitch. Pad the base with four straight stitches worked with the soft cotton thread in the large crewel needle.

2. Using one strand of the green thread, work nine single chain stitches evenly between the whipped spokes at the base of the flower head, then cover the base with satin stitch.

3. Work the stem in whipped chain stitch with two strands of green thread.

CHRISTMAS ROSE – FABRIC

Known as the Christmas rose, *Helleborus niger*, with its waxy white blooms, was introduced to the Southern Alps by the Romans and has been popular with gardeners since medieval times.

MATERIALS REQUIRED

- Calico (or quilter's muslin), 20 cm x 20 cm (8" x 8")

- 10 cm (4") embroidery hoop

- Wire: 30 gauge white covered, cut in 12 cm (4 3/4") lengths

- Mill Hill Petite Glass Beads 42011 (clear gold)

- Needles: Crewel 10
  Straw 9
  Chenille 18

- Threads: White stranded thread – Madeira Silk white
  Pale green stranded thread – DMC 3348
  Yellow stranded thread – DMC 744

1. Mount the calico into the hoop and trace the five petals. Using one strand of the white silk, couch the wire around each petal outline, leaving the tail ends free. Work buttonhole stitch over the wire (and through the calico), incorporating the couching stitches.

2. Work a row of long and short buttonhole stitch inside the petal, next to the wire. Embroider the petal in straight stitches, keeping the stitch direction towards the centre of the

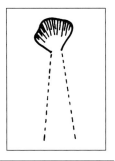

flower. Shade the centre edge of the petal with several straight stitches worked in the pale green thread. Carefully cut out the petals.

3. To apply the detached petals, use a chenille needle to make five holes and insert the petals around the centre outline. The wires for each petal are separate but *do* share a common hole with neighbouring petals. Bend the wires underneath the petal at the back of the work and secure. Trim the wires.

4. Work the centre of the Christmas rose with petite beads and yellow French knots (2 strands), with pale green French knots around the edge. Shape the petals with tweezers or fingers.

COTONEASTER

These hardy shrubs originated in China and the Himalayas. There are over fifty species available with berries ranging in colour from orange, yellow, purple and black to brilliant lacquer-red. They all bear small white rose-flowers in spring.

MATERIALS REQUIRED

- Beads: Mill Hill Glass Pebble Beads 5025 (ruby)
  Mill Hill Petite Glass Beads 42028 (rust)
  4 mm (3/16") glass beads (optional)

- Needles: Tapestry 26

- Threads: Orange stranded thread – DMC 922

With a long strand of the orange thread in a tapestry needle, and holding a 15 cm (6") tail, stitch over a pebble bead until it is covered. Thread on a petite bead and pass the needle through the pebble bead to form another tail. Use the tails of the thread to apply the berry to the main fabric.

To make smaller berries, use the 4 mm glass beads. (Check that they have a large enough hole to accommodate all the thread.)

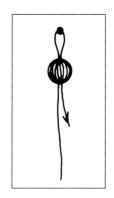

COTTAGE PINK

Cottage pinks are the wild cottage-garden species of the Dianthus genus with a delicious clove scent. They were also known as Sweet Johns, Sweet Williams and London pride (a speckled variety). 'Pink' also meant an exquisitely lovely person, the embodiment of perfection. 'He hath a pretty pinke to his own wedded wife.' (Nicholas Breton, 1602).

Cairo wall tile

MATERIALS REQUIRED

- Needles: Crewel 9 and 3
  Tapestry 26
  Straw 9

- Threads: Dark pink stranded thread – DMC 3712
  Medium green stranded thread – DMC 3347
  Green soft cotton thread – DMC Tapestry Cotton 2347

Petals

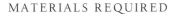

1. The cottage pink is worked in needleweaving. Trace the base onto the main fabric, then mark seven dots evenly around the top, as shown. Using two strands of the dark pink thread in

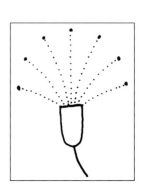

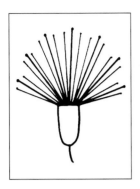

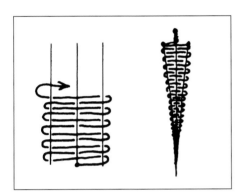

a size 10 crewel needle, work a straight stitch to each dot, then a slightly shorter straight stitch on each side of these seven stitches. Make sure that the straight stitches are well secured.

2. Each of the seven petals of the flower top is worked as follows:

(a) With one long strand of the dark pink thread in a tapestry needle, fill each group of three straight stitches with needleweaving, relaxing the tension gradually towards the top of the petal. When the end of the shorter spokes is reached, wrap the central spoke to the top.

(b) Finish the end of each straight stitch with a French knot (1 wrap) worked with two strands of thread in a straw needle.

Pink base

1. With one strand of the green thread, outline the base in backstitch. Pad the base with four straight stitches worked with the soft cotton thread in the large crewel needle.

2. Using one strand of the green thread, work a single chain stitch into the base of each petal, then cover the base with satin stitch.

3. Work the stem in whipped chain stitch with two strands of thread.

CRICKET

These lively little creatures foretell travel and good news. Embroiderers in the sixteenth and seventeenth centuries had a particular fondness for insects of all kinds. Queen Elizabeth's wardrobe included gowns 'glittering with flies, worms, grasshoppers and spiderwebs'.

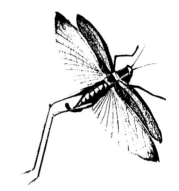

Copper engraving from Dru Drury's *Illustrations of Natural History*, 1770

MATERIALS REQUIRED

- Bronze organza ribbon, 15 cm (6") length, and scrap of paper-backed fusible web

- 8 cm (3") embroidery hoop

- Wire: 28 gauge uncovered, cut in 12 cm (4 3/4") lengths
  30 gauge green covered, cut in 12 cm (4 3/4") lengths
  34 gauge brass, cut in 12 cm (4 3/4") lengths

- Small piece of bronze snakeskin or kid leather

- Tweezers

- Mill Hill Petite Glass Beads 42011 (amber), 40374 (blue/black)

- Needles: Crewel 10 and 3
  Sharps 12
  Large yarn darner

- Threads: Bronze stranded thread in 3 shades – DMC 829 (dark), 831 (medium), 832 (light)
  Bronze soft cotton thread – DMC Tapestry Cotton 2831
  Nylon clear thread

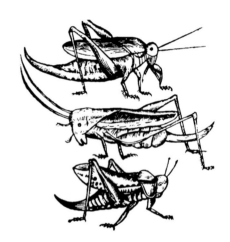

Detached wing

Mount the organza ribbon into the hoop. (This is easier to do if a strip of scrap fabric is stitched to each long side of the ribbon to make it wide enough.) Using one strand of the medium bronze thread in a size 10 crewel needle, overcast the uncovered wire around the wing shape, leaving the ends of the wire free. Cut out the wing carefully.

To embroider cricket body and head

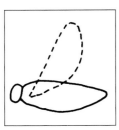

1. Trace the cricket body outline onto the main fabric, indicating the wing position with pins, not pencil. Cut the back wing shape out of the organza ribbon and fuse to the main fabric, using a scrap of paper-backed fusible web.

With one strand of the medium bronze thread, outline the wing, head and body in split backstitch.

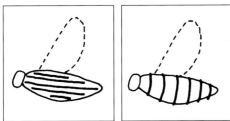

2. Using the soft cotton thread in the large crewel needle, pad the body with straight stitches. With one strand of the medium bronze thread, work couching stitches over the padded body, then cover with raised stem band worked on these couching stitches.

body sheath

3. Cut a piece of snakeskin or leather for the body sheath. Apply with stab stitches along the top of the abdomen, using the nylon thread in a sharps needle.

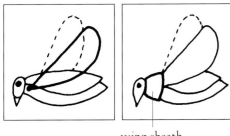

wing sheath

4. Insert the detached wing (using a large yarn darner) and secure. Cut a piece of snakeskin or leather for the wing sheath, making sure it is large enough to cover the body and wing. Apply with stab stitches (with the nylon thread) to the upper and lower edges of the body, hiding the wing 'insertion point'.

5. With one strand of the dark bronze thread, work the head in padded satin stitch including an 'oil-slick' bead for the eye. Work straight stitches at the lower edge of the head for the mouthparts.

Legs and antennae

The legs are made by wrapping the covered wire with one strand of the light-bronze thread, and using the amber beads for joints.

1. For the front and middle legs, bend the wrapped wire with tweezers and insert at the points shown, threading on a bead at the insertion points near the body. Secure at the back of the work with tiny stitches.

2. Work the back leg as shown:

(a) At A, wrap the end of the wire, thread on a bead, then bend the wire over the bead. Keep one end of the thread free to stitch the leg to the body.

(b) At B, with the other end of the thread, wrap the two wires together (making this part of the leg thicker) to C.

(c) At C, thread on a bead for the joint then wrap the remainder of the leg, bend the wire for the 'foot' and insert at a lower point. Secure at the back.

(d) Stitch the top of the leg (A) to the body with the free end of the thread.

3. Insert two pieces of brass wire into the top of the head for antennae. Secure at the back.

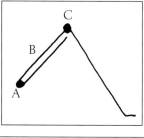

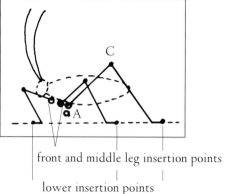

front and middle leg insertion points

lower insertion points

CURRANTS

Currants are among the most beautiful of small fruits and were very popular in the seventeenth century. William Lawson wrote of his garden, with borders on every side 'hanging and dropping with Feberries, Raspberries, Barberries, Currans . . . and Strawberries Red White and Green'.

MATERIALS REQUIRED

- Red currants: Mill Hill Glass Pebble Beads 5025 (ruby)
  Red stranded thread – DMC 75 (variegated) or 321

- Black currants: Mill Hill Glass Pebble Beads 5202 (amethyst)
  Dark purple stranded thread – Au Ver à Soie Soie d'Alger 3326

- White currants: Mill Hill Glass Pebble Beads 5147 (pearl)
  Pale green stranded thread – Au Ver à Soie Soie d'Alger 2131

- Tops of currants: either Mill Hill Antique Glass Beads 3024 (mocha)
  or brown stranded thread – DMC 898

- Needles: Tapestry 26
  Chenille (or sharp yarn darner) 18 or larger

- Green stranded thread for stalks – DMC 937

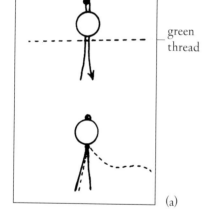

green thread

(a)

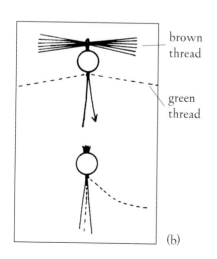

brown thread

green thread

(b)

1. With a long strand of thread in a tapestry needle, stitch through the hole in the pebble bead until covered.

There are two methods to form the top of a currant:

(a) Attach an antique bead and bring the thread through the pebble bead to the base and tie the ends together. Knot the ends over the middle of one strand of the green thread.

(b) To make a tuft, when the pebble bead is covered, attach six strands of the brown thread to the top of the currant by bringing the thread through the pebble bead to the base. Gently pull the six strands into the hole at the top to form a tuft, then tie the ends together and knot over the middle of one strand of green thread. Trim the tuft to the desired length.

2. To form a stalk, wrap both ends of the currant thread and one end of the green thread with the remaining green thread to the length desired. Secure.

3. Thread all the currant stalks into a large needle and apply through one hole. Let the currants hang loosely and at varying lengths. Secure the stalks at the back and trim.

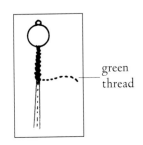

green
thread

DRAGONFLY

Moths, dragonflies, beetles, worms, snails, grasshoppers and flies were not only worked prolifically onto Stuart embroideries, but also borne as motifs on seventeenth-century coat-armour. The dragonfly, with its iridescent body and wing colours that often glisten like jewels in the sunlight, is the most elegant and lovely of these winged creatures.

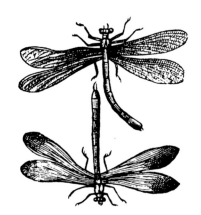

MATERIALS REQUIRED

- 10 cm (4") embroidery hoop

- Wire: 28 gauge uncovered, cut in 12 cm (4 3/4") lengths

- Mill Hill Glass Seed Beads 374 (dark teal)

- Needles: Crewel 10
  Straw 9
  Chenille 18

- Threads: Variegated metallic machine thread – Madeira No. 40 astro-1 or astro-3
  Gold/black metallic thread – Kreinik Cord 205c

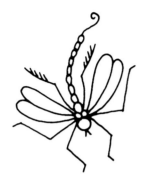

Aqua dragonfly

- Aqua organza ribbon, 15 cm (6") length

- Pearl metal organdie and paper-backed fusible web, 15 cm x 15 cm

- 4 mm (3/16") dark teal glass bead

- Threads: Aqua rayon machine embroidery thread –Madeira Rayon No. 40 col. 1045
  Teal stranded thread – DMC 3808
  Teal soft cotton thread – DMC Tapestry Cotton 2131
  Teal chenille thread

Bronze dragonfly

- Bronze organza ribbon, 15 cm (6") length

- Gold metal organdie and paper-backed fusible web, 15 cm x 15 cm

- 4 mm bronze glass bead

- Threads: Bronze stranded thread – DMC 830 or Madeira Silk 2114
  Bronze soft cotton thread – DMC Tapestry Cotton 2830
  Bronze chenille thread

Dragonfly wings

1. Remove the selvedges of the organza ribbon and fuse to the metal organdie using the paper-backed fusible web. Mount into the embroidery hoop, organza side up.

2. Bend the wire into a wing shape – do not cross the wires at *. Using one strand of either the rayon thread or the stranded thread, overcast the wire to the fabric, starting and

ending at * with a few stitches over both wires. Work four wings the same size.

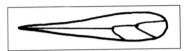

3. Using the variegated metallic thread in a straw needle, work the veins of the dragonfly wings in feather stitch. With sharp scissors, carefully cut around the wings.

Dragonfly abdomen

1. Trace the thorax and abdomen onto the main fabric. Pad the abdomen with two strands of the soft cotton thread, couched in place with one strand of the teal or bronze thread. With the same thread in a tapestry needle, cover the couching in raised stem band, working into the same holes at each end.

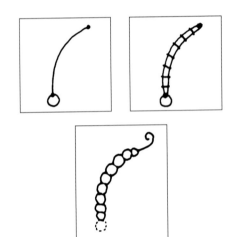

2. Couch again, firmly, over the raised stem band abdomen, placing couching stitches between the previous ones to form segments. Embroider the tail in small backstitches or with a fly stitch.

To apply wings and finish dragonfly

1. Using a chenille needle (or yarn darner), insert all the wings through one hole in the thorax, bend the wires and secure them to the back of the abdomen. Trim the wires. Work the thorax with three straight stitches in chenille thread (use a chenille needle and keep the stitches fairly loose).

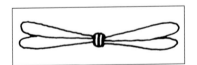

2. Apply a 4 mm bead for the head. To work the eyes, apply two seed beads together (from side to side), with two straight stitches, close to the head. Finish with one stitch between the beads towards the head – this makes the beads sit evenly.

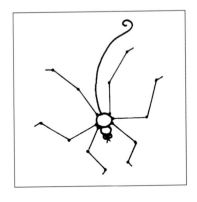

3. With two strands of the metallic thread in a straw needle, work three backstitches for each leg, stitching in the order and direction as shown for best results. Complete by working a fly stitch for the feelers with one strand of the metallic thread.

FENNEL

Fennel has been used in the kitchen since Roman times: the seeds as a spice, the young leaves as a herb, and the stems and bulbs as a vegetable. Fennel flowers are very decorative.

MATERIALS REQUIRED

- Mill Hill Petite Glass Beads 40123 (cream)

- Needles: Crewel 10
  Straw 9
  Sharps 12

- Threads: Medium green stranded thread – DMC 470
  Medium green silk thread – Cifonda Silk 522 or stranded cotton – DMC 470
  Pale yellow/green stranded thread – DMC 3047 or Au Ver à Soie Soie d'Alger 2131
  Pale yellow rayon thread – Madeira Decora 1426

1. Work the stem in chain stitch with one strand of the medium green thread.

2. Using one strand of the medium green silk or cotton, work the flower stalks in straight stitches, of varying lengths, into one central point at the top of the stem.

3. The flower head is formed by applying beads or French knots to the tip of each stalk, and then at random in the spaces in between. Work the French knots in a straw needle, with two strands of thread and two wraps. Make some knots in pale yellow/green thread and the others in pale yellow rayon.

FIG

Figs are not really fruit in the botanical sense. They are flowers, borne on the inside of a balloon-like stem and accessible to the outside world only through a hole at the base.

All the fields are full of figtrees, not small as with us, but as big in the body as some Appel-trees, and they have broad leaves. The fruite hath the forme of a long peare, and a blacke skinne, and a red juyce, being to be sucked like sugar in taste. Neither doe I thinke any fruite to bee more pleasant than this pulled from the tree, I say pulled from the tree, because the drie figges exported, are not in taste comparable thereunto.

FYNES MORYSON, An Itinerary, 1605–17

I must not forget to mention figs, which we have in vast quantities, and which everyone eats raw. We do not have many dried figs in my part of Italy, though they are common in other regions, and are very good indeed, particularly with almonds. Confectioners preserve them whole with peeled almonds in the shape of Dutch cheeses, a delicious sweetmeat, which they keep to eat during Lent.

GIACOMO CASTELVETRO, The Fruit, Herbs and Vegetables of Italy, 1989

MATERIALS REQUIRED

- Calico (or quilter's muslin), 20 cm x 20 cm (8" x 8")

- 10 cm (4") embroidery hoop

- Small amount of stuffing and saté stick

- Mill Hill Petite Glass Beads 42028 (ginger)

- Needles: Crewel 10
  Straw 8
  Sharps 12

- Threads: Plum/purple stranded thread in 2 shades –
  Au Ver à Soie Soie d'Alger 4636 (plum), 3326 (purple)
  Dark brown stranded thread – DMC 3371
  Green stranded thread – DMC 936
  Mid-brown stranded thread – DMC 433

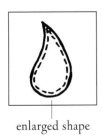

enlarged shape

Small fig

1. Mount the calico into the hoop and trace the slightly enlarged fig shape.

2. Outline the fig in split backstitch with one strand of the plum thread. Embroider the fig in straight stitches, starting at the base with dark brown, then blending in purple and plum to the top. Add a little green at the top of the fig.
    Cut out the embroidered shape, allowing a small turning.

3. Trace the fig shape onto the main fabric. Apply the embroidered fig with small stab stitches, turning in the raw edges as you go and following the pencil outline.
    Leave a small opening at the base of the fig. Insert a small amount of stuffing using the saté stick, then stitch the opening

closed. If necessary, cover the stab stitches with straight stitches, blending the colours.

4. Work a French knot (2 wraps) at the base of fig with two strands of the mid-brown thread in a straw needle.

Large split fig

1. Trace a slightly enlarged fig shape onto the calico. Draw the split as shown.

enlarged shape

2. With one strand of the plum thread, stitch each side of the split in small chain stitches, then cover these stitches with buttonhole stitch. Work the outline in split backstitch. Embroider the fig in straight stitches, starting at the base with dark brown, then blending in purple and plum to the top. Add a little green at the top of the fig.

3. Carefully cut out the split along the edge of the buttonhole stitches. Cut out the embroidered shape, allowing a small turning. Trace the fig shape onto the main fabric. Apply the embroidered fig with small stab stitches, turning in the raw edges as you go and following the pencil outline. (It is important to follow this outline as the embroidered shape is slightly larger to allow for stuffing.) If necessary, cover the stab stitches with straight stitches, blending the colours.

Using the saté stick, pad the sides of the fig through the split with a little stuffing. Stitch the beads into the fig, one at a time, with matching thread, until the shape is filled.

4. Work a French knot (2 wraps) at the base of the fig with two strands of mid-brown thread in a straw needle.

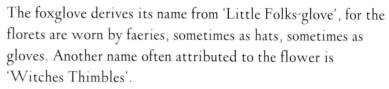

FOXGLOVE

The foxglove derives its name from 'Little Folks-glove', for the florets are worn by faeries, sometimes as hats, sometimes as gloves. Another name often attributed to the flower is 'Witches Thimbles'.

This favourite cottage garden plant was brought into English gardens, from its wild woodland source, in very early times. The foxglove, *Digitalis purpurea*, contains digitalis, a heart stimulant and 'source of wild dark excitement', so 'decline foxglove tea, for it is sinister'!

The tall spires of purple bells, usually with dark purple spots in their throats, are very evocative of high summer. Other colours that occur include white, pink and rose, with or without spots.

MATERIALS REQUIRED

- Calico (or quilter's muslin), 20 cm x 20 cm (8" x 8")

- 10 cm (4") embroidery hoop

- Wire: uncovered, cut in 12 cm (4 3/4") lengths

- Mill Hill Antique Glass Beads 3035 (aqua)

- Needles: Crewel 10
  Chenille 18

- Threads: Blue/green stranded thread in 3 shades – DMC 3768 (dark), 926 (medium), 927 (light)
  Medium green stranded thread – DMC 3346

1. Trace the foxglove outlines onto the main fabric. With one strand of the light blue/green thread, work each lower edge in long and short buttonhole stitch, covering the lower third of the shape.

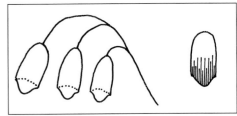

2. Mount the calico into the hoop and trace the upper foxglove outlines, enlarging them slightly at the sides to allow for the raised shape.

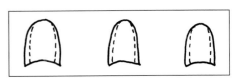

3. Couch, then buttonhole stitch the wire to the calico along the lower edge with the light blue/green thread (leaving the ends of the wire free), then work a row of long and short buttonhole stitch close to the wire.

Using one strand of blue/green thread, embroider the flower in long and short stitches, shading from light to dark. Carefully cut out the flower shape, leaving a small turning around the outside edge and cutting close to the wire at the base. (Do not cut off the wire ends.)

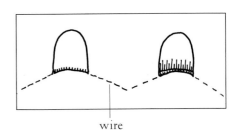

wire

To apply upper foxglove shape to main fabric

1. Insert the wires at the lower points using a chenille needle, and secure to the back of the work.

2. Stab stitch the outside edge in place, following the outline and turning in the raw edges as you go. Cover the stab stitches with straight stitches in blending colours, if required.

3. Using one strand of the green thread, embroider four detached chain stitches at the top of the flower to form the sepals. Use a saté stick to gently raise and shape the upper layer of the foxglove.

4. Complete by stitching six beads into each of the larger two flowers and three into the smallest.

FRUITING IVY

Ivy (*Hedera helix*) is an emblem of friendship, fidelity and affection. The foliage, branches and berries were much used decorative motifs in the art of the ancient Greeks and Romans. The ivy was considered sacred to Bacchus, the god of wine, an association embodied in the bunch of ivy leaves that often identified a Roman tavern.

MATERIALS REQUIRED

- Beads: Mill Hill Glass Pebble Beads 5202 (purple)
  Mill Hill Petite Glass Beads 42028 (rust)

- Needles: Tapestry 26

- Threads: Plum stranded thread – DMC 315 or Au Ver à Soie Soie d'Alger 4636
  Green twisted silk thread – Au Ver à Soie Soie Perlée 274

1. For the berries, thread a long strand of plum thread into a tapestry needle. Holding a 15 cm (6") tail, stitch over a pebble bead until it is covered, thread on a petite bead and bring the needle through the pebble bead to form another tail.

2. The berry cup is worked in raised cup stitch. With the twisted silk thread in a tapestry needle, make a triangle of three backstitches on the main fabric where the ivy berry is to be worked. Make three detached buttonhole stitches into each leg of the triangle to form the first row.

   Work rows of detached buttonhole stitch, increasing where necessary to allow the covered bead to be inserted, using the tails of thread. Secure at the back. Continue working rows of detached buttonhole stitch until the top edge of the bead is reached, decreasing where necessary to produce a 'snug' cup around the bead. Finish by easing the end of the thread between the bead and the cup through to the back.

MINIATURE GLOBE THISTLE

Miniature globe thistles are popular border plants that have spiny spherical flowers much loved by bees. The most common miniature globe thistle has bluish-mauve flowers, but there are light green and white varieties.

MATERIALS REQUIRED

- Mill Hill Petite Glass Beads 42024 (mauve)

- Needles: Crewel 9
  Straw 9
  Sharps 12

- Threads: Mauve stranded thread in 3 shades – Au Ver à Soie Soie d'Alger 3326 (dark), DMC 3740 (medium), 3041 (light)

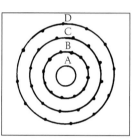

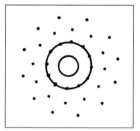

1. Trace all the circles onto tracing paper. Mark 12 dots around circle B and C, and 12 dots, in alternate spaces, around circle D as shown. Transfer circle A, circle B and all sets of 12 dots to the main fabric.

2. Work 24 detached chain stitches evenly around circle B with two strands of the medium mauve thread in a crewel needle.

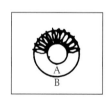

3. Work 12 detached chain stitches evenly around circle C with one strand of the medium mauve thread, making long tie-down stitches of varying lengths into circle D. Using two strands of the same thread in a straw needle, work French knots (2 wraps) at the end of these tie-downs.

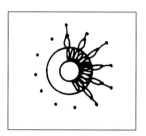

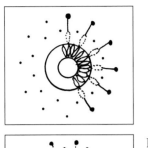

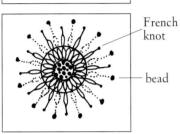

French knot

bead

4. Work 12 detached chain stitches evenly around circle C (between the previous chain stitches) with two strands of the light mauve thread, making long tie-down stitches to the edge of circle D. Stitch a petite bead at the end of each tie-down.

5. Fill centre A with French knots (2 strands, 2 wraps) in a mixture of dark mauve and medium mauve.

GOOSEBERRIES

Gooseberries were perhaps the most popular of the cottagers' berry fruits and were listed in 1862 in the following varieties: RED – Crown Bobs, Warringtons, Roaring Lion, Yellow Beauty, Nutmeg; YELLOW – Goldfinder, Gamecock, Sulphur; GREEN – Early Green Hairy, Adelaide, Favourite.

PETER CUFFLEY, COTTAGE GARDENS IN AUSTRALIA, 1983

Gooseberry – 'So called from the use that have a long time been made of them in the kitchen when green-geese are in season'. A fit dish for women with child, to stay their longings.

SARA MIDDA, IN AND OUT OF THE GARDEN, 1981

MATERIALS REQUIRED

- Felt and paper-backed fusible web, 5 cm x 8 cm (2" x 3")

- Needles: Crewel 10
  Straw 8 and 9

- Threads: Pale green stranded thread – DMC 3047 or 3013
  Fine silk or gold thread for veins – Cifonda Silk 44 or
  Madeira Metallic No. 40 gold 7
  Brown stranded thread – DMC 801

1. Using the paper-backed fusible web, cut three pieces of beige felt to pad the gooseberry – one piece the actual size and two pieces successively smaller.

2. With one strand of the pale green thread, apply the three layers of felt with stab stitches, starting with the smallest layer. Outline the shape with buttonhole stitch around the top layer of felt.

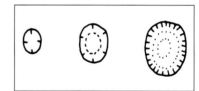

3. Using one strand of the pale green thread, cover the padded shape with satin stitch, covering the buttonhole outline. Concentrate the needle's entry and exit points at each end of the gooseberry to give a rounded shape.

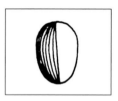

4. With the fine silk or the gold thread in a size 9 straw needle, embroider the veins in feather stitch, starting and ending each row at the same points at the top and the base of the gooseberry.

5. Work a tuft at the top of the gooseberry with a Turkey knot, using three strands of the brown thread in a size 8 straw needle.

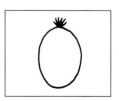

Gothic Vine Capital

Brussels Tapestry, early 16th century

GRAPES AND VINE

Along with the fig and the pomegranate, the grapevine has been a great favourite with designers from time immemorial. In ancient China it took the form of a realistic trail of grapes, leaves and tendrils. In Egypt it appeared in combination with the lotus, ivy and papyrus as an adornment to capitals, and a decoration on tomb ceilings.

The vine in the Brussels tapestry is merely a small piece of the border, six inches wide, of one of those huge 'triumphs' crowded with figures, animals, architecture and everything else which seemed to be so easy of accomplishment in those days. Kings, emperors, gods, saints and heroes march along or ride on gorgeously caparisoned horses or elephants, draperies are shot with colours innumerable, yet even the borders have a wealth of care and invention lavished upon them. The leaves are shaded in every tint of bluish and golden green. The grapes glow with purple, blue and gold, leading on to the next motif, a rose or some other contrasting form equally admirable in colour and design.

HERBERT COLE, HERALDRY, DECORATION AND FLORAL FORMS, 1988

Frieze of chimney piece, English, 17th century

MATERIALS REQUIRED

- Wire: 28 gauge uncovered

- Beads: Mill Hill Frosted Glass Beads 62056 (boysenberry)
  Mill Hill Frosted Glass Beads 60367 (garnet)
  Mill Hill Glass Seed Beads 367 (garnet)

- Needles: Crewel 10
  Large darning

- Thread: Green stranded thread in 2 shades – DMC 937
  (medium), 470 (light)
  Very dark plum stranded thread – Au Ver à Soie Soie
  d'Alger 4636

1. Trace the grape leaf onto the main fabric, then outline in split backstitch using one strand of the medium green thread. Embroider the leaf in long and short stitches, working the veins in the light green thread.

2. To form the grapes, stitch the boysenberry beads onto the leaf, one at a time, with one strand of the dark plum thread. Keep adding beads, on top of each other, until the desired shape is achieved, using a few of the garnet beads for highlights.

3. Make the stems and tendrils by wrapping the uncovered wire with one strand of the medium green stranded thread. For the stems, shape the wrapped wire and insert each end through to the back of the work and secure. To shape the tendrils, wind the wrapped wire around a darning needle to form a small coil. Insert one end through to the back of the grapes and secure.

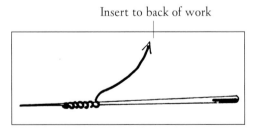

Insert to back of work

HEDGEHOG

A hedgehog makes a sweet-natured friend, and a little cream put out for it on a dish at night will ensure its nightly visits. Country folk call it the Urchin. It is a goodly little beast, and very affectionate. It knows when storms are brewing, and can tell the direction of the wind, building its nest in accordance with its wisdom. It is an animal of good omen.

CLAIRE NAHMAD, GARDEN SPELLS, 1994

MATERIALS REQUIRED

· Brown felt and paper-backed fusible web, 5 cm x 8 cm (2" x 3")

· Mill Hill Petite Glass Beads 42014 (black)

· Needles: Crewel 10
Straw 9

· Threads: Brown stranded thread in 3 shades – DMC 612 (light), 611 (medium), 610 (dark)
Brown fine silk thread in 3 shades – Cifonda Silk 497, 498, 222

felt

1. Trace the hedgehog onto the main fabric. Using the paper-backed fusible web, cut one piece of felt to pad the body and apply to the main fabric with stab stitches.

2. Embroider the hedgehog in long and short stitches, following the direction of 'hair growth' and using one strand

of the light brown thread. The 'spines' are worked in bullion knots (approximately 9 wraps) with one strand of thread in a straw needle. Start at the tail end of the hedgehog and work towards the neck, overlapping the spines as you go. Using all of the colours, work the first layer of bullion knots in the cotton thread, then highlight with finer silk spines on top.

To finish the hedgehog

1. The ear is a curved bullion knot in medium brown.

2. Work the nose in tiny satin stitches in black.

3. The claws are a straight stitch in dark brown.

4. Apply a petite bead for the eye.

HELLEBORE – NEEDLELACE

Hellebores have long been recorded in history and legend. The Winter rose, *Helleborus orientalis*, is native to Greece, and its name reflects the fact that it was reputed to be poisonous – in Greek, *helein* means 'to kill' and *bora* means 'food'. It comes in a sumptuous range of colours from speckled white and apple-green, through to plummy pinks to rich purple-black.

MATERIALS REQUIRED

• Pad for working detached buttonhole stitch (see General Instructions)

• Wire: 30 gauge white covered, cut in 12 cm (4 3/4") lengths

- Needles: Crewel 10
  Tapestry 26
  Straw 9
  Chenille 18

- Threads: White stranded thread – DMC white
  White Au Ver à Soie Soie Gobelins (optional)
  Mauve stranded thread – DMC 316
  Pale green stranded thread – DMC 472
  Yellow stranded thread – DMC 743, 744

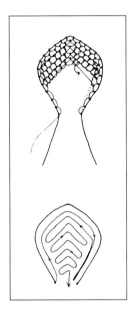

1. *To work detached petals:* Wrap the middle third of the wire with one strand of the white stranded thread. Tack the covered wire to the pad around the petal shape. With one strand of the white thread (or silk) in a tapestry needle, work the petal in detached buttonhole stitch (using method 3, p. 20). Work five petals.

2. Cut the tacking stitches and remove the petal from the pad. Embroider with small stitches in the mauve thread.

3. *To apply detached petals:* Using a chenille needle to make five holes, insert the petals around the centre outline. The wires for each petal are separate but *do* share a common hole with neighbouring petals. Bend the wires underneath the petal at the back of the work and secure with tiny stitches. Trim the wires.

4. The centre of the hellebore is worked in Turkey knots with two strands of the yellow thread (mix the yellows). Cut to the desired shape. With one strand of the pale green thread, work several straight stitches into the petals for shading, then embroider a circle of loose French knots (2 strands, 2 wraps) around the edge of the centre. Shape the petals with tweezers or fingers.

HOVERFLY

Hoverflies may be seen from the spring until late in the autumn. They live in woods, fields, parks, gardens and cemeteries, near water and in dry regions; in fact, hoverflies of some kind are to be found everywhere.

MATERIALS REQUIRED

* Bronze organza ribbon, 15 cm (6") length, and paper-backed fusible web

* Glass beads:
  Assortment of sizes in 'blue/black' colour for the body
  1 x large (3 mm, or 1/8") seed bead
  2 x medium seed beads – Mill Hill Glass Seed Beads 374
  4 x medium cut-glass seed beads
  3 x small seed beads – Mill Hill Petite Glass Beads 40374

  For the eyes
  2 x small beads – Mill Hill Petite Seed Beads 42028 (ginger)

* Needles: Straw 9
  Sharps 12

* Threads: 'Blue/black' metallic thread – Au Ver à Soie Metallic 050
  Nylon clear thread
  Orange rayon machine embroidery thread – Madeira Rayon No. 40 col. 1078
  Gold/black metallic thread – Kreinik Cord 205c

1. Iron the organza ribbon to the paper-backed fusible web. Trace and cut out the wing shape and fuse the ribbon to the main fabric (protect with GLAD Bake).

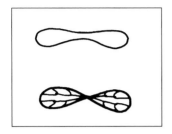

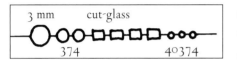

2. Couch one strand of the blue/black metallic thread around the wings with another strand of metallic thread in a straw needle. Work the veins in feather stitch.

3. Using a sharps needle, thread all the blue/black beads onto the nylon thread in the order shown and stitch to the main fabric with one long stitch, positioning the largest bead over the wings (for the thorax). Insert another long stitch through all the beads (for security), then couch between each bead, shaping the body into a curve as you go. (Make sure the original long stitch is longer than the beads to allow for the couching stitches.)

4. Using the orange thread, attach two ginger beads for the eyes, first stitching several times through both beads from side to side, then making one stitch between the beads towards the thorax.

5. Work the legs and feelers in straight stitches with one strand of the gold/black metallic thread.

LADYBIRD

If a ladybird settles upon your flesh or hair, good fortune is prophesied: you will have as many good months as there are spots.

A ladybird with seven spots on its back is a fairy's pet, and you may make three wishes before it flies away.

CLAIRE NAHMAD, GARDEN SPELLS, 1994

To the Ladybird

Bless you, bless you, burnie-bee,
Tell me when my wedding be;
If it be tomorrow day,
Take your wings and fly away.
Fly to the east, fly to the west,
Fly to him I love the best.

The ladybird, a symbol of fire and the sun, offers a great opportunity to introduce a flash of colour into your embroidery. Their wings (elytra) can be black with red or yellow spots, yellow with black spots, orange with black or yellow spots or the familiar red and black, with the number of spots ranging from two to twenty-two.

MATERIALS REQUIRED

- Red cotton (homespun), 20 cm x 20 cm (8" x 8")

- 10 cm (4") embroidery hoop

- Wire: 30 gauge red or orange covered, cut in 18 cm (7") length

- Black felt and paper-backed fusible web, small pieces

- Tweezers

- Mill Hill Glass Seed Beads 2014 (black)

- Needles: Crewel 10
  Large chenille or sharp yarn darner

- Threads: Red or dark orange stranded thread – DMC 817
  or 666 or 900
  Black stranded thread – DMC 310

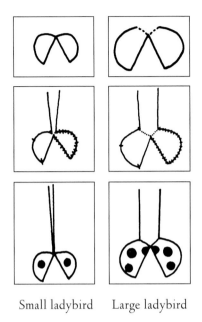

Small ladybird   Large ladybird

wire insertion points

Wings

1. Mount the cotton fabric into the hoop and trace the outline of the wings.

2. With one strand of the red thread, couch, then overcast the wire to the fabric around the outline, leaving the ends of wire free at the tops of the wings.

3. Pad stitch then satin stitch the wings, inside the overcasting.

4. With one strand of the black thread, embroider spots on the wings in satin stitch (across the wing stitches).

Body

1. To pad the ladybird, cut a body shape out of the black felt (using the paper-backed fusible web), and apply to the main fabric with stab stitches.

2. With one strand of black thread, cover the felt with satin stitch, worked from side to side.

To complete the ladybird

1. Cut out the wings and apply by inserting wires through • using a chenille needle. (Larger ladybird wings enter through two holes, small wings through one.) Bend the wires towards the tail of the ladybird and secure at the back of the work with a few stitches. Trim the wires.

2. With one strand of the black thread embroider the head in satin stitch, work the legs and antennae in straight stitches (small ladybird) or chain stitches (large ladybird). Apply the seed beads for the eyes. Gently shape the wings with tweezers.

Tiny ladybird

Embroider tiny ladybirds in padded satin stitch, with the eyes and spots worked in French knots.

ORANGE

The Italian poet Boccaccio (1313–75) gave a vivid description of orange trees in a medieval garden:

> In the midst of the garden a lawn of very fine grass, so green it seemed nearly black, coloured with perhaps a thousand kinds of flowers . . . shut in with very green citrus and orange trees bearing at the same time both ripe fruit and young fruit and flowers so that they pleased the sense of smell as well as charmed the eyes with shade.

MATERIALS REQUIRED

- Canvas or silk mesh (30 threads/inch), 5 cm x 10 cm (2" x 4")

- Calico, 15 cm x 15 cm (6" x 6")

- 10 cm (4") embroidery hoop

- Thin cardboard, small amount of stuffing and saté stick

- Needles: Tapestry 26
  Crewel 10

- Threads: Orange stranded thread in 3 shades – DMC 301 (dark), 3776 (medium), 402 (light)
  Green or brown stranded thread – (optional)

1. Machine stitch the silk mesh to the centre of the calico square, then carefully cut the calico away from behind the mesh. Mount the prepared mesh into the hoop.

2. Following the graph, embroider two orange shapes in tent (continental) stitch using two strands of thread. (The smaller orange is embroidered from the same graph but applied over a smaller template.)

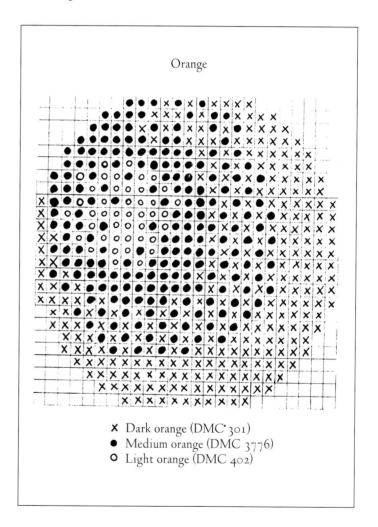

Orange

x Dark orange (DMC 301)
● Medium orange (DMC 3776)
○ Light orange (DMC 402)

Orange outlines

cardboard

3. Cut a cardboard template for each orange, making them 1 mm smaller than the outlines.

Cut out each embroidered orange with a small turning.

Run a gathering thread around the outside edge and insert a small amount of stuffing. Draw up over the cardboard shape and secure.

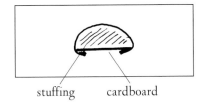

stuffing   cardboard

4. Apply the stuffed orange shapes to the main fabric with invisible stab stitches. When positioning the oranges, make sure that the direction of shading is the same for both.

5. If desired, work a French knot in the green or brown stranded thread near the top of the orange to form a little 'dimple'.

O W L

Because of its nocturnal activity, grave expression and strange haunting call, the owl has long been associated with mystery and magic, occupying a prominent place in mythology and folklore. It is said 'She can tell your future for you if you put your questions to her. One hoot is no, two mean yes'.

The Greeks made the owl sacred to Athena, the goddess of wisdom, and considered it a bird of prophecy – both of evil and good, depending on the circumstances of its appearance.

For heraldic purposes, the owl was used to signify watchfulness, vigilance, prudence and solitude.

Tawny owl: woodcut from
Ulisse Aldrovandi's *Ornithologiae*, 1599

There was an old owl lived in an oak,
The more he heard, the less he spoke;
The less he spoke, the more he heard
O, if men were all like that wise bird.

From *Punch*, vol. 68, 1875

MATERIALS REQUIRED

- Calico (or quilter's muslin), 20 cm x 20 cm (8" x 8")

- 10 cm (4") embroidery hoop

- Small amount of stuffing and saté stick

- Mill Hill Petite Glass Beads 42028 (ginger)

- Needles: Crewel 10
  Sharps 12

- Threads: Brown stranded thread in 3 shades – DMC 3787 (dark), 869 (medium), 3045 (light)
  Beige stranded thread in 2 shades – DMC 3032 (medium), 3033 (light)
  Black stranded thread – DMC 310
  Nylon clear thread

1. Mount the calico into the hoop and trace the slightly enlarged owl head and body. Outline in split backstitch in the medium brown thread.

2. Embroider the owl in straight stitches using one strand of thread and blending the colours as follows: the chest in the three lightest colours, the head in medium shades and the wings in the two darkest shades.
   Work the eyes in buttonhole wheel in the light beige thread, and the beak in straight stitches in black.

3. Cut out the owl, leaving a small turning. Apply to the branch with small stab stitches, turning in the raw edges as you go and leaving a small opening at the top through which to insert the stuffing.

Using the saté stick, stuff lightly, then stitch the opening closed. Make sure the owl is sitting 'straight' on the branch! Cover the stab stitches with straight stitches in blending shades, if required.

Stitch along the neck and wing lines with small stab stitches to 'sculpt' the owl body.

To finish the owl

1. The tail is embroidered in detached chain stitches in varying lengths (in medium and dark shades with one strand of thread).

2. Each 'ear' tuft is two detached chain stitches inside each other (in light and medium shades with one strand of thread).

3. The claws for each leg are two bullion knots worked over the branch (using one strand of black thread).

4. Each eye is a petite bead, applied on its side with three stitches worked in 'invisible' nylon thread. Stitch a French knot, with one strand of black, in the centre of each bead to complete the eyes.

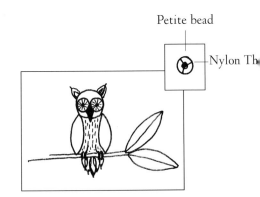

Petite bead

Nylon Th

Pansy

Pansies have long been grown in cottage gardens although originally in a much smaller form, Viola tricolour, known as Johnny-jump-up. Pansies as we know them were developed in the 1830s, and from 1841, show pansies had to meet rigid rules: a nearly perfect circular shape with the lower petals making up nearly one-half of the flower; clear yet deep colour; a well-defined margin and blotches. The eye had to be bright orange and clear-cut, not rayed or ragged. Pansies come in an amazing variety of sizes and colours – blue, yellow, purple, lavender, rust, pink, orange, bronze, white and even black – in single-coloured flowers as well as bicoloured and tricoloured ones. They may or may not have the blotches and rays that give them their 'faces'.

TOLLEY AND MEAD, A POTPOURRI OF PANSIES, 1993

Embroidered satin coverlet, English, early 17th century

There's rosemary, that's for remembrance; pray love,
remember: and there is pansies, that's for thoughts . . .

SHAKESPEARE, HAMLET, ACT 4, SCENE 5, 1601

MATERIALS REQUIRED

- Calico (or quilter's muslin), 20 cm x 20 cm (8" x 8")

- 10 cm (4") embroidery hoop

- Wire: 28 gauge uncovered, cut in 12 cm (4 3/4") lengths

- Needles: Crewel 9 or 10
  Large chenille or sharp yarn darner
  Straw 3

- Threads: Stranded threads for pansies
  Red pansy
  Very dark plum – Au Ver à Soie Soie d'Alger 4636
  Very dark red – Au Ver à Soie Soie d'Alger 2926
  Terracotta – DMC 3830
  Mauve/mustard – Minnamurra Stranded Cotton 110
  Mauve pansy
  Dark mauve – Au Ver à Soie Soie d'Alger 1316
  Mauve/mustard – Minnamurra Stranded Cotton 110
  Yellow thread for 'eye' of pansies – Cifonda Silk 174,
  DMC 742
  Green stranded thread – DMC 3345

Flowers

1. Mount the calico into the hoop and trace the pansy petals.
Number them as shown.

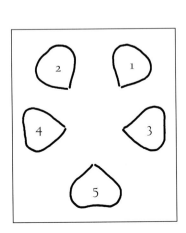

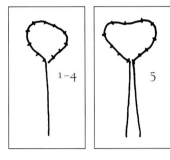

2. Using one strand of thread (*red – 3830, mauve – 1316*), couch the wire around the petal shape. For petals 1 to 4, leave one tail of wire with which to apply the petal. Leave two wire tails for petal 5. With the same thread, buttonhole stitch the wire to the calico, incorporating the couching stitches.

3. Work a row of long and short buttonhole stitch inside the petal, next to the wire, with one strand of thread (*red – 2926, mauve – 1316*).

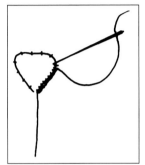

4. Embroider the petal in straight stitches, keeping the stitch direction towards the centre of the pansy (*red – 2926, 4636, mauve – 110*). Embroider the 'blotches' on the pansies (*red – 110, mauve – 110*).

5. Carefully cut out the petals, avoiding the wire. Using a chenille needle, apply the petals to the main fabric, all through one hole and in the order as numbered (petal 5 is applied last). Secure the wires at the back of the work with small stitches into the calico only (it is easier to secure each petal as you go). Trim the wires.

6. Using a straw needle, work a French knot (2 wraps) with six strands of yellow thread (3 silk and 3 cotton) for the eye (centre) of the pansy. (Keep the knot fairly loose.) Carefully shape the petals with tweezers or fingers.

Pansy bud

1. Trace the outline onto the main fabric. Work the lower edge of the outline in long and short buttonhole stitch with one strand of thread. Embroider the bud in straight stitches. (Use colours to match each pansy.)

2. Using two strands of the green thread, work four detached chain stitches at the top of the bud to form sepals.

Peas

Peas are the noblest of vegetables, especially the peas whose pods are good to eat as well. In Roman times peas were often dried, like lentils and chick peas, and were even used for making flour. Later, during the Renaissance, people began to eat them fresh. They were considered 'fit dainties for ladies' in Elizabethan days, as they were brought in 'at a cost' from Holland. Embroidered garments of the day often featured peapods that could be raised to reveal the tiny seed pearls within.

The pod or legume of the pea plant was known in the sixteenth and seventeenth century as a 'peascod', and a playfully dire curse of the day was 'A peascod on you!'.

'Peascod-wooing' – if you find a pod with nine peas in it, lay it on the lintel of the kitchen door. The first man to enter will be your love.

MATERIALS REQUIRED

- Calico (or quilter's muslin), 15 cm x 15 cm (6" x 6")

- 10 cm (4") embroidery hoop

- Wire: 28 gauge uncovered, cut in 12 cm (4 3/4") length

  30 gauge green covered

- Saté stick

- Mill Hill Glass Seed Beads 206 (violet)

- Needles: Crewel 10 and 6
  Chenille 18

- Threads: Green stranded thread in 5 shades – DMC 936, 469, 470, 471, 472
  Green Pearl (5) cotton thread – DMC 469
  White stranded thread

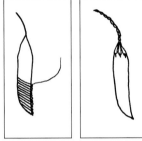

Closed peapod

This is worked in medium/light green thread (470).

1. Trace the outline onto the main fabric and outline in backstitch with one strand of thread. Pad the peapod by working three long stitches with the Pearl thread.

2. With one strand of thread, embroider the peapod with close buttonhole stitches, starting at the lower point of the pod.

3. Work the stems in whipped chain stitch with two strands of the dark green thread (936).

4. Embroider the sepals with single chain stitches in one strand of the light green thread (471).

Open peapods

These are worked in medium green thread (469).

1. Trace the outline onto the main fabric and outline in backstitch with one strand of thread.

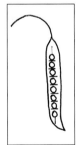

two strands of padding thread

2. Apply the beads with one long stitch down the centre of each pod, then couch between each bead to secure. (Make sure that there are not too many beads – allow for space to work the sepals at the top of the pod.) Pad the peapod sides with two (or three) long stitches of the Pearl thread on each side of the beads.

3. The peapod sides are worked with one strand of thread in buttonhole stitch, over the two (or three) strands of Pearl and through to the back of the work. Use the row of beads as a support for these stitches, which should be slightly raised from the surface. Start at the top of the pod and work in the direction as shown.

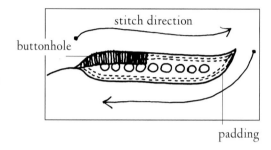

stitch direction

buttonhole

padding

Stitch the sides of the peapod together at the top and the bottom, with tiny stitches, to give the illusion that the peas are bursting the pods.

4. Work the stems in whipped chain stitch with two strands of the dark green thread (936).

5. Embroider the sepals with single chain stitches in one strand of the medium/light green thread (470).

Pea flower

1. Trace the flower outline onto the main fabric. With one strand of the white thread, work the edge of the top petal in long and short buttonhole stitch, keeping the stitch direction towards the centre edge of the petal, then embroider the petal in straight stitches. Work a few straight stitches in the light green (471) for shading.

2. Outline the lower petal in backstitch, pad stitch, then embroider in satin stitch in one strand of the white thread. Work a row of tiny backstitches around the edge of the lower half of the petal, in the very light green thread (472).

3. To work a detached petal, trace the upper petal onto the calico in the hoop. Couch, then buttonhole the uncovered wire around the outside edge with one strand of white thread, then

embroider the petal in straight stitches. Work a few stitches in light green for shading. Carefully cut out the petal.

4. Using a chenille needle to insert the wire, apply the petal to the main fabric at the points as shown, and secure the wires to the back. Work a few more shading stitches along the centre to hide the edge if necessary.

5. Work the flower stems in chain stitch with one strand of the dark green thread.

Pea flower bud

1. Work the bud with straight stitches in one strand of white thread.

2. Embroider the sepals with single chain stitches in one strand of medium/light green thread (470).

Pea tendrils

Wrap the covered wire with one strand of the dark green thread (937), starting at one end. Twist into a coil around a saté stick and apply through to the back of the work using a chenille needle. Stitch to secure.

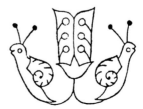

POMEGRANATE

In ancient Greece, the pomegranate was the symbol of Persephone and of the return of life in spring. With its countless seeds, the fruit stood for fertility and the unity in diversity of all creation.

The pomegranate, introduced from Islamic sources, was widely used in European design.

Chesterfield (coat-of-arms)

GILDED POMEGRANATES FOR CHRISTMAS

Cut a small hole in the base of a pomegranate and scoop the seeds out with a teaspoon. Fill the pomegranate with shredded newspaper to absorb moisture, and leave it in a warm place to dry.

When it is dry, spray the top of the pomegranate with gold paint. Lightly sprinkle sugar over the wet paint so that it adheres.

Dutch tile, first half 17th century

Persian

MATERIALS REQUIRED

- Calico (or quilter's muslin), 20 cm x 20 cm (8" x 8")

- 10 cm (4") embroidery hoop

- Mill Hill Glass Seed Beads 165 (pink/red)

- Small amount of stuffing and saté stick

- Needles: Crewel 10

- Threads: Pink/red stranded thread in 3 shades – DMC 350 (dark), 351 (medium), 352 (light)

Renaissance

Whole pomegranate

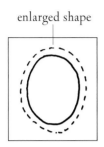

enlarged shape

1. Mount the calico into the hoop and trace the enlarged pomegranate shape. Outline in split stitch, with one strand of the medium red thread. Embroider in long and short stitches with one strand of thread, blending the three shades for a realistic look (lighter in the centre of the fruit).

2. Cut out the shape, allowing a small turning. Finger press.

3. Trace the pomegranate outline onto the main fabric. Apply the embroidered shape with stab stitches, easing the edge to fit the outline and leaving a small opening at the top. Insert the stuffing, then close the opening with stab stitches. If necessary, cover the stab stitches with straight stitches in blending shades.

4. Complete the pomegranate by working three single chain stitches at the top of the fruit, using two strands of thread (1 dark and 1 medium).

Split pomegranate

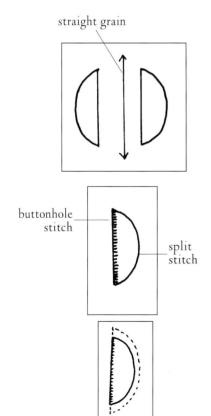

straight grain

buttonhole stitch

split stitch

1. Mount the calico into the hoop and trace the pomegranate shapes, with straight edges on the straight grain of the fabric.
   With one strand of the medium red thread, outline the shapes in split stitch, then work buttonhole stitch over the straight edges. Embroider the shapes in straight stitches using the three shades of thread. Work with one strand and blend the shades for a realistic look – lighter in the centre and darker at the edge.

2. Cut out the shapes close to the buttonhole edge and allowing a small turning around the outer edges. Finger press the turning.

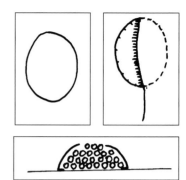

3. Trace the pomegranate outline onto the main fabric. Apply the embroidered shapes with stab stitches, following the outline and turning in the raw edges as you go. (The straight edge should bulge slightly.)

4. Stitch the beads into the pomegranate one at a time, with one strand of thread. Apply the bottom layer of beads first, then gradually fill the shape.

5. Using two strands of thread (1 dark and 1 medium), work three single chain stitches at the end of the fruit. If necessary, cover the stab stitches around the outside edge with straight stitches in blending shades.

POPPY (PAPAVER)

These brightly coloured flowers with tissue-like petals have long been used as decorative motifs. They were depicted as a cultivated plant, along with cornflowers, in an Egyptian tomb painting from about 1000 BC. The treasures buried for three thousand years in Tutankhamun's tomb included a casket with carved ivory panels showing the queen handing Tutankhamun two bouquets containing papyrus, lotus and gilded poppies. The frame of the panel is bordered with scarlet-flowered poppies, cornflowers and mandrake.

   After World War I, the poppy became the symbol of the tragedy of war and of the renewal of life, because poppies bloomed on many French battlefields.

In Flanders Fields

In Flanders fields the poppies blow
Between the crosses, row on row,
That mark our place; and in the sky
The larks, still bravely singing, fly
Scarce heard amid the guns below.

We are the Dead. Short days ago
We lived, felt dawn, saw sunset glow,
Loved and were loved, and now we lie
In Flanders fields.

Take up our quarrel with the foe:
To you from failing hands we throw
The torch; be yours to hold it high.
If ye break faith with us who die
We shall not sleep, though poppies grow
In Flanders fields.

JOHN McCRAE, 1915

MATERIALS REQUIRED

- Pad for working detached buttonhole stitch (see General Instructions)

- Wire: 30 gauge white covered, cut in 12 cm (4 3/4") lengths

- Felt and paper-backed fusible web, 5 cm x 8 cm (2" x 3")

- Needles: Crewel 10 and 6
  Tapestry 26
  Large chenille or sharp yarn darner

- Threads: Yellow stranded thread in 3 shades – DMC 742
  (dark), 743 (medium), 744 (light)
  Green Pearl (8) cotton thread – DMC 469, 472
  Green stranded thread – DMC 469
  Pale green stranded thread – DMC 472

1. *To embroider poppy petals on background:* Trace the poppy onto the main fabric. With one strand of the medium yellow thread, outline the petals in long and short buttonhole stitch. Work the stitches close together in random lengths, keeping the stitch direction towards the centre of the poppy.

Fill in the petals with long and short stitches, grading the colour to light yellow towards the centre. Leave a small gap (1 mm) between the embroidery and centre outline, in which to insert the detached petals.

2. *To work detached poppy petals:* Wrap the middle third of the wire with one strand of the light yellow thread. Tack the wrapped wire to the pad around the petal shape. With one strand of light yellow thread in a tapestry needle, work the petal in detached buttonhole stitch (using method 2, p. 32). changing to medium yellow towards the centre of the petal. Work five petals.

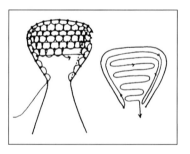

3. *To apply detached petals:* Using a yarn darner to make five holes, insert the petals around the centre outline. The wires for each petal are separate but *do* share a common hole with neighbouring petals. Bend the wires underneath the petal at the back of the work and secure with tiny stitches. Trim the wires.

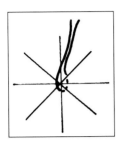

4. *To work centre of poppy*: This is worked in whipped spider web stitch. Using the Pearl thread (469), work four long stitches, crossing each other in the centre, to form a foundation for the whipping. Hold these threads together in the centre with a spare piece of thread. Work a whipped spider web over these foundation stitches with one strand of matching green stranded thread in a tapestry needle, pulling gently on the spare thread as you whip, causing the web to be slightly raised. (When filled, remove the spare thread.)

Embroider French knots (1 wrap), with two strands of the dark yellow thread, in the spaces between the spokes at the edge of the poppy centre.

Poppy seed pod

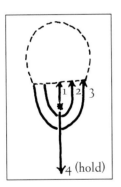

1. Using the paper-backed fusible web, cut two pieces of felt to pad the seed pod, one piece the actual shape of the pod and one slightly smaller. With one strand of the green thread, stab stitch the smaller shape in place, then apply and outline the larger shape with buttonhole stitch. Using the same thread, cover the seed pod with satin stitch, working the stitches closer together at the base to give a realistic shape.

2. The top of the seed pod is worked in whipped spider web stitch. Work three stitches with the Pearl thread (472) to form the five foundation spokes as shown, holding the Pearl thread at point * until the whipping is complete.

With one strand of the pale green stranded thread in a crewel needle, work the pod in whipped spider web stitch, starting at * and inserting the needle through the fabric at the beginning and end of each row. When filled, take the Pearl thread to the back of the work at point * and secure. Work a French knot (1 wrap) over point * with two strands of pale green thread.

ROSE

*The rose holds first place as the most beautiful of flowers,
be it the wild rose, dog rose, briar, the full blown red rose
of a Gothic illuminated initial letter, the delicate little tea roses
of a Chinese vase, or the ivory petals of one on a Japanese
lacquered screen.*

HERBERT COLE, *HERALDRY DECORATION AND FLORAL FORMS*, 1988

In heraldry, the rose is a conventional five-petalled flower, with sepals between the petals, sometimes with an inner circle of five or more petals. The heraldic Tudor rose was a combination of the red rose of Lancaster and white rose of York, symbolising the union of the two royal houses in 1485. The rose remains the royal badge of England.

Tapestry, 15th century

ROSEWATER

If you have access to a large number of rose petals, you can make a sweet-smelling lotion for a refreshing wash. Gather together a couple of kilograms (a pound) of scented rose petals, place them in a saucepan and cover with water. Bring to the boil and simmer for about 10 minutes. Strain and allow the rosewater to cool.

Tudor choir stall,
Henry VII's Chapel,
Westminster

Unlike the modern hybrid, the flower in old shrub roses is fuller blown and many petalled in soft, subtle colourations. They range from white and very pale pink to magentas and deep, deep purples that are almost black. Some are striped with pink or purple or fuchsia — almost as though an artist had coloured them.

Their history is a long one, and even the names — centifolia, gallica, alba, damask (which is thousands of years old and still grows in Bulgaria where attar of roses comes from today), cabbage, musk, china, and moss — evoke a sense of the past. These are the flowers that you often see printed on beautiful old chintzes and embroidered on old samplers. Many garden writers have compared these roses to old textiles and Ms Sackville-West says in her Garden Book that 'some of these traditional roses might well be picked off a Medieval tapestry or a piece of Stuart needlework. Indeed, I think you should approach them as though they were textiles rather than flowers'.

BARBARA MILO OHRBACH, THE SCENTED ROOM, 1986

ROSE – NEEDLELACE

MATERIALS REQUIRED

- Pad for working detached buttonhole stitch (see General Instructions)

- Wire: 30 gauge white covered, cut in 12 cm (4 3/4") lengths

- Needles: Crewel 10
  Tapestry 26
  Large chenille or sharp yarn darner

- Threads: Pink stranded thread in 3 shades – DMC 3713, 761, 760 or 225, 224, 223
  Green stranded thread – DMC 3346
  Yellow stranded thread – DMC 744

1. *To embroider rose petals on background:* Trace the rose onto the main fabric. With one strand of the palest pink thread, outline the petals in long and short buttonhole stitch. Work the stitches close together in random lengths, keeping the stitch direction towards the centre of the rose.

    Fill in the petal with long and short stitches, grading the colours to darkest pink at the centre. Leave a small gap (1 mm) between the embroidery and centre outline, in which to insert the detached petals.

2. *To embroider sepals:* With one strand of the green thread, work three single chain stitches inside each other, at the junction of the petals.

3. *To work detached rose petals:* Wrap the middle third of the wire with one strand of the palest pink thread. Tack a piece of

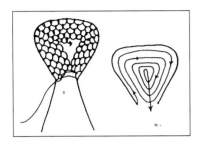

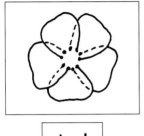

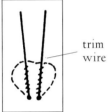

trim
wire

wire to the pad around the petal shape. With one strand of pale pink thread in a tapestry needle, work the petal in detached buttonhole stitch (using method 1, p.31), changing to darker shades towards the centre of the petal. Work five or nine petals.

4. *To apply detached petals:* Using a yarn darner to make the holes, insert the petals around the centre outline. The wires for each petal are inserted separately, and in such a manner as to allow the petals to overlap each other as desired. If applying nine petals, insert the first five petals just outside the centre circle, and the remaining four actually on the centre outline.

  To secure the detached petals, bend the wires underneath each petal at the back of the work and secure with tiny stitches. Trim the wires. (It is easier if each petal is secured before proceeding to the next.)

5. *To work centre of rose:* Embroider the centre of the rose in yellow or green in one of the following ways:

(a) Turkey knots (can be surrounded with French knots); or

(b) French knots (or a mixture of French knots and beads).

6. Bend the petals with tweezers or fingers into the desired shapes.

Two snails from Conrad Gessner's
Icones Animalium, 1560

Snail

Snails are symbols of unhurried patience and deliberation as their use in heraldry indicated: 'For albeit the snaile goeth most slowly, yet in time, she ascendeth the top of the highest tower'.

Snails peering out inquisitively from their shells were particular favourites with sixteenth- and seventeenth-century embroiderers, as they were the ideal shape to fill in spaces in stumpwork caskets and mirror frames.

MATERIALS REQUIRED

- Beige felt, organza and paper-backed fusible web, 5 cm x 8 cm (2" x 3")

- Mill Hill Petite Glass Beads 42028 (ginger)

- Needles: Crewel 10
  Tapestry 26
  Straw 9
  Chenille 18

- Threads: Beige stranded thread – DMC 3023
  Beige soft cotton thread for padding – DMC Tapestry
  Cotton 2647
  Dark beige stranded thread – 3022 (optional)
  Black stranded thread – DMC 310
  Brown (or variegated) stranded thread – Needle Necessities
  Overdyed Stranded 130
  Brown soft cotton thread for padding – DMC Tapestry
  Cotton 2610

Snail body

1. Outline the body in backstitch with one strand of the beige thread.
   Pad with three rows of the beige soft cotton thread, held in place with couching stitches worked over the outline stitches in the beige stranded thread.

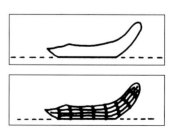

2. Starting at the tail, work raised stem band over the couching stitches using one strand of the beige thread in a tapestry needle. (Commence each row through the same point – the tail – and insert the needle at various points to form a rounded head.) If desired, work alternate rows of the dark beige thread near the top of the body to form stripes.

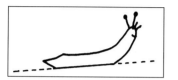

3. With one strand of the beige thread in a straw needle, work four tentacles in bullion knots (7 wraps for large and 5 wraps for small). Stitch a petite bead to the ends of the large bullion knots for eyes. The mouth can be worked with a straight stitch in the black thread.

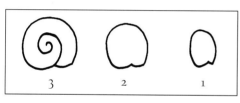

3   2   1

Snail shell

1. Trace the shell and two successively smaller shapes onto the organza, which has been fused to the paper-backed fusible web. Fuse the organza to the felt and cut out the shapes.

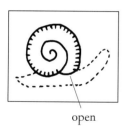

open

2. To pad the shell, stab stitch the first and second layers of felt in place (organza side up) with one strand of the brown thread. Apply the top layer with small buttonhole stitches, leaving an opening in the shell as shown. Make sure all layers are 'sitting' level with the top of the snail body.

3. Using a chenille needle, bring the soft cotton thread through at the middle of the shell and wrap closely with stranded cotton for about 3 mm (1/8"). Twist into a coil to start the shell, then secure. Bring up a second strand of soft cotton thread next to this.

To embroider the shell, buttonhole over both strands of soft cotton and through the felt, following the outline on the organza. Add a third strand of soft cotton at • as the shell widens, and stitch over the head of the buttonhole stitches of the previous coil.

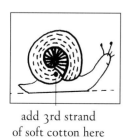

add 3rd strand
of soft cotton here

4. To finish, insert the soft cotton thread under the felt at the open edge and through to the back of the work.

SMALL SNAIL

MATERIALS REQUIRED

- Needles: Chenille 18
  Straw 9

- Threads: Rust soft cotton thread – DMC Tapestry Cotton
  2921
  Rust stranded thread – DMC 920 or 921
  Bronze/black metallic thread – Kreinik Cord 215c
  Beige stranded thread – DMC 3024
  Silver metallic thread – Madeira Metallic No. 40 silver
  (optional)
  Clear nylon thread (optional)

soft cotton   stranded thread

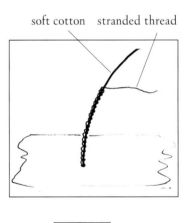

1. Using a chenille needle, bring the soft cotton through to the right side of work and wrap closely with the rust stranded thread for about 2.5 cm (1″).

2. Twist the wrapped thread into a coil, couching in place as you go with the metallic thread in a straw needle. Insert the end of the wrapped thread through to the back of the work and secure.

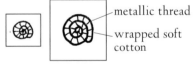

metallic thread
wrapped soft cotton

3. With one strand of the beige thread, work two bullion knots to form the snail body. Work two tentacles with straight stitches and eyes with French knots. (Eyes can be worked in bronze metallic thread if desired.)

A 'snail trail' can be embroidered by couching silver metallic thread in place with nylon clear thread.

S OLDIER-FLY

These two-winged insects with flattened bodies often have striking metallic colourings, and can be found hovering around flowering plants, especially dill and fennel.

MATERIALS REQUIRED

- Aqua or gold organza ribbon, 15 cm (6") length, and paper-backed fusible web

- Mill Hill Petite Glass Beads 40374 (blue/black)

- Threads: Variegated metallic machine thread – Madeira No. 40 astro-1 or astro-3
  Aqua or gold stranded thread – DMC 3765 or 3820
  Gold/black metallic thread – Kreinik Cord 205c

- Needles: Straw 9
  Crewel 10
  Sharps 12

1. Iron the organza ribbon to the paper-backed fusible web. Trace and cut out the wing shape and fuse the ribbon to the main fabric (protect the iron with GLAD Bake). Couch one strand of the variegated metallic thread around the wings with another strand of metallic thread in a straw needle. Work a fly stitch in metallic thread in each wing for veins.

2. With one strand of the aqua or gold thread, work satin stitches over the wings for the thorax. Outline the abdomen in small backstitches, pad stitch, then satin stitch across the body, covering the backstitches. (A rayon thread could be used, resulting in a shiny body.)
   Apply two petite beads for eyes. Embroider the legs in straight stitches with the metallic thread in a straw needle.

SPIDER

Spiders are lucky, so, 'If you wish to live and thrive, let the spider run alive'. In the house, it tells of prosperity and happiness; if it drops down upon you, that is money-luck; if it runs over your clothes, you will soon have beautiful new garments. To catch one and put it in your pocket for a moment (without harming it) is a charm to make your pocket jingle with silver.

CLAIRE NAHMAD, GARDEN SPELLS, 1994

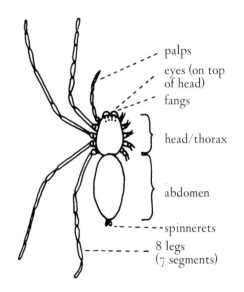

palps
eyes (on top of head)
fangs
head/thorax
abdomen
spinnerets
8 legs
(7 segments)

To make your spider look realistic, it helps to know the parts of a spider's body.

MATERIALS REQUIRED

· Needles: Crewel 10

· Threads: Black stranded thread – Cifonda Silk or DMC 310

1. With one strand of thread, work two padded satin stitch spots for the spider's thorax and abdomen. You can add a spot or stripe to the abdomen with metallic thread if desired. Work two small French knots for the eyes.

2. With one strand of thread, work the legs with straight stitches – either two or three stitches per leg, depending on the size of the spider.

Starting a web

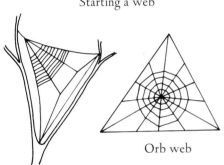

Orb web

The triangle spider builds a web between two twigs

SPIDER WEB

Web-spinning spiders live in caves, grass, shrubs or trees. The spiders that build the most beautiful and complicated of all webs are the orb-weavers. They weave their round webs in open areas, often between tree branches or flower stems. Threads of dry silk extend from an orb web's centre like the spokes of a wheel. Coiling lines of sticky silk connect the spokes, and serve as an insect trap.

MATERIALS REQUIRED

· Mill Hill Petite Beads 40161 (crystal)

· Needles: Straw 9

· Threads: Silver metallic thread – Madeira Metallic No. 40 silver

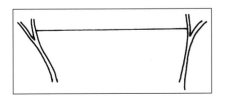
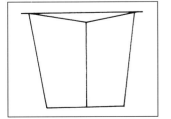

Spinning (or stitching) an orb web

1. A *bridge line*, or thread from which the web hangs, has to be established first.

2. Then establish foundation lines, which limit the area in which the spider spins the round insect trap. These foundation lines can extend over leaves or branches.

3. Work spokes into the web's central point – they look more realistic if they are not perfectly symmetrical.

4. Starting from the centre, work concentric rows of web, taking a tiny stitch through to the back of the work around each spoke. Make sure the rows are fairly close and parallel to each other for the best effect. If desired, a clear petite bead can be threaded on a row to represent a dew drop.

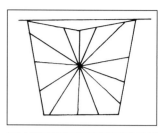

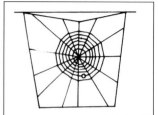

Strawberries

The strawberry's decorative habit of fruiting and flowering at the same time has made it a very popular subject with embroiderers through the ages. A symbol for fertility, the strawberry was gathered from hedgerows and woodlands, and was celebrated for its luscious taste. In medieval times strawberry leaves and berries were used medicinally to cool inflamed wounds and gums, and to clear the face of spots!

Wife unto thy garden and set me a plot
With strawberry rootes of the best to be got;
Such growing abroade among thornes in the wood
Well chosen and picked proove excellent good.

THOMAS TUSSER, c. 1580

MATERIALS REQUIRED

- Red felt and paper-backed fusible web, 5 cm x 8 cm (2" x 3")

- Needles: Crewel 10
  Tapestry 26

- Threads: Red stranded thread – DMC 321
  Red twisted silk thread – Kanagawa Silk 1000 denier col.
  4 or Au Ver à Soie Soie Perlée 779, 664 or 107
  Green stranded thread – DMC 937

1. Using the paper-backed fusible web, cut two pieces of red felt to pad the strawberry, one the actual shape of the strawberry and one slightly smaller.

2. Using one strand of the red thread, stab stitch the smaller shape in place. Apply the larger shape on top with buttonhole stitch. Work a row of small backstitches around the strawberry (close to the felt) in the twisted silk thread.

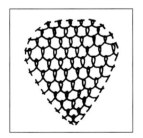

3. Using the twisted silk and a tapestry needle, embroider the strawberry in trellis stitch, working rows in alternate directions to produce the desired texture. Work the first row of trellis stitch into five backstitches at the top of the strawberry. At the end of each row, insert the needle through to the back of the work and bring it up again slightly below, to commence the next row. Increase or decrease stitches at the end of each row if required.

4. With the green thread, work three or four chain stitches at the top of strawberry to form sepals.

STRAWBERRY FLOWER

MATERIALS REQUIRED

- Needles: Crewel 10
  Straw 9

- Threads: White stranded thread
  Green stranded thread – DMC 3347
  Yellow stranded thread – DMC 743

1. With one strand of the white thread work five detached chain stitches to act as padding for the petals.

2. Each petal is embroidered with about eight buttonhole stitches, radiating in a curve from the same central point.

3. With one strand of the green thread, work a chain stitch between each petal.

4. The centre is worked in French knots (two wraps) with one strand of the yellow thread in a straw needle.

THISTLE

The thistle, with its bristly pink or purple flower heads, is the heraldic emblem of Scotland. It became known as the 'guardian thistle' during a fateful night attack upon Stirling Castle in the eighth century, when the attacking Danes stepped barefooted upon thistles growing around the castle and sounded an alarm with their cries of pain.

In medieval times, thistles were cultivated near to cloth and fustian mills as the head (or teasel), with its prickly, hooked spines, was used for carding or straightening out fibres before weaving and for raising the nap on the surface of the woven material. It has been claimed that thistledown was used by unscrupulous upholsterers to stuff cushions and beds. The thistle also seems to have been a popular plant with herbalists. The Roman writer Pliny said that the wild thistle boiled in water 'affects the womb in such a way that the male children are engendered'.

MATERIALS REQUIRED

· Grey felt and paper-backed fusible web, 5 cm x 8 cm (2" x 3")

· Eyebrow brush/comb

· Needles: Crewel 10
  Straw 9

· Threads: Green stranded thread in 2 shades – DMC 3051 (dark), 3053 (light)
  Terracotta stranded thread – DMC 356
  Stranded thread in 3 shades of preferred colour for thistle top:
  Cerise DMC 3607, 718, 917
  Pink/mauve DMC 3727, 316, 3726
  Mauve DMC 3042, 3041, 3740
  Violet DMC 340, 3746, 333

Thistle base

1. Using the paper-backed fusible web, cut three pieces of felt to pad the thistle base, one piece the actual size and two pieces successively smaller. (Pad the thistle bud with only two layers of felt.)

2. Using one strand of the light green thread, apply the three layers of felt with stab stitches, starting with the smallest layer. Outline the shape with buttonhole stitch around the top layer of felt.

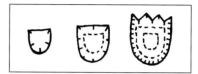

3. With the same thread, cover the thistle base with satin stitch, working the stitches close together at the base to give a realistic shape. (It is easier to start in the centre and work to the sides.)

4. Cover the satin-stitched base with lattice couching. With one strand of the dark green thread, make long, parallel stitches completely over the thistle base to form a lattice. Work small couching stitches (through to the back of the base) to hold the lattice stitches in place, using one strand of the terracotta thread.

Thistle top

1. Draw the outline of the top. Work the top in Turkey knots using two strands of thread in a straw needle. Start with two strands of the darkest shade in the 'valley' of the peaks of the thistle base, and work to the top, gradually changing to the lightest shade. (The number of rows worked depends on how large, or 'wild', you want your thistle head to be!)

2. Cut all the loops of the Turkey knots and comb. Cut the pile to the desired length, combing all the time. The more the pile is combed, the fluffier it becomes. For a really fluffy pile, use a suede brush (with care).

TULIP

From the moment they were brought from Constantinople to
Western Europe in 1554, tulips have attracted the keen
interest of garden enthusiasts and embroiderers alike. In the
sixteenth and seventeenth centuries the phenomenon of
'Tulipmania' occurred, particularly in the Netherlands. During
this period, the most popular tulips were striped in shades of
purple, red or vermilion, standing out sharply against a white
or yellow background. The most expensive tulips ever sold,
the purple-and-white 'Viceroy' and the red-and-white 'Semper
Augustus', fetched several thousand guilders.

   The tulip has much to inspire embroiderers, from the
exotic shape of the parrot tulips with their veined and
marbled petals, to the wonderful, and often surprising, colours
and 'stars' discovered in the tulip's throat.

MATERIALS REQUIRED

· Calico (or quilter's muslin), 20 cm x 20 cm (8" x 8")

· 10 cm (4") embroidery hoop

· Wire: 30 gauge white covered, cut in 12 cm (4 3/4")
  lengths
  28 gauge uncovered, cut in 12 cm lengths

· Needles: Crewel 10 and 9
  Large chenille (or sharp yarn darner)

· Threads: Coral stranded thread in 4 shades – DMC 948,
  754, 352, 351
  Dark brown stranded thread – DMC 3031
  Green stranded thread – DMC 936

1. *To work detached petals:* Mount the calico into the hoop and trace the petal outlines. With one strand of the pale coral thread, couch the covered wire to the calico around the outlines, then buttonhole around the wire, incorporating the couching stitches.

   For side petals, start the wire at *, leaving one wire end with which to apply the petal. For the central petal, leave two ends as shown. Embroider the petals in long and short stitch, shading as desired (either plain or variegated).

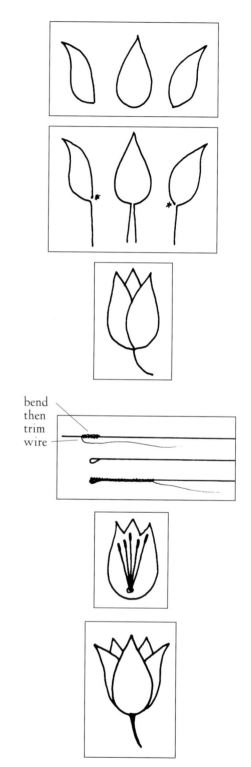

2. Trace the lower petals onto the main fabric and outline with pale coral thread in split backstitch. Embroider as for the detached petals.

3. Make the stamen by wrapping uncovered wire with one strand of the brown thread. To form a 'knob' on the end, wrap a small section of wire, bend this in half, then wrap both wires together for 2–3 mm (1/8"). Trim the short end of the wire, then continue wrapping over the single wire for 2 cm (3/4"). Tie off the thread. Make four or five stamen.

   Using a chenille needle, insert all the stamen through the same hole, over the embroidered petals, and secure to the back of the work.

4. Carefully cut out the detached petals. Using a chenille needle, apply the side petals first, through the same hole, then the central petal slightly below (covering the lower edges of the side petals). Secure at the back of the work, then trim the wires. Shape the petals with tweezers or fingers.

5. Embroider the stem in whipped chain stitch using two strands of the green thread. Work a few extra wraps at the base of the tulip to cover the wire's entry point.

Chapter 4 Field Flowers

Ye field flowers! the gardens eclipse you, 'tis true:
Yet, wildings of nature! I dote upon you,
For ye waft me to summers of old,
When the earth teemed around me with fairy delight,
And when daisies and buttercups gladdened my sight
Like treasures of silver and gold.

THOMAS CAMPBELL FIELD FLOWERS (1774-1844)

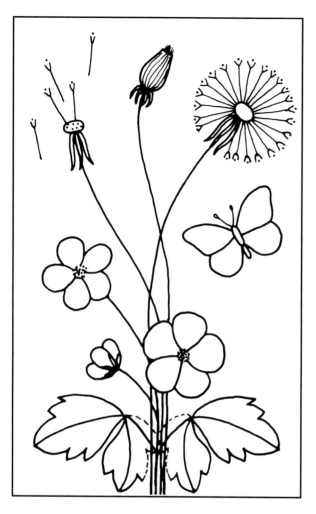

DANDELION AND BUTTERCUPS

Skeleton outline

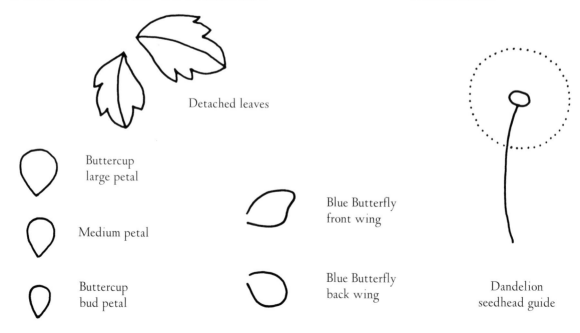

Detached leaves

Buttercup
large petal

Medium petal

Buttercup
bud petal

Blue Butterfly
front wing

Blue Butterfly
back wing

Dandelion
seedhead guide

Dandelion and Buttercups
<u>Plate 1. p. 145</u>

REQUIREMENTS

- Ivory satin (or fabric of choice) — 28 cm x 28 cm (11'' x 11'')

- Calico (or quilter's muslin) for backing —28 cm x 28 cm (11'' x 11'')

- 20 cm or 23 cm (8'' or 9'') embroidery hoop

- 'Blue' butterfly (see p.21)

- Buttercups (see p.14)

- Dandelion (see p.17)

ORDER OF WORK

1. Mount the main fabric and the backing fabric into the embroidery hoop.

2. Trace the skeleton outline onto the main fabric.

3. Buttercup stems.

4. Dandelion stems, bud and seed heads.

5. Butterfly.

6. Buttercups.

7. Detached buttercup leaves.

BUTTERCUPS

Buttercups or gold of the meadow are the gold-cups and cuckoo-buds of Shakespeare:

And cuckoo-buds of yellow hue
Do paint the meadows with delight.

Many children are introduced to the glossy yellow flower by having a blossom held beneath their chin the yellow reflection on the skin indicating that they love butter!

MATERIALS REQUIRED

- Calico (or quilter's muslin) 2 x (20 cm x 20 cm) (8'' x 8'')

- 10 cm (4'') and 15 cm (6'') embroidery hoops

- Wire: Fine flower wire, cut in 12 cm (5'') lengths
  30 gauge green covered, cut in 18 cm (7'') lengths

- Yellow marking pen to colour wire (optional)

- Fine tweezers to shape wire

- Needles: Crewel/embroidery 5-10
  Straw/milliners 3-9
  Chenille 18

- Thread: Dark yellow stranded thread (Cifonda 1116 or DMC 725)
  Medium yellow stranded thread (Cifonda 1115 or DMC 726)
  Pale green stranded thread (DMC 3819)
  Medium green stranded thread (DMC 469)
  Lighter green stranded thread (DMC 470)

Buttercup stems and detached leaves

1.   Work the stems in chain stitch with three strands of mixed green threads (2 x 470, 1 x 469)

2.   Work two pairs of detached leaves, on calico/muslin mounted in a hoop, as follows:
— couch then overcast the green wire down the central vein (470)
— couch then buttonhole the wire around the outside edge (469)
— work the side veins with stem stitch (470)
— embroider the leaf surface in straight stitches (469).

3.   Cut out and apply a pair of leaves to the ends of both leaf stems, using the chenille needle to insert the wires through to the back of the work. Secure then trim the wires.

Buttercup flowers

1.   Mount the calico/muslin into a 15 cm (6'') hoop and trace five large and five medium petals. Colour the flower wire with marking pen if desired. The petals are embroidered with one strand of thread.

2.   Using the dark yellow thread (1116 or 725), couch the wire to the calico around each petal shape leaving two tails of wire at the base of the petal, then stitch the wire to the calico with small, close buttonhole stitches, incorporating the couching stitches and working the buttonhole ridge on the outside edge of the petal.

   Using the same thread, embroider the top third of each petal with a row of long and short buttonhole stitch, worked close together and close to the inside edge of the wire. Keep the stitch direction towards the centre of the buttercup.

   Work the remainder of the petal in straight stitches with medium yellow thread (1115 or 726), keeping the stitch direction towards the centre of the petal.

3.   Using sharp scissors, cut out the petals close to the buttonholed edge, avoiding the wire tails. The buttercup petals are attached to the main fabric by inserting the wire tails

Large petal

Medium petal

through five holes in a circle (very close together) using a large chenille needle. Secure each petal by separating the wires and stitching to the back of the work, then bend the wire back and stitch again. Trim the wires. It is easier to secure each petal before proceeding to the next.

4.   Work the centre of each buttercup with French knots (two strands, one wrap) with a straw needle in pale green thread (3819). Carefully shape the petals with tweezers.

Buttercup bud

1.   To work three detached bud petals, mount calico/muslin into a hoop and trace three bud shapes. With one strand of dark yellow thread (1116 or 725), couch then buttonhole the wire to the calico around the outside edge of each petal. Leave two tails of wire for the centre petal, and one tail for the two side petals.

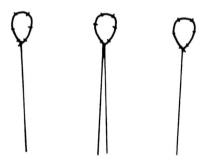

Work long and short buttonhole stitch inside the wire with medium yellow thread (1115 or 726). Add a few straight stitches at the base of the bud petals in pale green (3819).

2.   Embroider two bud petals on the main fabric. Work the top edges of the petals in long and short buttonhole stitch in dark yellow thread (1116 or 725) then the remainder of the petal in straight stitches in medium yellow thread (1115 or 726).

3.   The detached bud petals are applied to the main fabric, at the base of the embroidered petals, by inserting all the wire tails through one hole using a large chenille needle. Apply the two side petals first, then the centre petal. Secure each petal with small stitches at the back of the work.

4.   Carefully shape the bud petals with tweezers then work four sepals with detached chain stitches, (through to the back of the work), with two strands of green thread (470). Take care not to flatten the petals when stitching through them.

Plate 1

DANDELION AND BUTTERCUPS

Plate 2

HONESTY AND HEARTSEASE

Plate 3

ORIENTAL POPPY AND CORNFLOWERS

Plate 4

OWL BROOCH OR BOWL TOP

Plate 5

DEER AND PEAR TREE

DANDELION

The dandelion is a plant that is worth careful observation, for its life history abounds in interesting events. As a typical example of dandelion behaviour, watch the development of one single flower-head. At first the stalk is erect, holding up its bright yellow blossom, rich in nectar, for every insect to see. When the seeds have been fertilised, however, the blossom closes tightly, and the stalk lies down out of the way. Finally, when the seeds are ripe, the stalk rises to the vertical again. It has grown much longer during its retirement, and so is able to hoist its globular mass of silken parachutes high into the air.

RICHARD MORSE, THE BOOK OF WILDFLOWERS

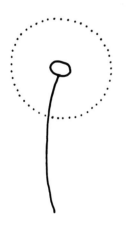

Dandelion
seedhead guide

In the language of flowers, dandelion means oracle, originating from the superstition that if you blow off all the seeds on the seedhead in one breath, your wish will come true. The name dandelion comes from the French *dent-de-lion*, for the jagged leaves resemble the teeth of a lion.

MATERIALS REQUIRED

· Beige felt and paper-backed fusible web 5 cm x 8 cm (3'' x 2'')

· Masking tape

· Tracing paper and silk tacking/basting thread

- Needles: Crewel/embroidery 5-10
  Sharps 10 (or 12 Appliqué)
  Chenille 18
  Tapestry 26

- Thread: Dark mauve/plum stranded (Au Ver à Soie
  d'Alger 4645 or DMC 3726)
  Medium mauve/plum stranded (Au Ver à Soie d'Alger
  4644 or DMC 316)
  Pale mauve/plum stranded (Au Ver à Soie d'Alger 4643 or
  DMC 778)
  Dark khaki green stranded (Au Ver à Soie d'Alger 2134 or
  DMC 3011)
  Medium khaki green stranded (Au Ver à Soie d'Alger
  2132 or DMC 3012)
  Beige fine silk stranded (Cifonda Silk 496)
  Mauve soft cotton thread for padding (DMC Tapestry
  Cotton 2113)

Dandelion stems

The stems are worked in Raised Stem Stitch Band over a
padding of soft cotton thread.

1.   To pad the stem, place one length of soft cotton thread
along the stem line inserting the ends through to the back at
the base and top of this line with the chenille needle.
Temporarily secure the ends of the soft cotton with masking
tape — trim away when the stem is worked.

2.   Couch the padding in place with stitches about 4 mm
(³/₈'') apart using one strand of thread in a crewel needle. To
ensure a rounded raised stem, enter and exit each couching
stitch from the same hole on the traced stem line, taking care
not to pierce the padding thread.

3.   To embroider the stem, cover the padding with four
rows of stem stitch worked over these couching stitches. All
the rows of stem stitch are worked in the same direction, each
row entering and exiting at the same points as the padding
thread. Changing colours where indicated, work with one
strand of thread in a tapestry needle so as not to pierce the
padding thread.

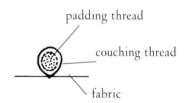

Cross-section of couching

padding thread

couching thread

fabric

Embroider the stems in the following order, working the rows of raised stem stitch in the colours and sequence indicated.

(A) SPENT DANDELION STEM:

— couch in medium green thread (2132 or 3012)

— rows of stem stitch —pale mauve/medium green/medium green/medium green.

(B) CLOSED DANDELION BUD STEM:

— couch in medium mauve/plum thread (4644 or 316)

— rows of stem stitch — dark mauve/medium mauve/medium mauve/pale mauve.

(C) OPEN DANDELION STEM:

(*Worked over all other stems*)

— couch in pale mauve thread (4643 or 778)

— rows of stem stitch — medium mauve/pale mauve/pale mauve/medium green.

Closed dandelion bud

1.   Using the paper-backed fusible web, cut three pieces of felt to pad the bud, one the actual size of the bud and two successively smaller.

2.   With one strand of dark green thread (2134 or 3011), stab stitch the smaller layers in place, then apply and outline the larger shape with buttonhole stitch, leaving the top edge open.

3.   Using the same thread, embroider the felt with rows of chain stitch (not too tight), staggering the starting point of every alternate row to achieve the effect of closed sepals around the bud. To prevent flattening the shape, most stitches are scooped through the top layer of felt, working loose stitches at the open top edge of the bud.

4.   Using two strands of beige silk thread (496) work long loops into the bud through the open top end, securing at the back of the work when necessary. Trim the loops close to the top edge of the bud to give the effect of fluffy seed heads about to burst open.

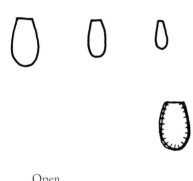

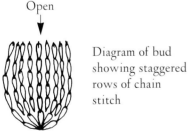

Open

Diagram of bud showing staggered rows of chain stitch

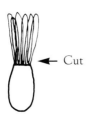

← Cut

5.   Work three small sepals (5 mm or ¼" long) in needleweaving at the base of the bud with one strand of medium green thread in the tapestry needle (See Stitch Glossary).

Open dandelion seedhead

1.   Outline the base in backstitch with one strand of medium green thread (2132 or 3012), then cover with padded satin stitch.

2.   Using the same thread in a tapestry needle, work three long sepals (1 cm or ⅜") in needleweaving under the base.

3.   Cut the seedhead guide out of tracing paper, hold over the stem and base and use as a template to stitch around with small running stitches in silk tacking/basting thread.

4.   Using the tacking/basting as a guide, work long fly stitches around the satin stitched base with one strand of beige silk thread (496) in a sharps needle. Remove the tacking/basting then embroider French knots in the space above each fly stitch.

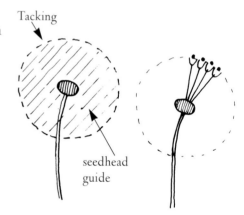

Tacking

seedhead
guide

Spent dandelion seedhead

1.   Outline the base in backstitch with one strand of medium green thread (2132 or 3012), then cover with padded satin stitch.

2.   Using the same thread in a tapestry needle, work three long sepals (1 cm or ⅜") in needleweaving under the base (See Stitch Glossary).

3.   Work small dots (one stitch) with one strand of dark green thread (2134 or 3011).

4.   With one strand of beige silk thread (496), work a long fly stitch with a small split stitch at the base and a French knot at the top for each seedhead. Place them at random — some attached to the base, others scattered.

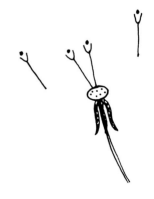

BLUE BUTTERFLY

The butterfly family Lycaenidae is found throughout the world and comprises several thousand small to medium-sized species. Most species have metallic upper side colouring, often shades of blue (the blues) but sometimes coppery orange-red (the coppers). The undersides are typically spotted or streaked in intricate patterns.

MATERIALS REQUIRED:

- Calico (or quilter's muslin) 20 cm x 20 cm (8'' x 8'')

- 10 cm (4'') embroidery hoop

- Wire: 30 gauge white covered or fine flower wire, cut in 12 cm (5'') lengths

- Fine tweezers to shape wire

- Needles: Crewel 10
  Straw 1 and 9
  Chenille 18

- Threads: Medium grey stranded silk (Cifonda 214)
  Pale grey stranded silk (Cifonda 212)
  Pale blue stranded silk (Cifonda 181)
  Copper stranded silk (Cifonda 102)
  Dark grey stranded silk (Madeira 1714)
  Black/multi metallic machine (Madeira Metallic No.40 colour 270)
  Copper metallic machine (Madeira Metallic No.40 colour 28)
  Slate/black metallic (Kreinik Cord 225c)
  Dark blue/brown variegated chenille (hunter/olive colour)

To embroider detached wings

1.   Mount the calico/muslin into the hoop and trace two front and two back wings. The wings are embroidered with one strand of thread using the colours as indicated on the diagrams.

Front wing

Back wing

2.   Couch, then buttonhole the wire to the calico around the wing outline, leaving a tail of wire at each end. Work buttonhole stitch in two colours, as shown, for front wing and one colour for back wing.

3.   Work a row of long buttonhole stitches inside the wire to fill the outer edge of the wing.

4.   Embroider the remainder of the wing with four rows of straight stitches blending into each other (encroaching satin stitch), blending the first row into the long buttonhole stitches.

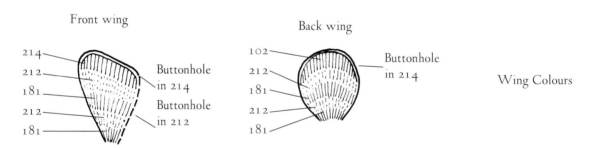

Front wing

214
212
181
212
181

Buttonhole in 214

Buttonhole in 212

Back wing

102
212
181
212
181

Buttonhole in 214

Wing Colours

5.   With one strand of black/multi metallic thread in the small straw needle, work the veins of the wing in fly stitch and buttonhole stitch, using the diagram as a guide. Embroider the spots where desired with one strand of copper metallic thread.

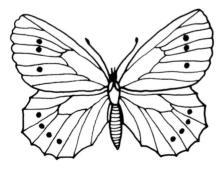

Veins of typical Blue Butterfly

Front wing veins showing direction of stitches

Back wing veins

To assemble and complete butterfly

1.   Make another dot between the two upper dots already marked on the fabric (now three dots for wings) — the lower dot indicates the length of the abdomen. Carefully cut out the wings and apply (back wings first) by inserting the wires through the three upper dots as shown, using the chenille needle. Secure the wires to the back of the work with tiny stitches. Trim the wires.

2.   To form the thorax, cover where the wings join with one stitch of the chenille thread.

3.   Work one bullion knot for the abdomen using eight strands of thread (4 x 214 and 4 x 1714) in the large straw needle, with as many wraps as necessary. Using the same thread, work a French knot (1 wrap) for the head.

4.   To work the antennae, make a small chain stitch for the knob with long tie-down stitch to the head, using the slate/black metallic thread in the small straw needle.

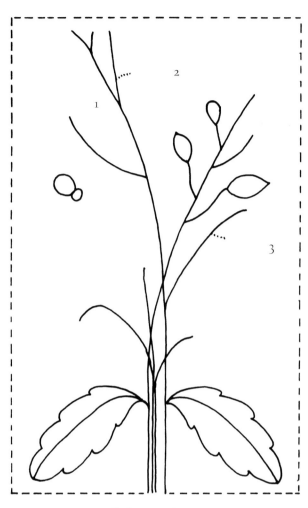

HONESTY AND HEARTSEASE

Skeleton outline

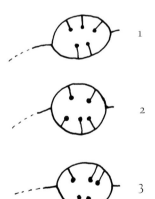

1

2

3

Dried honesty seed cases

Honesty flower petal

Heartsease petals

1 and 2

3 and 4

5

Tiny ladybird

Buff-tailed
bumble bee
wings

Honesty and Heartsease, Plate 2, p. 146

REQUIREMENTS

- Ivory satin (or fabric of choice) — 28 cm x 28 cm (11'' x 11'')

- Calico (or quilter's muslin) for backing — 28 cm x 28 cm (11'' x 11'')

- 20 cm or 22 cm (8'' or 9'') embroidery hoop

- Buff-tailed bumble bee (see p.166)

- Honesty (see p.158)

- Heartsease (see p.162)

- Tiny ladybird (see p.169)

ORDER OF WORK

1. Mount the main fabric and the backing fabric into the embroidery hoop.

2. Trace the skeleton outline onto the main fabric. Do not trace the dotted lines indicating the position of the dried honesty seed cases.

3. Honesty stems, green seed pods and bud.

4. Heartsease stems and surface leaves.

5. Buff-tailed bumble bee.

6. Honesty flowers.

7. Dried honesty seed cases.

8. Heartsease flowers.

9. Detached heartsease leaves and ladybird.

HONESTY

Honesty or Lunaria is named after the moon because its luminescent seed pods reflect the moonlight and in medieval times it was thought to have many occult powers. When the cases of the dried seed pods are removed, the inner membranes glow transparently in the light. This see-through nature of the plant may account for it being called honesty.

MATERIALS REQUIRED

- Honey-coloured sparkle mottled organza — 15 cm x 15 cm (6'' x 6'')

- Cream rayon lining fabric — 15 cm x 15 cm (6'' x 6'')

- Paper-backed fusible web — 15 cm x 15 cm (6'' x 6'')

- Calico (or quilter's muslin) — 20 cm x 20 cm (8'' x 8'')

- 10 cm (4'') embroidery hoop

- Wire: 28 gauge uncovered (cut in 12 cm (5'') lengths)
  Fine flower wire (cut in 12 cm (5'') lengths)

- Purple marking pen to colour flower wire (optional)

- Fine tweezers to shape wire

- Needles: Crewel/embroidery or sharps 5-10
  Sharp yarn darner 14

- Threads: Honey-coloured stranded thread — DMC 738
  Honey-coloured rayon machine thread — Madeira Rayon No.40 colour 1055
  Purple stranded thread — Cifonda 123 or DMC 552

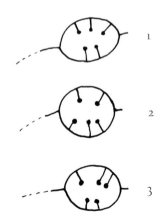

Dried honesty seed cases

Pale yellow stranded thread — DMC 744
Medium green stranded thread — DMC 3346
Light green stranded thread — DMC 3347

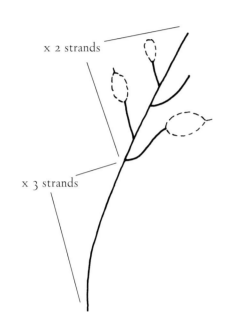

x 2 strands

x 3 strands

Honesty stems and seed pods

1.   The stems are worked in stem stitch with both shades of green in the needle. Start at the base with three strands of thread, then decrease to two strands to make the upper stems thinner.

2.   With one strand of 3347, embroider the seed pods with vertical satin stitches. With one strand of 3346, work the seed pod outline and point in back stitch, then work five or six straight stitches over the satin stitches for seed stalks.

Honesty flowers

1.   Mount the calico/muslin in the hoop and trace seven flower petals. Using one strand of purple thread, couch the flower wire to the fabric around each petal; six petals with one tail of wire, one petal (for the closed flower) with two tails of wire (see diagram). Work buttonhole stitch over the wire (and through the calico), incorporating the couching stitches. Embroider each petal inside the wire in long and short buttonhole stitch and straight stitches. Carefully cut out the petals.

Honesty flower petal

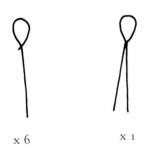

x 6   x 1

2.   *Open honesty flower.* Use a large needle to make four holes, in which to insert the wire tails of four petals, close together around a central point at the end of the stem. Bend the wires underneath each petal and secure to the back of the work with tiny stitches. Trim the wires. Work four small French knots, with two strands of pale yellow thread, to form the centre of the flower. Shape the petals with tweezers.

3.   *Closed honesty flower.* Embroider the edge of the petal on the main fabric with long and short buttonhole stitch then fill with straight stitches. Apply the two side petals by inserting both wires through one hole at the base of the petal on the main fabric, then insert the petal with two wire tails through the same hole and secure all wires to the back of the work with tiny stitches. Carefully embroider three sepals through the detached petals, with single chain stitches in two strands of mixed green threads.

Honesty flower bud

1.   Work the bud at the end of the stem with straight stitches in one strand of purple thread.

2.   Embroider the sepals with single chain stitches in two strands of mixed green threads.

Dried honesty stems

The stems are worked in stem stitch with honey-coloured stranded thread (738). Start at the base with three strands of thread, then decrease to two strands (then one strand) to make the upper stems thinner.

Dried honesty seed cases

1.   Mount the lining fabric in the hoop and trace the seed cases, seed stalks and seeds. Mark the position of the stems and seed case spikes. With one strand of 738, embroider each seed stalk with a straight stitch and the seeds with tiny satin stitch dots (six stitches).

spike

2.   Remove the lining fabric from the hoop, cover with the organza then mount both fabrics together in the hoop, taking care to maintain accurate seed case shapes.

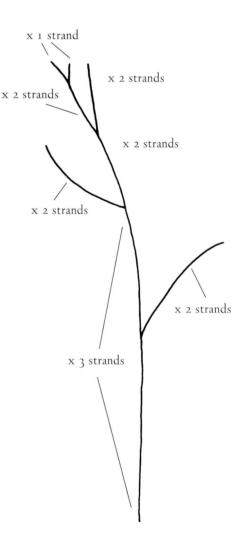

x 1 strand

x 2 strands

x 2 strands

x 2 strands

x 2 strands

x 2 strands

x 3 strands

spike

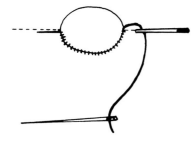

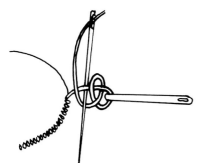

Enlarged detail of spike

3.   Using tweezers, shape the uncovered wire into an oval seed case, bending each wire tail at right angles to the oval to form the stem. The wire is attached to the seed case fabric sandwich with close overcast stitches, using one strand of rayon machine thread. Starting with stitches over both the wire bends at the stem end of the seed case, overcast until halfway around the oval, opposite the position for the seed case spike. Use the same thread to work the spike.

4.   To work a detached picot for the spike, insert another needle through both fabrics at the tip of the spike mark and bring that needle out again on the opposite side of the seed case. Slide the overcasting thread under the eye end of this needle, forming a small loop. Work detached buttonhole stitches over this loop with the overcasting thread, working from the tip of the spike back to the wire edge, thus forming a small buttonholed picot for the spike. Remove the needle, releasing the picot, then continue overcasting the wire to the fabric back to the stem end of the seed case. To form the stem, wrap over both wires (not through the fabric) for about ½ cm (³⁄₈'') with the overcasting thread, finishing with a knot.

5.   Carefully cut out the seed cases and apply to the stems on the main fabric by inserting the wire tails through to the back of the work, using a yarn darner. Secure the wires with tiny stitches. Trim excess wire.

HEARTSEASE

This much loved wild pansy (Viola tricolor), is one of the ancestors of all modern hybrids. Also known as Love-in-Idleness and Johnny-jump-ups, Heartsease grew wild in the fields providing materials for lovers' potions and medical cures, only disappearing from pharmacists' books in 1926.

MATERIALS REQUIRED

- Calico (quilters' muslin) — 2 x (20 cm x 20 cm)

- 15 cm (6'') embroidery hoop

- Wire: Fine flower wire, cut in 12 cm (5'') lengths
  30 gauge green covered, cut in 18 cm (7'') lengths

- Purple and yellow marking pens to colour wire (optional)

- Fine tweezers to shape wire

- Needles: Crewel/embroidery 10
  Chenille 18
  Sharp yarn darner 14

- Threads: Pale yellow stranded thread — DMC 744, 745
  Medium yellow stranded threads — Madeira Silk 113
  and 114
  Dark yellow stranded thread — DMC 741
  Mauve stranded threads — Au Ver à Soie d'Alger 3322
  and 3323
  Dark purple threads — Au Ver à Soie d'Alger 1336 and
  3336
  Dark purple fine silk machine thread — Silk Thread 50
  colour 24

Medium green thread — DMC 3346
Dark green thread — DMC 3345

Heartsease stems and leaves

1. Work the stems, in the order as shown on diagram, in chain stitch with two strands of 3345.

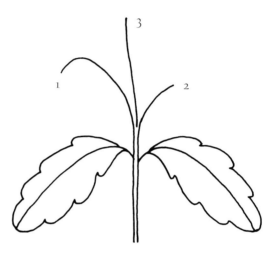

2. Embroider the leaves on the main fabric, with one strand of thread, as follows:
— central vein in chain stitch (3346)
— leaf surface in padded buttonhole stitch (3345)
— side veins with straight stitches (3346).

3. Work the detached leaves, on calico/muslin mounted in a hoop, as follows:
— couch then overcast the green wire down the central vein (3346)
— couch then buttonhole the wire around the outside edge (3345)
— embroider the leaf surface, inside the wire, in padded satin stitch (3345)
— work the veins with straight stitches (3346).

If desired, work a tiny ladybird with detached wings (see page 169) on the surface of the right hand leaf before you remove the detached leaves from the hoop. Carefully cut out the leaves.

Apply the detached leaves over the surface leaves, by inserting the wire tails through to the back of the work, using a yarn darner. Secure wires with tiny stitches then trim.

Heartsease flowers

1.   Mount the calico into the embroidery hoop and trace five petals for each heartsease. Number them from 1 to 5 as shown in diagram. The petals are embroidered with one strand of thread using the colours as indicated on the diagrams on page 33. Colour the flower wire with marking pen if desired.

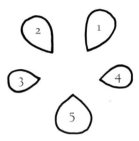

2.   Embroider the heartsease petals as follows:

(a) Starting at the base of the petal, couch the wire to the calico around the petal shape. For petals 1 to 4, leave one tail of wire with which to apply the petal. Leave two tails of wire for petal 5. Using the same thread, stitch the wire to the calico with small, close buttonhole stitches, incorporating the couching stitches and working the buttonhole ridge on the outside edge of the petal.

(b) The top third of each petal is covered by a row of long and short buttonhole stitches, worked close together and close to the inside edge of the wire. Keep the stitch direction towards the centre of the heartsease.

(c) Embroider the petal in straight stitches, keeping the stitch direction towards the centre of the heartsease.

(d) Embroider the base of the petal in straight stitches, then work purple rays with fine Silk Thread 50.

2.   Using sharp scissors, cut out the petals close to the buttonholed edge, avoiding the wire tails. The heartsease petals are attached to the main fabric by inserting the wire tails one at a time, through the same hole, using a large chenille needle. Apply the petals in the order as numbered (petal 5 is applied last), securing the wire tails with small stitches to the back of the work. It is easier to secure each petal before proceeding to the next. Trim the wires.

3. Work the centre of each heartsease with a French knot (one soft wrap) using the chenille needle and 6 strands of dark yellow thread (741). Carefully shape the petals with eyebrow tweezers or fingers.

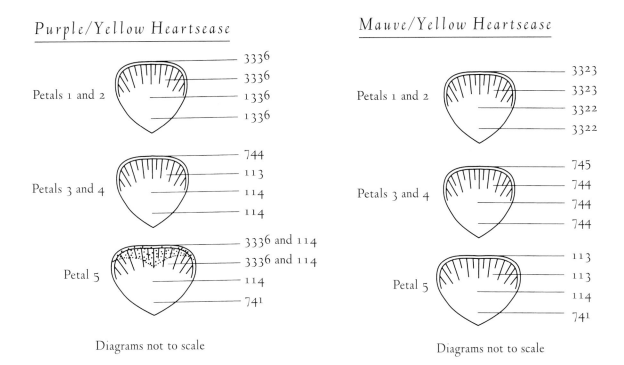

Purple/Yellow Heartsease

Petals 1 and 2
— 3336
— 3336
— 1336
— 1336

Petals 3 and 4
— 744
— 113
— 114
— 114

Petal 5
— 3336 and 114
— 3336 and 114
— 114
— 741

Diagrams not to scale

Mauve/Yellow Heartsease

Petals 1 and 2
— 3323
— 3323
— 3322
— 3322

Petals 3 and 4
— 745
— 744
— 744
— 744

Petal 5
— 113
— 113
— 114
— 741

Diagrams not to scale

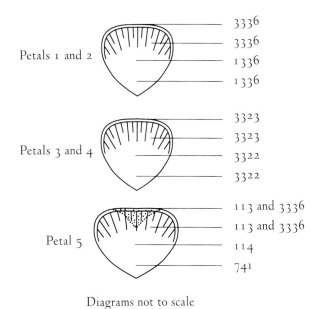

Purple/Mauve/Yellow Heartsease

Petals 1 and 2
— 3336
— 3336
— 1336
— 1336

Petals 3 and 4
— 3323
— 3323
— 3322
— 3322

Petal 5
— 113 and 3336
— 113 and 3336
— 114
— 741

Diagrams not to scale

BUFF-TAILED BUMBLE BEE

The Bombus terristris is very common in woods and gardens where they pollinate a great many plants, in particular cranberries, raspberries, sage, thistles and fruit trees. The queens emerge from hibernation at the beginning of spring to look for a suitable site for a nest; their search is accompanied by a deep buzzing. This species lives mostly in holes (often an abandoned mouse nest) as deep as 1 m (3 ft) in the ground, which the female bee lines with pieces of dry grass and leaves.

MATERIALS REQUIRED

- Wing fabric (cream crystal organza) — 15 cm x 15 cm (6'' x 6'')

- Cream nylon organza — 15 cm x 15 cm (6'' x 6'')

- Paper-backed fusible web — 15 cm x 15 cm (6'' x 6'')

- 10 cm (4'') embroidery hoop

- Wire: 28 gauge uncovered, cut in 12 cm (5'') lengths

- Fine tweezers to shape wire

- Eyebrow brush/comb

- Mill Hill Glass Seed Beads 374 (blue/black)

- Needles: Crewel/embroidery or sharps 10
  Straw/milliners 9
  Sharp yarn darner 14

Buff-tailed
bumble bee
wings

Threads: Dark brown/grey stranded thread — DMC 844
Copper stranded thread — DMC 921
Buff stranded thread — DMC 3033
Cream rayon machine thread — Madeira Rayon No.40 colour 1082
Gold metallic thread — Madeira Metallic No.40 colour gold 3
Bronze/black metallic thread — Kreinik Cord 215c

Thorax and abdomen

1.   Trace bee thorax and abdomen on to satin and outline with small back stitches with one strand of buff thread.

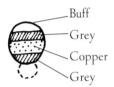

2.   Work the abdomen in Turkey knots using 2 strands of thread in a straw needle. Starting at the thorax end of the abdomen, aim to stitch 2 rows of Turkey knots in grey; 3 rows in copper; 2 rows in grey and 3 rows of buff for the tail. The number of rows may vary — it depends on the size of your stitches. The Turkey knots should pierce the back stitches but not protrude outside them.

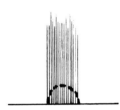

3.   Cut the loops between the knots and comb the threads upwards. Cut the threads in a curved shape, to form a velvety mound.

Wings

1.   Fuse the wing fabric to the nylon organza backing (one layer on the bias/cross grain if desired), using paper-backed fusible web, and mount in the hoop.

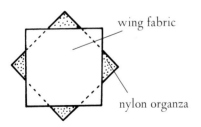

2.   Bend the wires into wing shapes, two large and two small, using the diagrams as a guide. Do not cross the wires at
*.

3.   Using one strand of rayon thread in a crewel or sharps needle, attach the wire to the fabric with small, close over-casting stitches, starting and ending at * with a few stitches over both wires. Work two large and two small wings, making sure that you have a right and a left side wing for each size. With one strand of gold thread in the straw needle, work a fly stitch in each wing for veins.

4.   With sharp scissors, carefully cut around the wings.

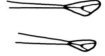

To apply wings and finish bee

1.   Using the yarn darner, insert two wings on each side of the thorax (they will be very close together within the stitched outline). Bend the wires to the sides (under the wings) and stitch to the muslin backing with tiny stitches. Trim the wing wires after the thorax has been stitched. Using two strands of thread, fill the thorax with Turkey knots, all in grey except for three knots in copper at the head end. Cut the Turkey knots to form a velvety mound.

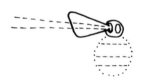

2.   To form the head/eyes, stitch two beads together (from side to side) close to the thorax. Finish with one stitch between the beads towards the thorax — this makes the beads sit evenly to form the head.

3.   With two strands of bronze metallic thread in the straw needle, work three back stitches for each leg. Complete by working a fly stitch for the mouth parts, with one strand of metallic thread.

TINY LADYBIRD

Ladybird, ladybird! Fly away home.
Your house is on fire.
Your children do roam.

This little rhyme has interesting origins. It started in England where the hop vines are burned after harvesting is over. These vines were usually covered with aphids and young ladybirds that were feeding on the aphids. When the hop vines were burning these small spotted beetles would take to wing and the larvae would crawl rapidly away from their homes that were now in flames.

MATERIALS REQUIRED

- Red cotton (homespun) — 20cm x 20 cm (8'' x 8'')

- 10 cm (4'') embroidery hoop

- Wire: Fine flower wire, 18 cm (7'') length

- Red marking pen to colour wire if desired

- Fine tweezers to shape wire

- Mill Hill Petite Glass Beads — 42014 (black)

- Threads: Red stranded thread (Madeira Silk 210 or DMC 349)
  Black stranded thread (Madeira Silk or DMC 310)

- Needles: Crewel/embroidery 10
  Sharps 12
  Sharp yarn darner 14

tiny ladybird

Ladybird wings

1.   Mount the red fabric into the hoop and trace the outline of the wings.

2.   With one strand of the red thread, couch, then overcast the wire to the fabric around the outline, leaving the ends of wire free at the top of the wings.

3.   Pad stitch then satin stitch the wings, inside the overcasting.

4.   With one strand of black thread, embroider a satin stitch spot on each wing.

Diagrams not to scale

Ladybird body

With one strand of black thread, work the ladybird body in padded satin stitch, either on to the detached leaf surface or on to the background fabric.

To complete the ladybird

1.   Cut out the wings and apply by inserting both wires through • using a yarn darner. Bend the wires towards the tail of the ladybird and secure at the back of the leaf (or background fabric) with a few stitches. Trim the wires.

2.   With one strand of the black thread embroider the head in satin stitch, work the legs and antennae in straight stitches (small ladybird) or chain stitches (large ladybird). Apply the seed beads for the eyes. Gently shape the wings with tweezers.

Oriental Poppy and Cornflowers

Plate 3. p. 147

REQUIREMENTS

- Ivory satin (or fabric of choice) — 28 cm x 28 cm (11'' x 11'')

- Calico (or quilter's muslin) for backing — 28 cm x 28 cm (11'' x 11'')

- 20 cm or 23 cm (8'' or 9'') embroidery hoop

- Caterpillar (see p.183)

- Cornflowers (see p.178)

- Damselfly (see p.180)

- White Oriental Poppy (see p.173)

- Spider and Web (see p.130)

ORDER OF WORK

1.   Mount the main fabric and the backing fabric into the embroidery hoop.

2.   Trace the skeleton outline onto the main fabric.

3.   Poppy stems and surface leaves.

4.   Poppy bud and seed pod.

5.   Cornflower stems and leaves.

6.   Cornflowers.

7.   Caterpillar.

8.   Spider and web.

9.   Poppy flower.

10.   Damselfly.

11.   Detached poppy leaves.

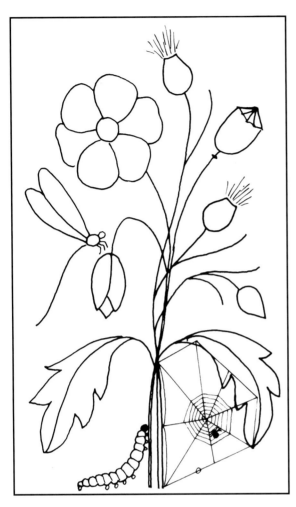

ORIENTAL POPPY AND
CORNFLOWERS

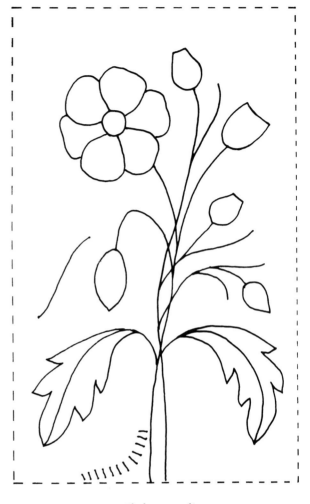

Skeleton outline

Detached poppy petal

Damselfly wings
templates

Upper wing

Poppy bud sheath

Lower wing

White Oriental Poppy (Perry's White)

Showiest of the poppy genus are the many hybrids of Papaver orientale, the gigantic Oriental Poppy from Armenia. These enormous blooms shrug away their hairy sepals to unfold wrinkled crepe-like petals which may take days to reach their full diameter of up to 30 cm (12'') as a silken cup, brimming with purple-black stamens that protect the exotic seed capsule. The cultivar 'Perry's White' was developed in Britain by Amos Perry in 1913.

MATERIALS REQUIRED

- Calico (or quilter's muslin) — 3 x (20 cm x 20 cm) (8'' x 8'')

- 10 cm (4'') embroidery hoop

- Wire: Fine flower wire, cut into 12 cm (5'') lengths 30 gauge green covered, cut in 18 cm (7'') lengths

- Fine tweezers to shape the wire

- Grey felt and paper-backed fusible web — 5 cm x 8 cm (3'' x 2'')

- White felt and paper-backed fusible web — 5 cm x 8 cm (3'' x 2'')

- Needles: Crewel/embroidery 5-10 Straw/milliners 3-9

Tapestry 26
Chenille 18 or sharp yarn darner

- Thread: Petals — White stranded (Madeira Silk white or DMC white)
Deep pink stranded (Au Ver à Soie d'Alger 3024 or DMC 3350)
Dark purple or black stranded (Au Ver à Soie d'Alger 3326 or DMC 310)
Centre — Dark plum stranded (Au Ver à Soie d'Alger 4636 or DMC 3802)
Green Pearl (8) thread (DMC 472)
Stems — Dark green stranded (DMC 3345)
Leaves — Mid and light green stranded (DMC 3346 and 3347)
Seed pod top — Pale green stranded (DMC 472)

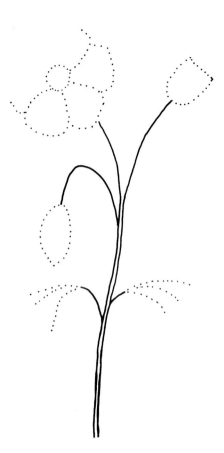

Oriental poppy stems and leaves

1.　The poppy stems are worked in stem stitch using two strands of dark green thread (3345). Starting at the base with two rows of stem stitch side by side (only one line is drawn on the skeleton outline) — work one row to the flower and one to the seed pod. Then work the stems to the poppy bud and to the leaves as shown on the diagram.

2.　Embroider the leaves on the main fabric with one strand of thread as follows:
— central vein in chain stitch (3347)
— leaf surface in rows of stem stitch (3346), starting at the base and working to edge points of leaf as shown.

3.　Work the detached leaves, on calico/muslin mounted in a hoop, as follows:
— couch then overcast the green wire down the central vein (3347)
— couch then buttonhole the wire around the outside edge (3346)
— work split back stitch on either side of the central vein and inside the wire edge to provide a foundation into which the leaf surface can be stitched.

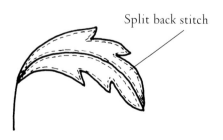

Split back stitch

— embroider the leaf surface, inside the wire, in rows of stem stitch (3346), as for the leaf on the main fabric.

Oriental poppy flower

1.   With one strand of white thread, embroider the outside edge of the poppy petals on the main fabric in long and short buttonhole stitch (work the stitches close together, keeping the stitch direction towards the centre of the poppy). Embroider the petals in white with long and short stitches, leaving a space for the blotch at the base. Work the blotch in deep pink with a dark purple edge. Leave a small gap (1mm) between the embroidery and the centre outline, in which to insert the detached petals.

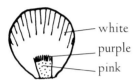

white
purple
pink

2.   To work the detached poppy petals, mount calico/muslin into a hoop and trace six petal outlines (they are easier to work if the outside edge of the petal points towards the edge of the hoop). With one strand of white thread, couch then buttonhole the flower wire around outside edge of the petal, leaving two tails of wire. Work a row of long and short buttonhole stitch inside the petal, close to the wire (work stitches close together, keeping the stitch direction towards the centre of the poppy). Embroider each petal and the blotches as for the petals on the main fabric.

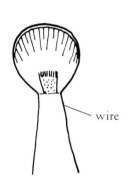

wire

3.   Carefully cut out the detached petals and apply to the main fabric, inserting the wires from each petal through two holes, using the chenille needle. As poppy petals occur in pairs, apply the petals, two at a time, opposite each other around the centre outline in the order indicated on the diagram. Bend the wire underneath each petal at the back of the work and secure with tiny stitches. Trim wire.

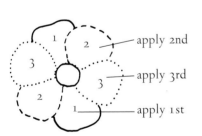

apply 2nd
apply 3rd
apply 1st

4.   The centre of the poppy is worked in whipped spider web stitch (p. 389). Using the pearl thread (472), work four long stitches, crossing each other in the centre and extending into the petals, to form a foundation (spokes) for the whipping. Hold these threads together in the centre with a spare piece of thread. Work a whipped spider web over these foundation stitches with one strand of dark plum thread in the

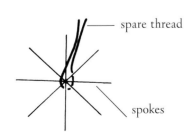

spare thread
spokes

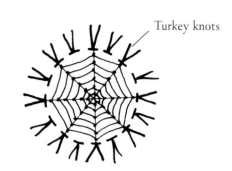

Turkey knots

tapestry needle, pulling gently on the spare thread as you whip, causing the web to be slightly raised. When whipping is complete, remove the spare thread revealing the small green centre point. With two strands of dark purple or black thread (or one of each), work sixteen Turkey knots around the whipped centre for stamen (one knot at the end of each spoke and one in between), then cut to the desired length. Shape the petals with tweezers.

Oriental poppy seed pod

1.   Using paper-backed fusible web, cut three pieces of grey felt to pad the seed pod, one the actual shape of the pod and two successively smaller. With one strand of green (3347) thread, stab stitch the smaller shapes in place, then apply and outline the larger shape with buttonhole stitch. Using the same thread, cover the pod with satin stitch, working the stitches closer together at the base to give a realistic shape.

2.   The top of the pod is worked in whipped spider web stitch. Work three stitches with the pearl thread (472) to form the five foundation spokes into the satin stitched base as shown, holding the pearl thread at point * until the whip-ping is complete. With one strand of pale green (472) strand-ed thread in a crewel needle, work the pod in whipped spider web stitch, starting at * and inserting the needle through the fabric at the beginning and end of each row. When filled, take the pearl thread to the back of the work at point * and secure. Work a French knot over point * with pale green thread if desired.

3.   To form a ridge at the base of the pod, work a bullion knot with one strand of green (3347) thread in a straw needle.

Oriental poppy bud

1.   Using paper-backed fusible web, cut three pieces of white felt to pad the bud, one the actual shape of the bud and two slightly smaller. With one strand of white thread, stab stitch the smaller shapes in place, then apply and outline the

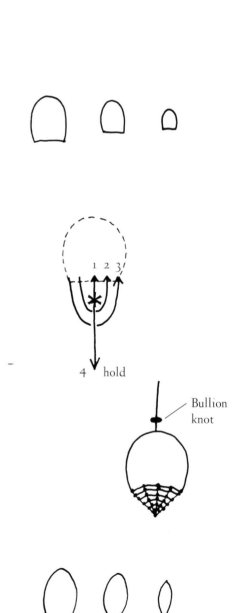

Bullion knot

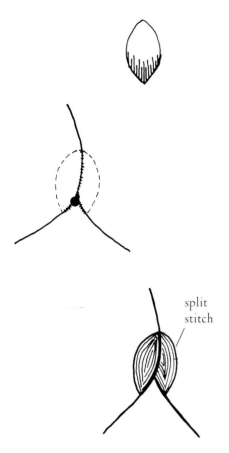

split
stitch

larger shape with buttonhole stitch. Using the same thread, embroider the lower edge of the bud with long and short buttonhole stitch, covering the outline stitches and working into the felt. Fill the lower half of the bud in long and short stitch (work the stitches softly so as not to flatten the padding).

2.   Mount calico/muslin into a hoop and trace the poppy bud sheath. With one strand of pale green (3347) thread, couch then overcast two pieces of flower wire across the lower edges of the sheath as shown, inserting one tail at •, thus leaving three tails of wire. Using the same thread, embroider the sheath with split stitch, working in rows from the tip of the bud to the base.

3.   Cut out the bud sheath with a small seam allowance around the outside edge, and close to the wired lower edge, taking care not to cut the wire tails.

4.   Apply the sheath over the embroidered bud. Using a chenille needle, insert the top wire first, then the lower wires at either side of the bud. Secure the wires at the back, then stab stitch the outside edge of the sheath in place, turning in the seam allowance with the point of the needle as you go. Cover the stab stitched edges with a few straight stitches if required.

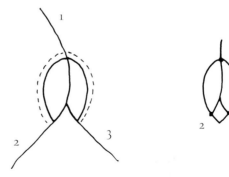

CORNFLOWERS

The cornflower, with its heavenly blue-purple petals, was believed to exert a magical influence over the fortunes of lovers, consequently, young men often carried it in their pockets. The botanical name, Centaurea, comes from the Greek, named after the learned centaur Chiron, who is said to have discovered the flower. The medicinal uses of cornflower were well known, the writings of Pliny recounting at least twenty remedies prepared from Centaurea.

MATERIALS REQUIRED

- Grey felt and paper-backed fusible web — 5 cm x 8 cm (3" x 2")

- Eyebrow brush/comb

- Needles: Crewel/embroidery 9-10

- Thread: Green stranded (DMC 3362)
  Blue/purple stranded (DMC 791, 792 and/or Madeira Silk 903)

Cornflower stems and leaves

1.   The cornflower stems are embroidered in chain stitch with two strands of green thread. Work two rows of chain stitch, together or slightly apart, each row crossing the poppy stems and ending at the base of a cornflower. Then work the stem to the cornflower bud, starting at the flower stem.

stem stitch
leaves

2.   With one strand of green thread, work the leaves in stem stitch (quite long and a little slanted).

Cornflowers

1.   Using paper-backed fusible web, cut two layers of grey felt to pad each cornflower base — one the actual size and one slightly smaller. With one strand of green thread, stab stitch the smaller layer of felt in place, then apply and outline the larger shape with buttonhole stitch.

2.   Starting at the top of the base (straight edge), cover the felt (and outline) in corded detached buttonhole stitch with one strand of green thread in a crewel needle. The laid threads (cord) are worked from left to right (using the point of the needle), and the detached buttonhole stitches are worked from left to right (using the eye of the needle), as shown in the diagram. Increase or decrease stitches at the beginning and end of rows as required. A sliver of card inserted temporarily between the stitches and the felt will facilitate the working of this covering.

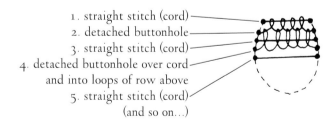

1. straight stitch (cord)
2. detached buttonhole
3. straight stitch (cord)
4. detached buttonhole over cord
and into loops of row above
5. straight stitch (cord)
(and so on…)

3.   Work the cornflower petals in Turkey knots (about six to eight rows), using two strands of thread, mixing the colours randomly. Cut and comb the pile to achieve the desired effect.

Cornflower bud

1.   Using paper-backed fusible web, cut one layer of grey felt to pad the cornflower bud. With one strand of green thread, apply and outline the shape with buttonhole stitch.

2.   Cover the felt (and outline) in corded detached buttonhole stitch as for the cornflowers, working the first laid thread (cord) a little way down from the tip of the bud. Embroider the tip of the bud with straight stitches in green or purple thread, or work a few Turkey knots.

DAMSELFLY

Small, graceful damselflies have slender bodies and narrow gauze-like wings which are held almost parallel to the body when at rest. They have large compound eyes which look like beads, and six legs which are held together to form a basket to capture insects as they fly through the air.

MATERIALS REQUIRED

- Bronze organza — 15 cm x 15 cm (6'' x 6'')

- Wing fabric (pearl metal organdie) — 15 cm x 15 cm (6'' x 6'')

- Paper-backed fusible web (Vliesofix) — 15 cm x 15 cm (6'' x 6''), and another small piece

- 10 cm (4'') embroidery hoop

- Wire: 28 gauge uncovered, cut in 12 cm (5'') lengths

- Fine tweezers to shape wire

Small piece of bronze snakeskin (or kid)

·   Beads: Mill Hill Small Bugle Beads 72053 (nutmeg)
Mill Hill Petite Glass Beads 42024 (nutmeg)
Mill Hill Petite Glass Beads 40374 (dark teal)
4 mm ($^3/_{16}$'') dark teal glass bead (Hot Spotz SBXL-449)

Damselfly wings
templates

Upper wing

·   Needles: Crewel/embroidery 10
Sharps 12 (or beading needle)
Straw/milliners 9
Chenille 18 (or sharp yarn darner)

Lower wing

·   Thread: Bronze/black metallic (Kreinik Cord 215c)
Bronze rayon machine embroidery (Madeira Rayon No.40
colour 1057)
Peacock green metallic filament (Kreinik Blending
Filament colour 085)
Nylon clear thread

Detached damselfly wings

1.   Fuse the organza to the wing fabric using the paper-backed fusible web. Mount the wing sandwich into the embroidery hoop, bronze side up.

2.   Bend the wires into the two wing shapes, using the template as a guide — do not cross the wires. Using one strand of the rayon thread, overcast the wire to the fabric, starting and ending at • with a few stitches over both wires. Work both wings.

Upper wing

Lower wing

3.   Using the blending filament in a straw needle, work the veins of the wing in feather stitch. Carefully cut out wings, reserving fabric scraps for the wings on the main fabric.

Damselfly wings on main fabric

1.   Iron a piece of Vliesofix to the wrong side of the scrap of wing sandwich. Cut out an upper and lower wing, using the template as a guide. Fuse to the main fabric at the top of the body line, protecting the wings and embroidery from the iron with a piece of GLAD Bake.

2. Work a row of split backstitch to outline the edge of the fused wings, using one strand of the rayon thread. Using the blending filament in a straw needle, work the veins of the wings in feather stitch.

To apply wings and work damselfly body

1. Using a chenille needle, insert both the wings through one hole at A, bend the wires under the applied wings and secure to the back with small stitches. Trim the wires.

2. The abdomen is worked with beads. With one strand of black/bronze metallic thread in a Sharps 12 (or beading needle), bring the needle up at A and thread on 4 small bugle beads (72053) and 2 petite beads (42024) and insert the needle at B (make sure the length of the stitch is longer than the combined length of the beads so that the beads sit smoothly). Bring the needle up at C, then couch between each bead back to B. Work a fly stitch for the tail and bring the tie-down thread back through all the beads to A (you may need tweezers to pull the needle through).

3. With nylon thread in the Sharps needle, apply a small piece of bronze snakeskin over the bead-end and wires at A to form the thorax. Apply the large teal bead for the head and the small teal bead for the eye. Using the bronze/black metallic thread, work the feelers with a fly stitch and the legs with straight stitches.

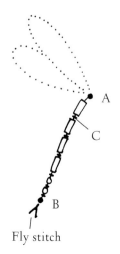

Fly stitch

Snakeskin

CATERPILLAR

The caterpillar (butterfly larva) has a head and thirteen segments. The head is a hardened round capsule bearing a prominent pair of toothed jaws (mandibles), a pair of short stubby antennae and six small black simple eyes on each side. The first three segments form the thorax, and each bears a pair of short, jointed legs which end in a single claw. The abdomen has ten segments, five of these bearing a pair of false legs or pro-legs. These soft, jointless structures are present on the third to sixth segments. A final pair of legs, claspers, occur on the last segment.

MATERIALS REQUIRED

- Mill Hill Antique Bead — 3036 (cognac)

- Needles: Chenille 18
  Tapestry 26
  Crewel 10
  Straw 6

- Thread: Pale lime green stranded (DMC 3819)
  Medium lime green stranded (DMC 581)
  Orange stranded (DMC 900)
  Lime green soft cotton thread (DMC Tapestry Cotton 2142)

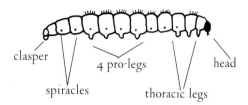

clasper

spiracles

4 pro-legs

thoracic legs

head

1.   The caterpillar body is worked in raised stem stitch. Using the chenille needle, pad the body with three lengths of the soft cotton thread. Secure the padding with 12 soft couching stitches worked in places as marked, with one strand of green thread (3819).

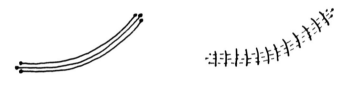

2.   Using a tapestry needle, proceed to cover the padding by working rows of stem stitch over the couching stitches. Work four rows in pale lime green, one row in orange, then about five rows in alternate greens to give a striped effect. All the rows are worked in the same direction, and enter and exit through the same two points.

3.   Work the eight legs with French knots (1 wrap) using three strands of medium lime green thread (581).

4.   Apply an antique bead for the head.

Chapter 5 Wild Life

Wild beasts were a part of the embroidered gardens too. Lions with meticulously curled and waved manes sit smiling on grassy hummocks, or stand twirling their tails opposite spotted leopards, both equally disinterested in the docile unicorns, stags and camels on the surrounding slopes. The embroiderer chose these wild and mythical animals to inhabit the garden from the patterns available in books. And whether she was aware of it or not, she was following a tradition that goes back to the menageries attached to royal palaces, like the one in Oxfordshire where Henry I kept 'lyons, leopards, strange spotted beasts, porcupines, camells and such like animals.'

THOMASINA BECK, EMBROIDERED GARDENS, 1979.

DEER AND PEAR TREE

Dear and Pear Tree, Plate 5. p. 148

REQUIREMENTS

- Ivory satin — 28 cm x 28 cm (11'' x 11'')
- Calico (or quilter's muslin) — 28 cm x 28 cm (11'' x 11'')
- 23 cm (9'') embroidery hoop
- Mound (see p.189)
- Pear tree (see p.191)
- Owl (see p.197)
- Beehive (see p.199)
- Tiny bees (see p.200)
- Spider and web (see p.193)
- Deer (see p.201)
- Pears (see p.193)

ORDER OF WORK

1. Mount the main fabric and the backing fabric into the embroidery hoop.

2. Trace the skeleton outline onto the main fabric.

3. Work the mound in rococo stitch on canvas and apply to the main fabric.

4. Tree trunk, branches and leaves on the main fabric.

5. Owl.

6. Beehive and tiny bees.

7. Spider and web.

8. Deer.

9. Detached pear tree leaves

10. Pears

11. Apply antlers.

Skeleton Outline

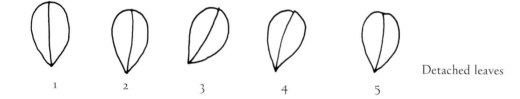

Detached leaves

1   2   3   4   5

MOUND

MATERIALS REQUIRED

- Mono canvas 12 threads to 1 inch — 10 cm x 18 cm (4'' x 7'')

- Blue water-soluble marking pen

- Masking tape

- Needles: Crewel/embroidery 3-10
  Tapestry 24

- Threads: Olive green in 3 shades (DMC 731, 732, 733)

Note: Before commencing work, bind the raw edges of the canvas with masking tape. The stitching is done in the hand, not in a frame.

1. Trace the mound outline onto the canvas with marking pen, checking that the side and lower edges of the mound line up with the threads (grain) of the canvas.

2. Work the mound in rococo stitch with three strands of thread (one each of 731, 732 and 733) in a size 24 tapestry needle. The rows must all be worked diagonally, starting in the top right hand corner. Extend the stitches beyond the marked side and lower lines to avoid the gaps left when working rococo stitch.

3. Place the completed mound face down on a soft towel and lightly press with a steam iron, pulling gently into shape if distorted. Leave to dry.

4. Trim excess canvas away from all edges of the mound leaving a 7mm ($^1/_4$'') allowance. Press the top edge under, along the worked outline, keeping the side and lower edges flat.

5. Pin the mound to the main fabric, lining up all worked edges with the skeleton outline. Using one strand of olive thread, stab stitch the top edge of the mound to the satin.

Tack/baste the side and lower edges in place (after the deer is applied, these stitches can be removed if the mound needs to be retensioned, then restitched).

6.   With the three shades of olive thread in a crewel needle, work straight stitches (imitating rococo stitch) into the top edge of the mound, to fill any gaps left in the canvas.

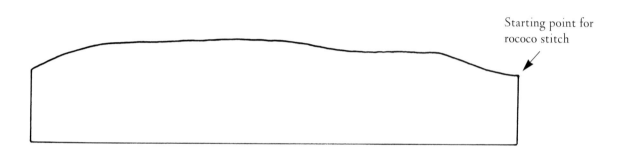

Starting point for
rococo stitch

PEAR TREE

MATERIALS REQUIRED

- Calico (quilter's muslin) — 20 cm x 20 cm (8'' x 8'')

- 10 cm (4'') embroidery hoop

- Wire: 30 gauge green covered, cut in 10 cm (4'') lengths

- Fine tweezers to shape wire

- Needles: Crewel/embroidery 5-10
  Chenille 18
  Sharp yarn darner 14

- Threads: Leaves — Green stranded — DMC 469 (medium), 470 (light)
  Tree trunk — Brown stranded in 2 shades — DMC 610, 611
  — soft cotton for padding — DMC Soft (Tapestry) Cotton 2610
  Web — Silver metallic thread — Madeira Metallic No.40 silver
  Spider — Black stranded DMC 310 or Cifonda Silk — black

Tree trunk

The tree trunk is embroidered in raised stem stitch band, worked over a padding of couched, soft cotton thread.

1.   Start by couching a line of soft cotton thread around the outline of the tree (tapering to one strand at the tip of the branches), inserting this thread through to the back of the work, using a chenille needle, whenever necessary. Work the couching stitches (with one strand of brown stranded thread) as close together as needed to obtain an accurate outline.

2.   Continue to couch layers of thread on top of each other, one strand at a time, to build up the contours of the branches,

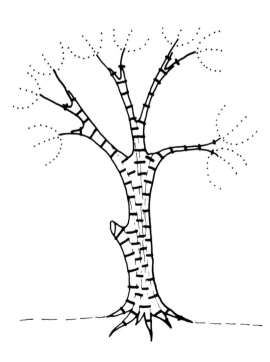

tree trunk and roots into the mound (as if working a sculp-ture). The trunk can be as smooth or gnarled as desired.

3.   Establish a grid for the raised stem band by working longer couching stitches over several threads, at regular inter-vals, along the desired contours of the trunk. These stitches should be about 3-4 mm ($^1/_8$'') apart and not too tight. Stagger the rows of couching stitches (and work short rows when nec-essary), to achieve a more realistic effect.

4.   With one strand of the darker brown thread in a tapes-try needle, cover the trunk with rows of raised stem band (using short rows when necessary for shaping), working each row in the direction of growth, i.e. from the tree roots to the tips of the branches. Include some rows in the lighter brown thread for highlights. The original couching stitches can also be used when required.

Pear tree leaves

1.   Embroider the leaves on the main fabric with one strand of thread as follows:
— the central vein in chain stitch (470)
— work the leaf surface in padded buttonhole stitch (469)
— the veins in straight stitches (470)

2.   Work five detached leaves, on calico/muslin mounted in a hoop, as follows:
— couch then overcast the green wire down the central vein (470)
— couch then buttonhole the wire around the outside edge (469)
— work split back stitch on either side of the central vein and inside the wire edge to provide a foundation into which the leaf surface can be stitched.
— embroider the leaf surface, inside the wire, in padded satin stitch (469)
— work the veins with straight stitches (470)

3.   Carefully cut out the detached leaves and apply over the surface leaves (as indicated), by inserting the wire tails

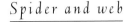

through to the back of the work, using a yarn darner. Secure the wires with tiny stitches, then trim.

Spider and web

1.   Work a fly stitch and a straight stitch in silver thread, to form the web.

2.   With one strand of black thread, work two satin stitch spots (at the end of the silver thread) for the spider's thorax and abdomen, and two small French knots for the eyes. Work eight legs, each with two straight stitches.

Pears

The pears (red Corella) are worked in needlelace over a mould of plastic modelling clay. The same technique could be used for a variety of fruits.

MATERIALS REQUIRED

·   Plastic modelling material (e.g. Fimo, Polyclay, Cernit) — to match pear colour

·   Needles: Tapestry 26
Straw/milliners 8

·   Threads: Twisted silk thread, e.g. Kanagawa 1000 denier (colour 98)
or Kanagawa Silk Stitch 30 (colour 98)
or russet stranded cotton (DMC 355)
Brown stranded cotton (DMC 801)

Pear moulds

Knead the modelling clay until it is pliable, then break off small pieces and shape into pears. Make an assortment of shapes and sizes, some with flattened backs so that they will lie flat on the main fabric if desired. Insert a needle through the length of the pear to make a hole, then bake in an oven, on a sheet of foil, following the directions supplied with the modelling material.

FIMO — bake at 100°C-130°C (212°F-265°F) for 20-30 minutes

POLYCLAY — bake at 150°C (300°F) for 15 minutes

CERNIT — bake at 150°C (300°F) for 15-30 minutes

Select five pears of similar size, approximately 9 mm (3/8'') long — the size is your choice!

If modelling clay is unavailable, pears can be successfully made from felt, in a blending colour, rolled and stitched into shape.

To cover a pear mould with needlelace

The moulds are to be covered with a mesh of needlelace, either detached buttonhole stitch or trellis stitch, with the thread of your choice (the pears in the model are worked in trellis stitch with a fine twisted silk thread). The pears have proved to be one of the most challenging projects in classes, so the following information (gathered from these classes) is offered to enable choices to be made!

Threads: almost any thread can be used to work needlelace although some are easier to stitch with than others. The choices are:
— Twisted silk thread (1000 denier) — easiest to work, but quite coarse.
— Twisted silk thread (30 or 50 thread) — the finer the thread the more challenging it becomes! The result, however, is worth the effort.
— Stranded thread (1 or 2 strands) — is quite easy to use, and is available in variegated colours which can look very effective.

Work some samples to determine which thread you prefer. Use a fine tapestry needle and a long length of thread, as joins are to be avoided.

Work the detached buttonhole stitch (or trellis stitch), in one of the following ways (experiment and choose the method that works for you):

Method 1

(a)   Attach the pear mould to the main fabric with a long stitch through the shape and secure at the back of the work.

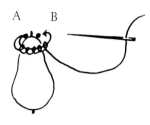

(b)   Take a long length of thread and tie a knot 15 cm (6'') from one end. Bring both ends up on the left side of the pear at A. Holding the short thread taut, work about 7 buttonhole stitches over it with the longer thread. Insert both threads through to the back of the work at B but do not pull tight until several rows have been stitched.

(c)   Cover the pears with buttonhole stitch, working the rows from left to right and going through to the back of the work at the end of each row. Increase at the sides of each row when necessary.

(d)   Start decreasing at the end of the pear until a circle of buttonhole stitches is formed at the base. Finish by inserting the needle through the base hole to the top of the pear, then through to the back of the work. Tighten up all the loops at the back of the work to make the mesh sit snugly around the mould.

Method 2 (worked in the hand)

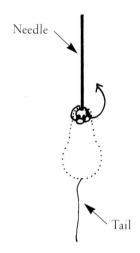

Needle

Tail

(a)   Bring the thread through the pear, leaving a short tail at the base. Form a loose loop in the thread around a large straw needle (or saté stick) inserted into the top of the pear.

(b)   Work 8-10 buttonhole stitches around the loop (the loop will be tightened later, by pulling the tail of thread at the base).

(c)   Continue working rounds of buttonhole stitch, increasing if necessary at the back of the pear.

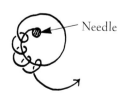

Needle

View from above

(d)   Decrease in the last rows at the base of the pear and, after pulling the base tail of thread to tighten the top of the pear, insert the needle from the base through to the top. Use both threads (or the top thread only) to apply the pear to the main work, at the base of a leaf.

Method 3 (worked in the hand)

(a)   Bring the thread through the pear to wrap three or four times (leaving a tail at the base), and secure by inserting a large straw needle or sate stick into the top of the pear.

(b)   Make a loop at the top of the pear, underneath the wrapped threads. Work 8-10 buttonhole stitches around this loop.

(c)   Continue working rounds of buttonhole stitch, increasing if necessary at the back of the pear.

(d)   Decrease in the last rows at the base of the pear and insert the needle from the base through to the top. Use both threads (or the top thread only) to apply the pear to the main work, at the base of a leaf.

All Methods:

Using two strands of dark brown thread, bring the needle out at the top of the pear then through to the base. Work a French knot at the base of the pear (2 wraps) then bring the needle back through to the top of the pear where the threads can be used to form a wrapped stalk, if desired.

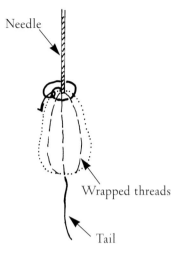

Needle

Wrapped threads

Tail

Owl

MATERIALS REQUIRED

- Calico (or quilter's muslin) — 20 cm x 20 cm (8'' x 8'')

- 10 cm (4'') embroidery hoop

- Small amount of stuffing and saté stick

- Mill Hill Petite Glass Beads 42028 (ginger)

- Needles: Crewel/embroidery 5-10
  Sharps (or beading) 12

- Threads: Beige stranded in 2 shades DMC 3032 (medium), 3033 (light)
  Brown stranded in 3 shades DMC 3045 (light), 869 (medium), 3787 (dark)
  Black stranded DMC 310
  Nylon clear thread

1. Mount the calico into the hoop and trace the slightly enlarged owl head and body. The owl is embroidered using one strand of thread.

2. Embroider the breast of the owl in long and short stitch blending the three lightest colours (3033, 3032, 3045).

3. The wings are filled with rows of Roumanian couching worked with the two darkest shades (3787, 869). The direction of the rows can be either of the examples shown.

4. Embroider the head with straight stitches in medium shades, then work each eye with a buttonhole wheel in light beige thread (3033), and the beak with straight stitches in black.

To apply the owl to the main fabric

5.   Run a gathering thread 1mm away from the outside edge of the owl (not the base) then cut out, leaving a small turning allowance. Turn in the lower edge, then gently pull the gathering thread to ease the remaining turning allowance to the inside. Apply the owl body (below the head) to the branch with small stab stitches (make sure the owl is sitting straight on the branch!) and stuff lightly using a saté stick. Stab stitch the head in place, leaving a small gap at the top to insert the stuffing, then stitch the opening closed. Cover the stab stitches with straight stitches in blending shades, if required. Stitch along neck and wing lines with small stab stitches to sculpt the owl body.

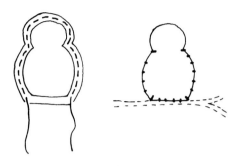

To complete the owl

1.   The tail is embroidered in detached chain stitches of varying lengths in medium and dark shades.

2.   Each ear tuft is two detached chain stitches (one inside the other) in light and medium shades.

3.   The claws for each leg are two bullion knots, worked over the branch with black thread.

4.   Each eye is a petite bead, applied on its side with three stitches worked in nylon thread, in the middle of each buttonhole wheel. Stitch a French knot, with black thread, in the centre of each bead to complete the eyes.

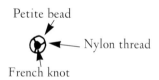

Petite bead

Nylon thread

French knot

BEEHIVE

MATERIALS REQUIRED

· Beige felt, paper-backed fusible web and organza —
5 cm x 8 cm (2'' x 3'')

· Threads: Straw yellow stranded in 2 shades — DMC 729
(light), 680 (medium)
Brown stranded — DMC 3371

· Needles: Crewel/embroidery 10

1. Iron fusible web to organza (protect iron with GLAD
Bake). On organza side, trace beehive outline (and all internal
lines) and two smaller shapes for padding. Remove the paper
and fuse the organza to the felt. Cut shapes out carefully.

2. With one strand of the light yellow thread, stab stitch
the padding layers in place, starting with smallest layer and
keeping organza side uppermost. Stitch upper layer of beehive
in place with stab stitches at the end of each round as shown.

3. Embroider the hive entrance in satin stitch with one
strand of brown thread.

4. Using the pencil lines on the organza as a guide, embroider
each round of the beehive as follows:
— work 10 long satin stitches in 729
— work 2 long satin stitches on either side in 680
— couch all in place with 680 (keep within the pencil lines)

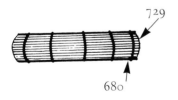

Repeat for each round, staggering couching stitches to form a
brick pattern.

TINY BEES

MATERIALS REQUIRED

- Black stranded thread (DMC 310)

- Yellow stranded thread (DMC 783)

- Silver/black metallic thread (Kreinik Cord 105c)

- Needles: Crewel 10

1.   With one strand of black thread, work seven small satin stitches into the same two holes to pad the body.

2.   Using one strand of thread, work satin stitches over padded body, in black and yellow (two stitches in each colour — three black stripes and two yellow).

3.   With one strand of black thread, work a French knot (2 wraps) for the head.

4.   Using metallic thread, work two detached chain stitches for the wings.

Deer

The stag, 'royal beast of the chase', has always been a popular motif, both with embroiderers and as an image in heraldry, where it signified 'a man who is wise and politicke, who well foresees his times and opportunities, endowed with exceeding speed of foot, to flie from danger when it approacheth'.

MATERIALS REQUIRED

- Calico (or quilter's muslin) — 20 cm x 20 cm (8'' x 8'')

- 10 cm (4'') embroidery hoop

- Wire: 28 gauge uncovered, cut in 15 cm (6'') lengths

- Fine tweezers to shape wire

- Mill Hill Petite Bead 42014 (black)

- Stuffing and saté stick

- Needles: Crewel/embroidery 10
  Sharps (or beading) 12
  Sharp yarn darner 14

- Threads: Cream stranded in 2 shades — DMC 739 (light), 738 (medium)
  Tan stranded in 3 shades — DMC 437 (light), 436 (medium), 435 (dark)
  Dark brown stranded — DMC 801

1.   Mount the calico into the embroidery hoop and trace the deer outline and the two reference points for the mound.

2.   The deer is embroidered in long and short stitch using one strand of thread (imagine that you are stroking the animal when determining the stitch/hair direction). The antlers, hooves, tail, back ear and facial features are all worked after the deer is applied to the main fabric.

A guide to the order of working and the shades used is as follows:

(a) belly and chest — medium and light cream (739, 738)

(b) spots — light cream (739)

(b) background legs — dark and medium tan (436, 435)

(c) foreground legs — dark (edges), medium and light tan (435, 436, 437)

(d) back and neck — medium cream, light and medium tan (436, 437, 738)

(e) head — light and medium cream and tan (739, 738, 436, 437).

To apply the deer to the main fabric

1.   Cut out the deer, leaving a turning allowance of 5 mm (3/8'') above the reference points, 3 mm (1/8'') below the reference points, and no turning allowance at the base of the unembroidered hooves. Finger press the turnings to the inside (and tack/baste if desired).

2.   Pin the deer to the mound, lining up the reference points with the top edge of the mound and making sure that the deer is sitting straight.

3.   Turning in the raw edges as you go, stab stitch the lower half of the deer to the mound (1), leaving the hooves unturned and unstitched. Stitch around the internal edges of the background legs (to prevent the stuffing entering). Using a saté stick and polyester filling, lightly stuff the foreground legs of the deer.

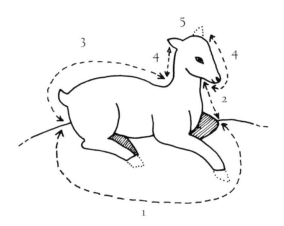

4.   Continue stab stitching the deer to the main fabric, working in the order (1–5) as shown. Stuff lightly as you go (allowing for quilting/sculpting later). Embroider the tail in light and medium cream thread.

5.   Shape (sculpt) the body of the deer with small stitches along the edges of the foreground limbs, under the head and near the tail. Hide any stab stitches that might show around the outside edge with straight stitches, worked in the direction of the hair and in blending colour/s.

To complete the deer

1.   Using one strand of dark brown thread, embroider the hooves in padded satin stitch and work the nose and mouth in straight stitches.

2.   With one strand of dark tan thread, outline the front ear with a fly stitch and work the back ear with two detached chain stitches (one inside the other). Apply a petite bead for the eye, pulling the thread firmly, then work a detached chain stitch around it.

3.　The antlers are made by wrapping uncovered wire with dark brown thread. As the antlers are fragile, do not apply to the work until all the other embroidery is complete.

Using fine tweezers, bend the wire into three branches as shown (do not curve the branches into shape until the wrapping is complete). Wrap the wire with one strand of dark brown thread (801), in the following sequence:

Tie a knot at 1, leaving a short thread tail. Wrap to 2, enclosing the tail of thread.

Take the thread to 3 and tie a knot. Wrap to 4.

Take the thread to 5, tie a knot then wrap back to 4.

Wrap the wire tails to a length longer than required for the antler, then secure the thread.

Shape the wrapped antlers and, using the yarn darner, insert the wire ends at the top of the deer's head between the ears. Secure to the back of the work and trim.

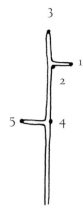

Owl Brooch or Bowl Top

This little owl makes a lovely gift when mounted into an oval brooch or pendant, or into the lid of a small porcelain box.

REQUIREMENTS

- Ivory satin — 20 cm x 20 cm (8" x 8")

- Calico (or quilter's muslin) — 20 cm x 20 cm (8" x 8")

- 10 cm (4") embroidery hoop

- Mill Hill Petite Beads 42012 (dark pink berries)

- Owl (see p.197)

- Tiny bee (see p.200)

- Needles: Crewel 5-10
  Straw 9
  Sharps (or beading) 12

- Threads: Medium green stranded (DMC 469)
  Dark green stranded (DMC 936)
  Nylon clear thread

ORDER OF WORK

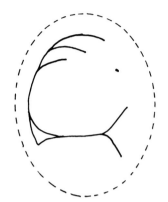

Skeleton outline

1.   Mount the satin and calico backing into the embroidery hoop. Trace the oval outline on to the calico backing, then tack/baste around this line with rayon machine thread.

2.   Trace the skeleton outline of the design on to the satin, inside the tacked oval outline.

3.   *Branch*: Embroider the branches in stem stitch with one strand of dark green thread, working two or three rows for the lower branch. Work the tree trunk in long and short stitch.

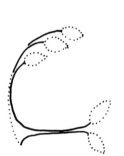

4.   *Leaves*: Embroider the leaves in fishbone stitch with one strand of medium green thread.

5.   *Owl* (see p.197). Embroider the owl then apply to the branch to complete.

6.   *Tiny bee* (see p.200).

7.   *Berries*: Using nylon thread, apply three petite beads at the end of the lower branch.

8.   To mount the embroidery into an oval frame:
— cut satin leaving a 5 mm (³⁄₈'') seam allowance outside the tacked outline
— cut the calico slightly smaller than the oval cardboard backing board
— gather the satin over the cardboard backing and secure
— insert into the frame and secure

Parrot and Boysenberry Bush

Plate 12. p. 215

REQUIREMENTS

- Ivory silk or satin — 20 cm x 20 cm (8'' x 8'')

- Calico (or quilter's muslin) — 20 cm x 20 cm (8'' x 8'')

- 15 cm (6'') embroidery hoop

- Boysenberry bush and mound (see p. 209)

- Parrot (see p. 212)

- Detached beaded boysenberries (see p. 364)

ORDER OF WORK

1.   Mount the silk and the calico backing into the embroidery hoop and mark a 10 cm (4'') circle on the calico backing. Tack/baste around this circle with rayon machine thread.

2.   Trace the skeleton outline of the design onto the main fabric, within the tacked circle.

3.   Mound.

4.   Boysenberry bush trunk and leaves on the silk.

5.   Parrot.

6.   Work two beaded detached boysenberries with wrapped stalks. Apply to the branch, using a chenille needle, and secure to the back of the work.

7.   Detached leaves.

PARROT AND BOYSENBERRY BUSH

detached leaves

detached wing

Skeleton outline

BOYSENBERRY BUSH AND MOUND

MATERIALS REQUIRED

- Calico (or quilter's muslin) — 2 squares each 20 cm x 20 cm (8'' x 8'')

- 10 cm (4'') embroidery hoop

- Wire: 30 gauge green covered, cut in 10 cm (4'') lengths

- Needles: Crewel/embroidery 5-10
  Straw/milliners 3
  Tapestry 26
  Chenille 18
  Sharp yarn darner 14

- Threads: Mound - fine crewel wool in shades of green — DMC Broder Médicis 8414, 8415, 8416 or Needle Necessities Over-dyed Wool colour 33
  Tree trunk — brown stranded cotton in 3 shades — DMC 433, 801, 898
  — soft cotton for padding — DMC Soft (Tapestry) Cotton 2801
  Leaves — green stranded cotton — DMC 3345 (dark), 3346 (medium)

Mound

1. Mount a square of calico into the embroidery hoop and trace the mound outline.

Mound outline

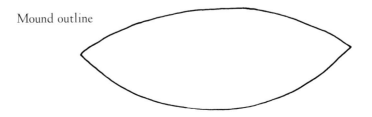

2.　With one strand of wool in the straw needle, embroider the mound in French knots (one wrap), selecting the shades randomly, unless using the variegated overdyed wool.

3.　Remove the worked mound from the embroidery hoop and trim away excess calico, leaving a turning allowance of 5mm (3/8'') around all edges. Press the turning allowance to the wrong side.

4.　Pin the mound to the main fabric, lining up the worked edges with the skeleton outline and tacked circle. Stitch the mound in place with small slip stitches using one strand of dark green cotton (3345), allowing the mound to bulge slightly.

Boysenberry bush trunk

The tree trunk is embroidered in raised stem stitch band, worked over a padding of couched, soft cotton thread.

1.　Couch a line of soft cotton thread from the mound to the base of each leaf, taking the thread ends through to the back of the work with a chenille needle. Work the couching stitch-es about 3 mm (1/8'') apart, using one strand of mid-brown thread (801).

2.　Couch several layers of soft cotton thread on top of each other, one strand at a time, to build up the contours of the trunk, taking some threads into the mound for roots.

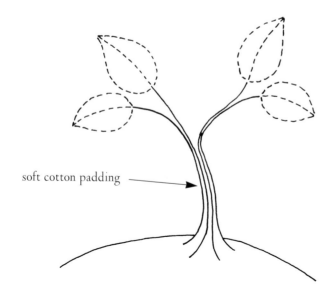

soft cotton padding

3.   Establish a grid for the raised stem band by working longer couching stitches over several threads, at regular intervals, along the trunk. These stitches should be about 3-4 mm apart and not too tight. Stagger the rows of couching stitches (and work short rows when necessary), to achieve a more realistic effect.

4.   With one strand of brown thread in a tapestry needle, cover the trunk with rows of raised stem band (using short rows when necessary for shaping), working each row in the direction of growth, i.e. from the tree roots to the tips of the branches. Work some rows in the darker brown at the edges for shading, and in the lighter brown for highlights. The original couching stitches can also be used when required.

Boysenberry bush leaves

1.   Embroider the leaves on the main fabric with one strand of thread as follows:
— central vein in chain stitch (3346)
— work the leaf surface in padded buttonhole stitch (3345)
— side veins with straight stitches (3346).

2.   Work two detached leaves, on calico/muslin mounted in a hoop, as follows:
— couch then overcast the green wire down the central vein (3346)
— couch then buttonhole the wire around the outside edge (3345)
— work split back stitch on either side of the central vein and inside the wire edge to provide a foundation into which the leaf surface can be stitched
— embroider the leaf surface, inside the wire, in padded satin stitch (3345)
— work the veins with straight stitches (3346).

3.   Carefully cut out the detached leaves and apply by inserting the wire at the base of the leaves on the main fabric, using a yarn darner. Secure the wire at the back of the work, then trim.

PARROT

This brilliantly coloured, talkative bird is part of a large family, Psittacidae, which includes cockatoos, lorikeets, macaws, love-birds and parakeets. Native to the tropics, parrots have been popular as caged pets for thousands of years.

MATERIALS REQUIRED

- Calico (or quilter's muslin) — 20 cm x 20 cm (8'' x 8'')

- 10 cm (4'') embroidery hoop

- Cream felt, paper-backed fusible web and organza —
  5 cm x 8 cm (2'' x 3'')

- Wire: Fine flower wire 10 cm (4'') length

- Teal marking pen to colour wire (optional)

- Mill Hill Petite Bead 42028 (ginger)

- Needles: Crewel/embroidery 5-10
  Straw/milliners 3-9
  Sharps 12
  Tapestry 26

- Threads: Red/orange stranded in 3 shades — DMC 900,
  606, 608
  Orange/yellow stranded in 3 shades — DMC 740, 741,
  742
  Bright green stranded in 2 shades — DMC 905, 906
  Teal stranded in 3 shades — DMC 3808, 3809, 3765
  Electric blue stranded — DMC 995
  Electric blue metallic — Madeira Metallic No.40
  colour 37

Plate 6

DEEP RED PANSY AND BEETLE

Plate 7

MAUVE PANSY/VIOLA AND BEE

Plate 8

RING OF PANSIES

Plate 9

ORANGE RUSSET PANSY BROOCH

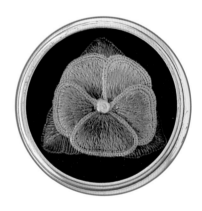

Plate 10

VIOLET PANSY BROOCH

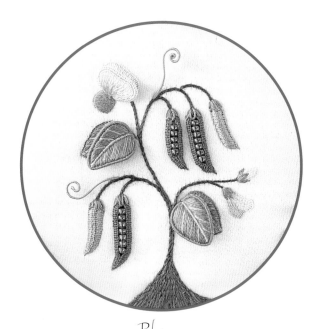

Plate 11

PEA FLOWER ROUNDEL

Plate 12

PARROT AND BOYSENBERRY BUSH

Plate 13

ELIZABETHAN ROUNDEL WITH BUMBLEBEE

Plate 14

ELIZABETHAN ROUNDEL WITH LADYBIRD

Black stranded — DMC 310 or Cifonda Art Silk — black
Nylon clear thread

1.   Iron the fusible web to the organza (protect the iron
with GLAD Bake). On the organza side, trace the parrot outline (and all internal lines), and the three smaller shapes for
padding. Remove the paper and fuse the organza to the felt.
Cut the shapes out carefully. Cut away the shaded areas on
the smaller two layers of felt to allow for the branch.

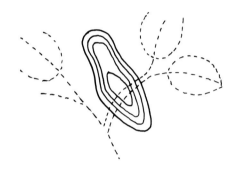

cut away

2.   With one strand of an orange thread, stab stitch the
padding layers in place, starting with the smallest layer (on
either side of the branch), keeping the organza side uppermost. Outline the top layer of felt with buttonhole stitch
(stitches 2 mm apart), using an orange thread for the lower
side of the body, and teal thread for the upper side.

3. Using one strand of thread, embroider the parrot body
with straight stitches taken through to the back of the work
(do not make these stitches too tight or they will flatten the
padding). Work the stitches and blend the colours as follows:

   (a) Starting at the tail with dull orange thread (900), work
the lower half of the body (and under the wing) with straight
stitches, shading from dull orange to red/orange (606 and
608), then orange to yellow (740, 741 and 742) for the lower
head.

   (b) Starting at the tail with dark teal thread (3808), work
the upper half of the body with straight stitches, shading
from dark teal to electric blue (3809, 3765 and 995), then
bright greens (905, 906) for the upper head.

4. The tail feathers are worked in needleweaving over a loop of thread as follows:

(a) Using two strands of thread, bring the needle out at the tail end of the body, go down 2 mm away and secure at the back of the work, leaving a loop the length of the feather. Pass a strand of scrap thread through the loop and hold it taut with the left hand while the weaving is being done.

(b) Using the suggested thread/s in a fine tapestry needle, fill the loop with needleweaving, taking the needle *over* the thread and *into* the loop (from right to left, then left to right and so on), so that the woven thread finishes on the *underside* of the feather end.

(c) Remove the scrap thread, then insert the tail of the woven thread (loosely) through to the back of the work at the lower end of the feather and secure to the calico backing.

Work the tail feathers in the following order, using the suggested threads.

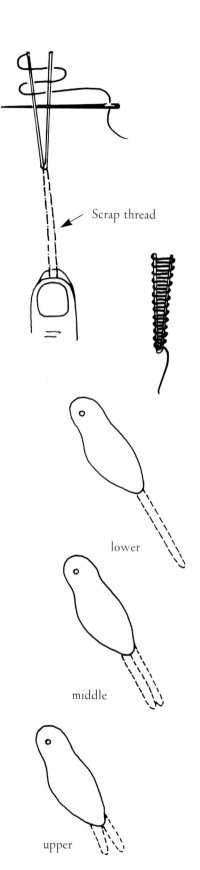

Scrap thread

lower

middle

upper

LOWER TAIL FEATHER:
— make a loop 24 mm (1'') long with 2 strands of teal thread (3808)

— weave with 2 strands of thread: 1 dark teal (3808) and 1 blue metallic (37).

MIDDLE TAIL FEATHERS:
— make both loops 17 mm (³/₄'') long with two strands of dark teal thread (3808)

— weave the upper feather with 2 strands of thread: 1 electric blue (995) and 1 blue metallic (37)

— weave the lower feather with 2 strands of thread: 1 orange (900) and 1 blue metallic (37).

UPPER TAIL FEATHERS:
— make the upper loop 10 mm (¹/₂'') long with two strands of electric blue (995), and weave with one strand of the same thread.

— make the lower loop 8 mm ($\frac{1}{3}$'') long with two strands of orange (900), and weave with one strand of the same thread.

5.   The detached wing is worked with one strand of thread as follows:

(a) Mount the calico into the embroidery hoop and trace the detached wing outline. Colour the wire with marking pen if desired. Using dark teal thread (3808), couch the wire to the calico around the wing outline, leaving two tails of wire. Do not stitch the small loop at the end of the wing.

(b) Overcast the lower edge of the wing to the calico with dark teal thread (3808). Buttonhole stitch the upper edge of the wing to the calico with electric blue thread (995). Do not stitch the small loop at the end of the wing — fill this with needleweaving using electric blue thread in a fine tapestry needle.

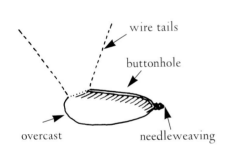

wire tails

buttonhole

overcast   needleweaving

(c) Work a row of long buttonhole stitches inside the wire, along the upper edge of the wing. Embroider the remainder of the wing with straight stitches blending in to each other (encroaching satin stitch) and into the buttonhole stitches. Use a mixture of the blue stranded threads (3808, 3809, 3765, 995) with highlights worked in the electric blue metallic thread.

(d) Carefully cut out the wing around the wire (take care not to snip the loop of needleweaving) and close to the unwired edge. Apply the wing to the parrot body by insert-ing the wires through two holes made with a yarn darner (secure to the back of the body with tiny stitches). Cover the calico wing edge (and attach the wing) with straight stitches in colours to blend with the body.

6.   Embroider the beak with straight stitches with one strand of black thread. The legs are made with bullion knots, using two strands for the leg and one strand for the claws. The eye is a petite bead applied on its side with three stitch-es worked in nylon thread. Stitch a French knot, with one strand of black thread, in the centre of the bead to complete the eye.

Chapter 6   Roundels

Roundel or Roundle: any circular panel that adorns a surface or an ornamental circular inset of stained glass in a window. Carved roundels were a favourite form of ornament on medieval boarded chests, and glass roundels bearing heraldic devices, set in lead-glazed windows, were known from the 15th to the 19th centuries.

DORA WARE & MAUREEN STAFFORD,
AN ILLUSTRATED DICTIONARY OF ORNAMENT, 1974.

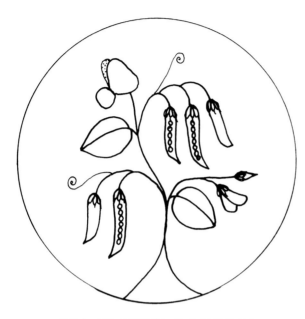

PEA FLOWER ROUNDEL

Skeleton outline

Detached leaves and petal

Pea Flower Roundel, Plate 11, p. 215

REQUIREMENTS

- Ivory satin — 20 cm x 20 cm (8'' x 8'')

- Calico (or quilter's muslin) — 2 pieces (20 cm x 20 cm) (8'' x 8'')

- 10 cm (4'') embroidery hoop

- Wire: 30 gauge green covered, cut in 12 cm (5'') lengths
  28 gauge uncovered, cut in 12 cm (5'') lengths
  Fine flower wire 12 cm (5'')

- Mill Hill Glass Beads — 206 (violet)

- Needles: Crewel 3-10
  Chenille 18

- Threads: Green stranded thread in 5 shades — DMC 936, 469, 470, 471, 472
  Green Pearl (5) cotton thread — DMC 469
  Pink stranded thread in 3 shades — DMC 223, 224, 225

ORDER OF WORK

1. Mount the satin and a piece of muslin for backing into the embroidery hoop.

2. Trace the skeleton outline onto the main fabric.

3. Stems and mound.

4. Pea leaves on main fabric.

5. Pea flower buds.

6. Closed peapods.

7. Open peapods.

8. Pea flower.

9. Detached leaves.

10. Pea tendrils.

11. A tiny bee (see p.200) can be embroidered near the pea flower if desired.

Stems and mound

These are worked with two strands of the darker green threads (one each of 936 and 469).

1. Starting at the base of the mound, work the stems and mound outline in stem stitch. Use one strand of either thread for the stems of the buds and leaves.

2. Starting at the top, work the mound in long and short stitch.

Pea leaves on main fabric

These are worked with one strand of medium/light green thread (470 and 472).

1. Work the central vein in chain stitch (472).

2. Pad the leaf inside the outline with long stitches (470).

3. Working from the base to the tip, embroider the leaf with long buttonhole stitches (470).

4. Work the veins with straight stitches (472).

Pea flower buds

These are worked with one strand of thread (223, 224, 225 and 470, 471).

1. Work the closed flower bud with straight stitches in pale pink thread (225).

2. Embroider the sepals with detached chain stitches in light green thread (471)

3.   Work the lower edges of the open flower bud petals in long and short buttonhole stitch, then embroider in straight stitches (lower petal in medium pink 224, upper petal in pale pink 225).

4.   Embroider the sepals with detached chain stitches in green thread (470).

Closed peapods

These are worked with one strand of medium/light green thread (470 and 471).

1.   Outline the pods in backstitch (471). Pad the peapods by working three long stitches, inside backstitch outline, using six strands of thread (471).

2.   Embroider the right peapod with close buttonhole stitches, starting at the lower end of the pod, and covering the backstitch outline. Work one straight stitch at the lower end of the pod to form a point.

3.   Embroider the left peapod with two rows of close buttonhole stitches, covering the backstitch outline and each buttonhole edge being side by side down the centre of the pod. Work one or two straight stitches at the lower end of the pod to form a point.

4.   Embroider the sepals with three detached chain stitches (470).

Open peapods

These are worked with one strand of medium green thread (469 and 470).

1.   Outline the pods in backstitch (469).

2.   Apply the beads with one long stitch down the centre of each pod, then couch between each one to secure. (Make sure that there are not too many beads — allow for space to work the sepals at the top of the pod.)

3. Pad the peapod sides with two long stitches of pearl thread on each side of the beads.

4. The peapod sides are worked in buttonhole stitch (469), over the two strands of pearl thread (for padding) through to the back of the work. Use the row of beads as a support for these stitches which should be slightly raised from the surface. Start at the top of the pod and work in the direction as shown. Stitch the sides of the peapod together at the top and the bottom (if necessary) with tiny stitches, to give the illusion that the peas are bursting the pods. Work one or two straight stitches at the lower end of the pod to form a point.

5. Embroider the sepals with three detached chain stitches (470).

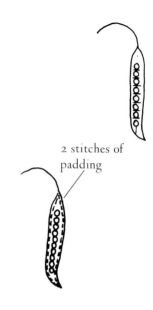

2 stitches of padding

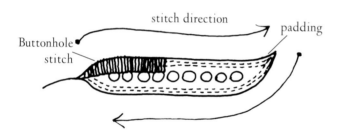

stitch direction

padding

Buttonhole stitch

Pea flower

This is embroidered with one strand of pink thread (225, 224, 223).

1. Work the edge of the upper petal in long and short buttonhole stitch, using pale pink thread (225) and keeping the stitch direction towards the centre edge of the petal. Embroider the petal in long and short stitch in pale pink, changing to medium pink (224) at the base of the petal.

2. Using dark pink thread (223), outline the lower petal in backstitch, pad with straight stitches then embroider in satin stitches to cover the outline.

Note: The detached upper petal is worked on calico/muslin mounted in a hoop (trace the outlines and work the detached leaves at the same time).

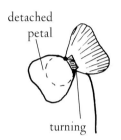

detached
petal

turning

3. Trace the upper petal shape on to calico. Couch then buttonhole the flower wire to the calico around outside edge with pale pink thread (225). Work a row of long and short buttonhole stitch inside the top edge of the wire, keeping the stitch direction towards the centre edge of the petal. Embroider the petal in long and short stitch in pale pink, changing to medium pink (224) at the base of the petal. Carefully cut out the petal, leaving a small turning (2 mm) of fabric at the lower edge (between the wires).

4. Using a chenille needle to insert the wires, apply the petal to the main fabric at the points as shown, keeping the petal face down over the lower petal. Secure the wires to the back of the upper petal. Stitch the turning to the upper petal with medium-pink thread, then curve the petal right side up to cover the turning.

Detached leaves

These are worked on calico/muslin with one strand of medium/light green thread (470 and 472).

1. Mount muslin in a hoop and trace detached leaves and pea flower upper petal (see Pea flower instructions).

2. Couch and overcast green-covered wire down central vein (472).

3. Couch and overcast (or buttonhole) the wire around the outside edge (470).

4. Work split backstitch next to the wire around all the inside edges then pad the leaf surface with long straight stitches (470).

5. Embroider the leaf in satin stitch (470).

6. Work the veins with straight stitches (472).

7. Carefully cut out the leaves and apply by inserting the wire at the base of the leaves on the main fabric, using a chenille needle. Secure the wire at the back of the work, then trim.

padding

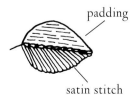

satin stitch

Pea Tendrils

The pea tendrils are made by wrapping wire with one strand
of light green thread (471 or 472). Either uncovered or green-
covered wire can be used — the uncovered is finer, the green-
covered is easier. (Refer p.33)

1. Knot the thread 1 cm (³/₈'') from the end of the wire.
Wrap over the wire (enclosing the thread tail) to the required
length. Knot again, leaving a tail of thread and wire.

2. Twist wrapped wire into a coil around a saté stick or
large knitting needle to form a tendril.

3. Using a chenille needle, insert the wire and tail of thread
through to the back of the work and secure.

4. Cut the unwrapped 1 cm (³/₈'') of wire close to the knot.

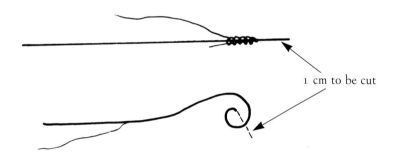

1 cm to be cut

Elizabethan Roundels

The *ELIZABETHAN ROUNDELS* were designed for a submission to the Embroiderers' Guild of America for its Seminar in San Francisco in 1996, and were inspired by the scrolling floral designs found in the embroideries of the Elizabethan period. These consisted of an all-over pattern of coiling stems enclosing flowers, birds and insects, worked in silk and metal threads, and decorated with spangles.

Garden flowers, rose, cornflower, borage, pansy, crown imperial lily, columbine, daffodil, carnation; wild flowers, thistle, convolvulus, honeysuckle, foxglove, daisy; fruit and berried plants, pear, nut, pomegranate, strawberry, grape, acorn; the peascod, transparent or open to show the peas, raindrops, birds and animals are but a few from a large repertoire freely used with the scroll.

BARBARA SNOOK, ENGLISH EMBROIDERY, 1960.

Two variations are given here, but many motifs from my first book could be used in this design.

I have very happy memories of my time spent on the west coast of the US (and Canada) in 1996.

ELIZABETHAN ROUNDEL WITH BUMBLE BEE

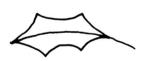

Skeleton outline

Detached leaves

Elizabethan Roundel with Bumble Bee, Plate 13. p. 216

REQUIREMENTS

- Black or ivory satin — 20 cm x 20 cm (8'' x 8'')

- Calico (or quilter's muslin) — 2 x (20 cm x 20 cm) (8'' x 8'')

- 10 cm (4'') and 15 cm (6'') embroidery hoops

- Wire: 30 gauge green covered wire, cut in 12 cm (5'') lengths

- 3 mm (¹/₈'') gold sequins

- Grapes (see p. 96).

- Thistles (see p. 134).

- Acorns (see p. 47).

- Bee (see p. 55).

- Needles: Crewel/embroidery 3-10
  Straw/milliners 3-9
  Tapestry 26
  Chenille 18
  Sharp yarn darner 14

- Threads: Vine and leaves — 469, 937
  Gold thread — DMC light gold thread (Art No. 282)
  Grapes — 902
  Thistle base — 3051, 3053, 356
  Thistle top — 3607, 718, 917 (cerise)
  or 316, 3726, 3727 (dusty pink)
  or 3042, 3041, 3740 (soft mauve)
  or 340, 3746, 333 (violet)
  Acorn kernel — 3045
  Acorn base — Au Ver à Soie Perlée 455
  Bumble bee — 783, 310 (black)

White rayon machine thread (Madeira No.40 colour
1001)
Gold/black metallic thread — Kreinik Cord 205c
Sequins — Nylon clear thread

ORDER OF WORK

1.   Mount the satin and a piece of calico/muslin for backing
into the 15 cm (6'') hoop.

2.   Trace the skeleton outline onto the satin using dressmaker's carbon paper for black fabric or tracing paper (GLAD
Bake) and lead pencil for ivory fabric.

3.   *Vine.* The vine is embroidered in interlaced chain stitch:
— work the chain stitches with three strands of green thread
(937) until the branches are reached, then in two strands
— whip both sides of main vine and one side only of branches
with the gold thread (undivided) in a tapestry needle.

4.   Grape leaf, grapes and tendrils.

5.   Thistles.

6.   Acorns.

7.   Bee.

8.   *Detached leaves.* These are worked on calico/muslin mounted in a hoop, with one strand of green thread and green covered wire.

OAK LEAF:
— couch then overcast the wire down the central vein (469)
— couch then buttonhole the wire around the outside edge
(937)
— work split back stitch on either side of the central vein
and inside the wire edge to provide a foundation into which
the leaf surface can be stitched
— embroider the leaf surface inside the wire in padded satin
stitch (937)
— work the veins in straight stitches with one strand of gold
thread.

THISTLE LEAF:

— couch then overcast the wire down the central vein (469)
— couch then buttonhole the wire around outside edge (937)
— embroider the leaf surface in stem stitch filling (937)
— work the veins with straight stitches in gold (optional).

Carefully cut out the leaves and apply, using a large yarn darner or chenille needle. Secure wires to the back of the vine and trim.

9. Apply sequins at random with nylon clear thread.

ELIZABETHAN ROUNDEL WITH LADYBIRD

Skeleton outline

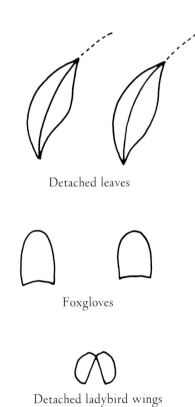

Detached leaves

Foxgloves

Detached ladybird wings

Elizabethan Roundel with Ladybird, Plate 14. p. 216

REQUIREMENTS

- Ivory satin — 20 cm x 20 cm (8'' x 8'')

- Calico (or quilter's muslin) — 2 pieces (20 cm x 20 cm) (8'' x 8'')

- 10 cm (4'') and 15 cm (6'') embroidery hoops

- Wire: 30 gauge green covered wire, cut in 12 cm (5'') lengths

- 3 mm (1/8'') gold sequins

- Carnation (see p. 71)

- Foxgloves (see p. 369 — substitute Mill Hill Antique Beads 3036)

- Strawberries (see p. 132)

- Ladybird (see p. 102 — substitute Mill Hill Petite Beads 42014 for eyes)

- Needles: Crewel/embroidery 3-10
  Straw/milliners 3-9
  Tapestry 26
  Sharps (or beading) 12
  Chenille 18
  Sharp yarn darner 14

- Threads: Vine and leaves — 469, 937
  Gold thread — DMC light gold thread (Art No. 282)
  Ladybird — 900 or 666 and black
  Foxgloves — 3740, 3041, 3042, 937
  Carnation — 470, 3825 or Madeira 2307
  Green soft cotton thread (DMC Soft Cotton 2470)
  Strawberries — 321, 469
  Red twisted silk thread — Kanagawa 1000 denier — Colour 4 or Au Ver à Soie Perlée 779 or 664 or 107
  Sequins — Nylon clear thread

ORDER OF WORK

1.   Mount the satin and a piece of calico/muslin for backing into the 15 cm (6'') hoop.

2.   Trace the skeleton outline onto the satin.

3.   *Vine.* The vine is embroidered in interlaced chain stitch:
— work the chain stitches with three strands of green thread (937)   until the branches are reached, then in two strands
— whip both sides of main vine and one side only of branches with the gold thread (undivided) in a tapestry needle.

4.   Carnation.

5.   Foxgloves (substitute Mill Hill Antique Beads 3036).

6.   Strawberries.

7.   Ladybird (substitute Mill Hill Petite Beads 42014 for eyes).

8.   *Detached leaves.* These are worked on calico/muslin mounted in a hoop, with one strand of green thread and green covered wire.

STRAWBERRY LEAF:
— couch then overcast the wire down the central vein (469)
— couch then buttonhole the wire around the outside edge (937)
— work split backstitch on either side of the central vein and inside the wire edge to provide a foundation into which the leaf surface can be stitched
— embroider the leaf surface inside the wire in padded satin stitch (937)
— work the veins in straight stitches with one strand of gold thread.

CARNATION LEAF:
— couch then overcast the wire down the central vein (469)
— couch then buttonhole the wire around outside edge (937)
— embroider the leaf surface in stem stitch filling (937)
— work the veins with straight stitches with one strand of gold thread.

Carefully cut out the leaves and apply, using a large yarn darner or chenille needle. Secure wires to the back of the vine and
trim.

9.   Apply sequins at random with nylon clear thread.

Chapter 7 Just Pansies

Before the cultivation of what we know as pansies, wild pansies or heartsease were familiar to the Elizabethans. These tiny, fragile flowers delighted the English and Europeans who found great charm in their 'faces'. Queens and empresses grew pansies in their gardens, including Elizabeth I of England and, later, in the eighteenth century, the Empress Josephine of France, who grew heartsease in her famous garden at Malmaison.

JENNIFER ISAACS,
THE SECRET MEANING OF FLOWERS, 1993.

Pansy

Apply pansies to your choice of background fabric, either in a bunch or as part of a garland. A single pansy makes a lovely gift when mounted in a brooch or on top of a small bowl or box.

REQUIREMENTS

- Calico (or quilter's muslin) — 20 cm x 20 cm (8'' x 8'')

- 10 cm (4'') embroidery hoop

- Wire: Fine flower wire, cut in 12 cm (5'') lengths

- Marking pens to colour wire (optional)

- Fine tweezers for shaping wire

- Needles: Crewel/embroidery 10
  Chenille 18

- Threads: see requirements for individual pansies

To embroider detached pansy petals

1.   Mount the calico into the hoop and trace the pansy petals. Number them from 1 to 5 as shown. The petals are embroidered with one strand of thread using the colours as indicated on the individual pansy diagrams. Colour the flower wire with marking pen if desired.

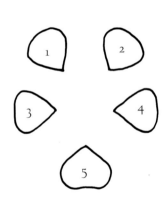

2.   Embroider each pansy petal as follows:

(a)   Starting at the base of the petal, couch the wire to the calico around the petal shape. For petals 1 to 4, leave one tail of wire with which to apply the petal. Leave two tails of wire for petal 5. Using the same thread, stitch the wire to the calico with small, close buttonhole stitches, incorporating the couching stitches and working the buttonhole ridge on the outside edge of the petal.

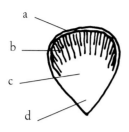

(b)   The top third of each petal is covered by a row of long and short buttonhole stitches, worked close together and close to the inside edge of the wire. Keep the stitch direction towards the centre of the pansy.

(c)   Embroider the petal in straight stitches, keeping the stitch direction towards the centre of the pansy.

(d)   Embroider blotches and/or rays at the base of the petals.

To apply the detached petals

1.   Using sharp scissors, cut out the petals close to the buttonholed edge, avoiding the wire tails.

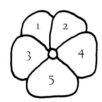

2.   The pansy petals are attached to the main fabric by inserting the wire tails one at a time, through the same hole, using a large chenille needle. Apply the petals in the order as numbered (petal 5 is applied last), securing the wire tails with small stitches to the back of the work. For petal 5, spread and stitch the two wire tails separately to give support to the petal. It is easier to secure each petal before proceeding to the next. Trim the wires.

3.   Work the centre of the pansy with a French knot (two wraps) using a chenille needle and 6 strands of thread (keep the knot fairly loose). Carefully shape the petals with fine tweezers or fingers.

GOLD/PURPLE PANSY

THREADS

Au Ver à Soie d'Alger 3326 (dark purple), 1336 (bright purple)

Madeira Stranded Silk 113, 114 (two shades of bright yellow)

DMC Stranded Cotton 740 (orange), 741 (orange/yellow)

1.   Follow the general instructions to work the detached pansy petals, using the colours as indicated on the diagram.

2.   Apply the detached petals to the main fabric.

3.   Work the centre with 6 strands of thread (3 each of 740 and 741).

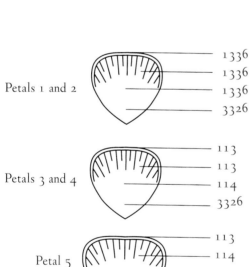

Petals 1 and 2
1336
1336
1336
3326

Petals 3 and 4
113
113
114
3326

Petal 5
113
114
741
3326

Diagrams not to scale

GOLD/YELLOW PANSY

THREADS

Au Ver à Soie d'Alger 4636 (very dark plum)

Au Ver à Soie d'Alger 611, 612 (two shades of orange/yellow)

DMC Stranded Cotton 3830 (terracotta), 742 (dark yellow)

Cifonda Silk 174 (orange/yellow)

1.   Follow the general instructions to work the detached pansy petals, using the colours as indicated on the diagram.

2.   Apply the detached petals to the main fabric.

3.   Work the centre with 6 strands of thread (3 each of 742 and 174).

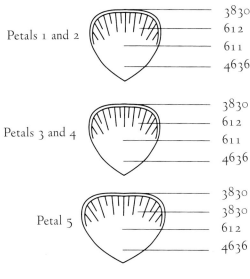

Petals 1 and 2
3830
612
611
4636

Petals 3 and 4
3830
612
611
4636

Petal 5
3830
3830
612
4636

Diagrams not to scale

Mauve Pansy/Viola

THREADS

Au Ver à Soie d'Alger 1316 (bright purple/mauve)

DMC Stranded Cotton 550 (dark violet), 742 (dark yellow)

Minnamurra Stranded Cotton 110 (variegated mauve/yellow)

Cifonda Silk 174 (orange/yellow)

1. Follow the general instructions to work the detached pansy petals, using the colours as indicated on the diagram.

2. Apply the detached petals to the main fabric.

3. Work the centre with 6 strands of thread (3 each of 742 and 174).

Petals 1 and 2 — 1316 / 1316 / 550 / 110

Petals 3 and 4 — 1316 / 1316 / 550 / 110

Petal 5 — 1316 / 1316 / 550 / 110

Diagrams not to scale

ORANGE RUSSET PANSY

THREADS

Au Ver à Soie d'Alger 3326 (dark purple), 616 (rust)

Au Ver à Soie d'Alger 645, 646 (two shades of orange)

DMC Stranded Cotton 742 (dark yellow)

Cifonda Silk 174 (orange/yellow)

1.   Follow the general instructions to work the detached pansy petals, using the colours as indicated on the diagram.

2.   Apply the detached petals to the main fabric.

3.   Work the centre with 6 strands of thread (3 each of 742 and 174).

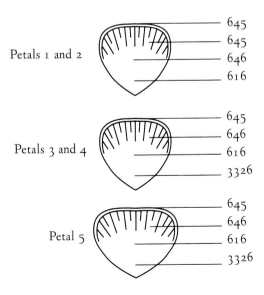

Petals 1 and 2 — 645, 645, 646, 616

Petals 3 and 4 — 645, 646, 616, 3326

Petal 5 — 645, 646, 616, 3326

Diagrams not to scale

DEEP RED PANSY

THREADS

Au Ver à Soie d'Alger 2926 (very dark red)

Au Ver à Soie d'Alger 4636 (very dark plum)

DMC Stranded Cotton 3830 (terracotta), 742 (dark yellow)

Minnamurra Stranded Cotton 110 (variegated mauve/yellow)

Cifonda Silk 174 (orange/yellow)

1. Follow the general instructions to work the detached pansy petals, using the colours as indicated on the diagram.

2. Apply the detached petals to the main fabric.

3. Work the centre with 6 strands of thread (3 each of 742 and 174).

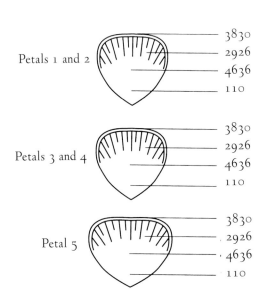

Petals 1 and 2 — 3830 / 2926 / 4636 / 110

Petals 3 and 4 — 3830 / 2926 / 4636 / 110

Petal 5 — 3830 / 2926 / 4636 / 110

Diagrams not to scale

ROYAL PURPLE PANSY

THREADS

Au Ver à Soie d'Alger 1336 (bright purple)

DMC Stranded Cotton 939 (dark navy blue), 742 (dark yellow)

Cifonda Silk 125 (purple), black, 174 (orange/yellow)

1. Follow the general instructions to work the detached pansy petals, using the colours as indicated on the diagram. Embroider rays in black silk at the base of the petals.

2. Apply the detached petals to the main fabric.

3. Work the centre with 6 strands of thread (3 each of 742 and 174).

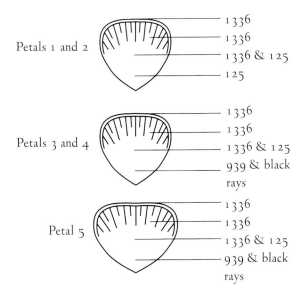

Diagrams not to scale

VIOLET/PURPLE PANSY

THREADS

Au Ver à Soie d'Alger 3326 (dark purple)

Au Ver à Soie d'Alger 1343, 1344, 1345 (three shades of violet)

DMC Stranded Cotton 741 (orange/yellow)

Cifonda Silk 174 (orange/yellow)

1.   Follow the general instructions to work the detached pansy petals, using the colours as indicated on the diagram.

2.   Apply the detached petals to the main fabric.

3.   Work the centre with 6 strands of thread (3 each of 741 and 174).

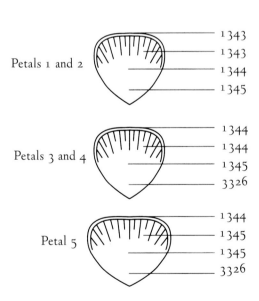

Petals 1 and 2
— 1343
— 1343
— 1344
— 1345

Petals 3 and 4
— 1344
— 1344
— 1345
— 3326

Petal 5
— 1344
— 1345
— 1345
— 3326

Diagrams not to scale

Single Pansy Brooch

Detached pansy petals are applied over embroidered leaves, then mounted into a purchased brooch form, bowl or box.

REQUIREMENTS

- Ivory satin (or fabric of choice) — 20 cm x 20 cm (8'' x 8'')

- Calico (or quilters' muslin) — 20 cm x 20 cm (8'' x 8'')

- 10 cm (4'') embroidery hoop

- Detached pansy petals of choice

- Needles: Crewel/embroidery 10
  Chenille 18

- Threads: Green stranded thread for leaves (DMC 3345)

ORDER OF WORK

1. Mount the main fabric and calico/muslin backing into the embroidery hoop.

2. Trace the outline of leaves onto the main fabric.

3. The leaves are embroidered with one strand of green thread as follows:
— Work the central vein in chain stitch.
— Pad the leaf surface with straight stitches.
— Embroider each side of the leaf in buttonhole stitch, inserting the needle close to the central vein, with the button-holed edge forming the edge of the leaf. Work the stitches from the base of the leaf to the point, at an angle, and very close together.

4. Following the instructions for single pansies (see p.104), apply the petals over the leaves, then work the pansy centre.

5. This project can be mounted into a Framecraft brooch,

rosewood bowl or porcelain box, with the following alter-
ations to the assembly procedure:
— trim the calico backing to a circle slightly smaller than the
cardboard template/backing plate supplied
— with a small seam allowance, gather the main fabric only
over the cardboard, the calico backing becoming an additional
padding layer
— insert the pansy into the empty frame — the acetate supplied will not be used.

Ring of Pansies

This garland of pansies (Gold/yellow pansy,
Gold/purple pansy and Royal purple pansy) looks pretty
mounted into a gilt pincushion. Substitute your own colours
or use any combination of the seven pansies provided.

Skeleton outline

REQUIREMENTS

- Ivory satin —20 cm x 20 cm (8'' x 8'')

- Calico (or quilter's muslin) — 2 pieces, 20 cm x 20 cm (8'' x 8'')

- 10 cm (4'') embroidery hoop

- Wire: 28 gauge uncovered or fine flower wire, cut in 12 cm (5'') lengths

- Marking pens to colour the wire if desired

- Needles: Crewel/embroidery 5-10
  Straw/milliners 1 or 3
  Chenille 18

- Threads: Stems and leaves — dark and medium green stranded (DMC 3345, 3346)
  Pansies — see individual directions for threads and colours

ORDER OF WORK

1. Mount the satin and one piece of calico/muslin for backing into a 10 cm (4'') embroidery hoop.

2. Trace the skeleton outline onto the satin.

3. *Stems.* Work the stems in whipped chain stitch with dark green thread (3345). Use three strands for the central ring and two strands for the pansy bud stems.

4. *Leaves.* The leaves are embroidered with one strand of thread:
— work the central vein in chain stitch (3346)
— pad the leaf surface with straight stitches (3345)
— embroider each side of the leaf in buttonhole stitch, inserting the needle close to the central vein, with the buttonholed edge forming the edge of the leaf. Work the stitches from the base of the leaf to the point, at an angle and very close together (3345)
— the veins are worked with straight stitches (3346), if desired.

5.   *Pansy Buds.* The buds are worked with one strand of thread in colours to match each pansy:
— work the lower edge in long and short buttonhole stitch, then embroider the bud with straight stitches in desired colour/s
— using two strands of green thread, work three detached chain stitches at the base of each bud to form the sepals.

6. *Pansy Petals.* Mount the remaining piece of calico into a hoop and trace pansy petals (5 petals for each pansy):
— follow individual instructions to work the five detached petals for each of the three pansies
— using small, sharp scissors, cut out the petals close to the buttonholed edge, avoiding the wire tails
— the pansy petals are attached to the main fabric by inserting the wire tails, one at a time, through the same hole, using a large chenille needle. Apply the petals in the order as numbered (petal 5 is applied last), securing the wire tails to the calico backing with small stitches. Secure each petal before proceeding to the next. Trim the wires
— work the centre of each pansy with a French knot (two soft wraps) using a chenille (or straw) needle and 6 strands of thread (3 each of both yellows)
— carefully shape petals with eyebrow tweezers or fingers.

Finishing

The finished piece can be mounted into the lid of a Framecraft Gilded Pincushion 8 cm (3'') following the enclosed directions.

Another option is to convert the pincushion into a frame, using only the gilded metal base and rim:
— cut out embroidery with a 2 cm (1'') seam allowance and gather over a circle of cardboard the same size as the pincushion
— insert into the base of the pincushion, securing with a little glue if desired
— glue a circle of perspex or glass inside the rim and secure to the base
— a small brass ring can be glued to the back of the base to enable the frame to be hung.

Pansy and Beetle, Plate 6. p. 213

This design can be worked with any coloured pansy, and a bee instead of a beetle if desired. When mounted in a small paperweight it makes a lovely gift.

REQUIREMENTS

- Ivory satin — 20 cm x 20 cm (8'' x 8'')

- Calico (or quilter's muslin) — 2 pieces (20 cm x 20 cm) (8'' x 8")

- 10 cm (4'') embroidery hoop

- Wire: 30 gauge green-covered, 12 cm (5'') length

- Pansy (see p.240)

- Beetle (see p.256)

- Small snail (see p.128)

- Needles: Crewel/embroidery 5-10
  Straw/milliners 3-9
  Chenille 18
  Sharp yarn darner 14

- Threads: Stems and leaves — three shades of green (DMC 3346, 3345, 895)
  Beetle — blue/grey (DMC 930 or Cifonda Silk 215)
  Pansy — choice of colour — see individual pansy directions for threads
  Snail — own choice of stranded threads for body and shell

Skeleton outline

ORDER OF WORK

1.   Mount the satin and a piece of calico/muslin for backing into the hoop.

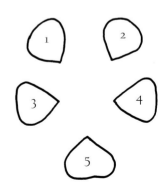

Detached pansy petals

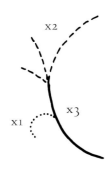

2.   Trace the skeleton outline onto the satin.

3.   *Stems.* Embroider the stems with whipped chain stitch in dark green thread (895). Work the chain stitches and the whipping with the number of threads indicated on the diagram.

4.   *Leaf on main fabric.* This leaf is worked with one strand of green thread:
— work the central vein in chain stitch (3346)
— pad the leaf surface inside the outline with long stitches (3345)
— working from the base to the tip, embroider the leaf with long buttonhole stitches (3345)
— work the veins in straight stitches (3346).

5.   *Pansy bud.* The bud is worked with one strand of thread in colours to match the pansy.
— work the lower edge in long and short buttonhole stitch, then embroider the bud in straight stitches
— using two strands of green thread (3345), work three detached chain stitches at the base of the bud to form the sepals.

6.   Small Snail.

7.   Beetle.

8.   Pansy.

9.   *Detached leaf.* This is worked on calico mounted in a hoop with one strand of green thread and green-covered wire:
— couch then overcast the wire down the central vein (3346)
— couch then buttonhole the wire around outside edge (3345)
— pad stitch leaf and work split backstitch around inside edge of wire (3345)
— work leaf in satin stitch (3345)
— work veins in straight stitches (3346).

10.   Assemble into paperweight if desired.

Detached pansy leaf

BEETLE

Never kill a beetle, but leave him to go about his important work in the garden. If a black beetle crawls over your shoe, it is a warning against illness which bids you to take better care of your health. Many nocturnal flying beetles predict fine weather.

CLAIRE NAHMAD, GARDEN SPELLS, 1994.

MATERIALS REQUIRED

· Pad for working detached buttonhole stitch (see p. 29)

· Wire: 28 gauge uncovered, 15 cm (6'') length
(or 30 gauge blue-covered wire is easier to manage)

· Fine tweezers to shape wire

· Grey felt and paper-backed fusible web — 5 cm x 8 cm
(3'' x 2'')

· Blue/bronze snakeskin — small piece

· Mill Hill Petite Glass Beads — 40374 (blue/black)

· Needles: Crewel 3-9
Tapestry 26
Chenille 18
Sharps needles 12

· Thread: Blue/grey stranded (DMC 930 or Cifonda Silk
215)
Slate blue metallic thread (Kreinik Cord 225c)
Nylon clear thread

Detached wings (elytra)

1.   Wrap the middle 5 cms (2'') approximately of the wire with one strand of the blue/grey thread, leaving a tail at each end.

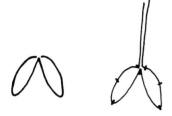

2.   Transfer the wing outline to the buttonhole pad and cover with self-adhesive plastic (see p. 29). Tack the wrapped wire around the wing outline, leaving two tails of wire (mostly not wrapped) as shown.

3.   With one strand of metallic thread in the tapestry needle, work a row of buttonhole stitch over the wire around the inside of one wing, then work about three rows of corded detached buttonhole stitch to fill the wing. Repeat for the other wing. Remove the tacking stitches to release the wings.

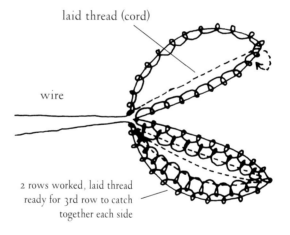

laid thread (cord)

wire

2 rows worked, laid thread ready for 3rd row to catch together each side

Abdomen

1. Using the paper-backed fusible web, cut two pieces of grey felt to pad the abdomen; one the actual shape of the abdomen and one sightly smaller.

2. With one strand of the blue/grey thread, stab stitch the felt in place (applying the smaller shape first), then cover the felt with satin stitch, worked from side to side to represent the segments of the abdomen.

To apply detached wings and complete beetle

1. Insert the wires and any thread tails at • using a chenille needle (or large yarn darner), bend under the abdomen and secure at the back with a few small stitches.

2. With blue/grey thread, work a few satin stitches at • for padding under the head. The head is cut from snakeskin and applied with nylon thread in a sharps needle. Cut the snakeskin a little larger than the head shape, then trim to size as you apply — make sure it is wide enough to cover the top of the wings.

Attach the snakeskin head at five points as follows:
— work the first two stitches on either side of the wings (1 and 2)
— make one stitch at centre front (3)
— on either side of the centre apply two petite beads for the eyes with 2-3 stitches into the snakeskin (4 and 5).

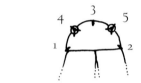

3. With two strands of the metallic thread in a straw needle, work three backstitches for each leg. Complete by working a fly stitch for the feelers with one strand of metallic thread.

eye — 3 stitches

Chapter 8 Fruits, Flowers and Insects

These projects vary in degree of difficulty from simple brooches using one element to the more time consuming 'mirror frames'. It will be helpful to read the points on this page before embarking on a project.

- Ivory duchess satin, with a backing of quilter's muslin, has been used as the main fabric for most of the projects. Almost any fabric can be substituted as long as it has a suitable backing.

- At the beginning of each project, a list of Suggested Threads is given. These are DMC stranded cottons unless otherwise indicated. Colours and threads can be changed if desired. Nearly all the embroidery is worked with one strand of thread in a size 10 crewel needle.

- The Order of Work is cross-referenced to the Individual Elements chapter, which gives instructions and the materials required for all the elements. Any variations in colours or materials are specified in each project. Almost any element in a project can be replaced by a preferred element if desired.

- Directions for leaves and stems are cross-referenced to the General Instructions chapter. These are suggestions only and can be replaced by a preferred method.

Brooches

Individual elements can be embroidered on their own to make charming brooches. They can be mounted into purchased brooch forms, or gathered over cardboard and attached to a pin (see p.44)

Ladybird Stickpin. Plate 15. p. 265

Embroider a ladybird (see p. 101) on satin, gather over thin cardboard and glue to a purchased stickpin base. Try this project with a bee!

Grape Brooch. Plate 16. p. 265

Embroider a grape leaf, grapes and tendrils (p.95) on satin and mount into a purchased brooch form.

Pansy Brooch. Plates 19 and 20. p. 268

Detached pansy petals are applied over embroidered leaves, then mounted into a purchased brooch form.

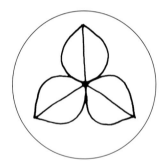

SUGGESTED THREADS

- Leaves: 3345

- Pansy: Petals – Au Ver à Soie Soie d'Alger 1343, 1344, 1345, 3326
  Centre – 741, Cifonda Silk 174

ORDER OF WORK

1. Mount dark green/black silk (or ivory satin) and calico backing into a small hoop.

2. Trace the outline of the leaves with white or orange dressmaker's carbon paper.

3. Embroider the leaves in buttonhole stitch (method 4, p.36).

4. Embroider the pansy petals (p. 109) with the violet/purple threads.

5. Apply the petals over the leaves, then work the pansy centre.

6. Mount the finished embroidery into a purchased brooch form (p. 44). An individual pansy would also make a pretty top for a tiny gift box.

Rose, Pomegranate and Strawberries, Plate 24. p. 288

SUGGESTED THREADS

- Strawberry: 321, Kanagawa Silk 1000 denier col. 4 or Au Ver à Soie Soie Perlée 779, 664 or 107
  Sepals – 937

- Split pomegranate: 350, 351, 352

- Stems: 869, 830 or 730

- Stem leaves: 937

- Rose:
  Petals in 3 shades – (3713, 761, 760) or (225, 224, 223) or (745, 744, 743)
  Centre – 744, 745 or 3347 or 471
  Stem – 830, Tapestry Cotton 2830
  Thorns – 937, or Kreinik Cord 215c

- Leaf: (937, 470) or (3345, 3346)

Pomegranate pattern

Skeleton outline

Rose, Pomegranate and Strawberries

- Soldier-fly:
  Body – 3765 or 3820
  Wings and legs – Madeira No. 40 astro-1 or astro-3,
  Kreinik Cord 205c

- Bee: Body – 310 (black), 783
  Wings and legs – Madeira Rayon No. 40 col. 1001,
  Kreinik Cord 205c

ORDER OF WORK

1. Mount the main fabric and backing fabric (both 20 cm x 20 cm, or 8" x 8") into a 15 cm (6") hoop.

2. Trace the skeleton outline onto the main fabric.

3. Strawberries (p. 132).

4. Split pomegranate (p. 117).

5. With two strands of the brown thread, work the stems of the strawberries and pomegranate in rows of stem stitch, as indicated on the diagram.
   Using one strand of the green thread, and a detached chain stitch with a straight stitch inside, embroider the small stem leaves.

6. Needlelace rose (p. 124).

7. To work the rose stem, wrap two strands of soft cotton thread with one strand of green/brown thread (method 7, p. 37). Work the thorns with either stranded or metallic thread.

8. On the main fabric, starting at the point of the leaf, outline each side in single feather stitch. Embroider the leaf with long and short stitch (method 2, p. 35).

9. Work the detached leaf in long and short stitch (method 2, p. 34).

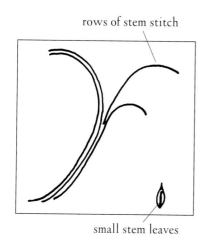

rows of stem stitch

small stem leaves

10. Soldier-fly (p. 129).

11. Bee (p. 55).

Rose and Bee. Plate 22. p. 286

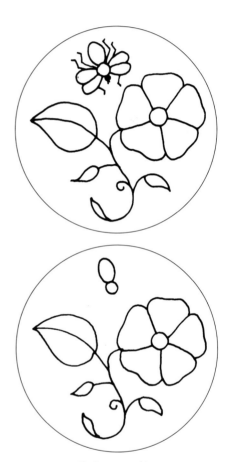

Skeleton outline

SUGGESTED THREADS

- Stems: 936 or 830 or 935

- Stem leaves: 470 or 3346

- Leaf: (937, 470) or (3345, 3346)

- Rose: Petals in 3 shades – (3713, 761, 760) or (225, 224, 223) or (745, 744, 743)
  Centre – 744, 745 or 3347 or 471

- Bee: Body – 310 (black), 783
  Wings – Madeira Rayon No. 40 col. 1001
  Legs – Kreinik Cord 205c

ORDER OF WORK

1. Mount the main fabric and backing fabric (both 20 cm x 20 cm, or 8" x 8") into a 10 cm (4") hoop.

2. Trace the skeleton outline onto the main fabric.

3. Work the stems in whipped chain stitch, using two strands of thread for the main stem and one strand for small stems. The tiny leaves are embroidered in padded satin stitch.

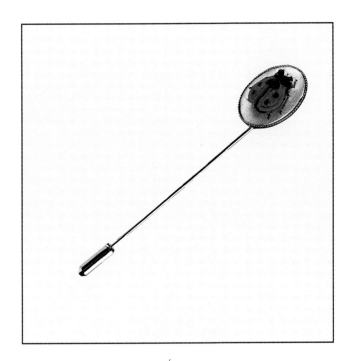

Plate 15

LADYBIRD STICKPIN

Plate 16

GRAPE BROOCH

Plate 17

BERRIES BROOCH

Plate 18

MEDIEVAL MIRROR FRAME 1

Plate 19

VIOLET/PURPLE PANSY BROOCH

Plate 20

ORANGE/RUSSET PANSY BROOCH

4.   On the main fabric, starting at the point of the leaf, outline each side in single feather stitch. Embroider the leaf with long and short stitch (method 2, p. 35).

5.   Work the detached leaf in long and short stitch (method 2, p. 34).

6.   Needlelace rose (p. 124 – replace method 1 with method 2 if desired).

7.   Bee (p. 55).

8.   Make into a paperweight or small box top (p. 42 or 43).

Acorn, Thistle and Bee. Plate 21. p. 285

SUGGESTED THREADS

- Leaves: Thistle – 3051, 3052
  Oak – 937, 470

- Stems: Thistle – 612, 611
  Oak – 370

- Thistle: Base – 3053, 356
  Top: (3726, 316, 3727) or (3607, 718, 917) or (3042, 3041, 3740) or (340, 3746, 333)

- Acorn: Kernel – 3045
  Base – Au Ver à Soie Soie Perlée 580 or 455 or 274

- Bee: Body – 310 (black), 783
  Wings – Madeira Rayon No. 40 col. 1001
  Legs – Kreinik Cord 205c

Skeleton outline

Acorn, Thistle and Bee

ORDER OF WORK

1. Mount the main fabric and backing fabric (both 20 cm x 20 cm, or 8" x 8") into a 15 cm (6") or 10 cm (4") hoop.

2. Trace the skeleton outline onto the main fabric.

3. Outline the thistle leaves in split backstitch. Work the veins in chain stitch, finishing each vein with a long securing stitch to form a spike. Embroider the leaves in long and short stitch (method 2, p. 35).

4. Using two strands of the brown thread, work the thistle stem with 2 1/2 rows of stem stitch, as shown in the diagram. With one strand of the darker brown thread, work the spikes in straight stitches and a detached chain stitch at the end of the stem.

5. For the oak leaves on the main fabric, work the central veins in chain stitch. Embroider each leaf in buttonhole stitch (method 4, p. 36).

6. Work the oak stems in whipped chain stitch, using three strands of thread for the main stem and two strands for the smaller branches. Stitch over the thistle stem.

7. Thistle flowers (p. 134).

8. Acorns (p. 47).

9. Work the detached oak leaves (p. 30).

10. Bee (p. 55).

11. Work the anniversary numbers, date or initials, or a small snail (p. 128) in the lower space, if desired.

Acorn, Thistle and Butterfly

Plate 23, p. 287

SUGGESTED THREADS

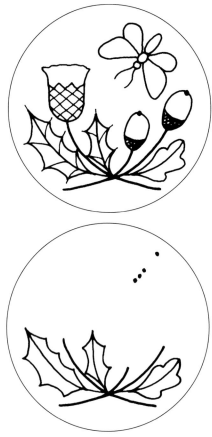

Skeleton outline

- Leaves: Thistle – 3051, 3052
  Oak – 937, 470

- Stems: Thistle – 611
  Oak – 370

- Thistle: Base – 3053, 356
  Top – (3726, 316, 3727) or (3607, 718, 917) or (3042, 3041, 3740) or (340, 3746, 333)

- Acorn: Kernel – 3045
  Base – Au Ver à Soie Soie Perlée 580 or 455 or 274

- Small butterfly: Wings – 744, 743, 3808, Madeira No. 40 astro 3
  Body – 3371, chenille thread

ORDER OF WORK

1. Mount the main fabric and backing fabric (both 20 cm x 20 cm, or 8" x 8") into a 10 cm (4") hoop.

2. Trace the skeleton outline onto the main fabric.

3. Outline the thistle leaves in split backstitch. Work the veins in chain stitch, finishing each vein with a long securing stitch to form a spike. Embroider the leaves in long and short stitch (method 2, p. 35).

4. Using two strands of the brown thread, work the thistle stem with 2 1/2 rows of stem stitch (see diagram on p. 270).

5. For the oak leaf on the main fabric, work the central vein in chain stitch, and embroider the leaf in buttonhole stitch (method 4, p. 36).

6. Work the oak stems in whipped chain stitch, using three strands of thread for the main stem and two strands for the smaller branches. Stitch over the thistle stem.

7. Thistle (p. 134).

8. Acorns (p. 47).

9. Work the detached oak leaf (p. 30).

10. Small butterfly (p. 68).

11. Make into a small box top or paperweight (p. 42 or 43).

Butterfly and Berries. Plate 31. p. 294

SUGGESTED THREADS

*   Stems: Blackberry – 801
    Orange – 610, 611

*   Leaves: Orange – 470, 469
    Red currant – 469, 3051
    Blueberry – 470, 937
    Gooseberry – 3052, 3362
    Blackberry – 3052, 3051

*   Gooseberries: 3013, 801, Cifonda Silk 44 or Madeira
    Metallic No. 40 gold 7

*   Blackberries: 902, 815, 304, 347, 3328, 3712, 760, 754,
    3013

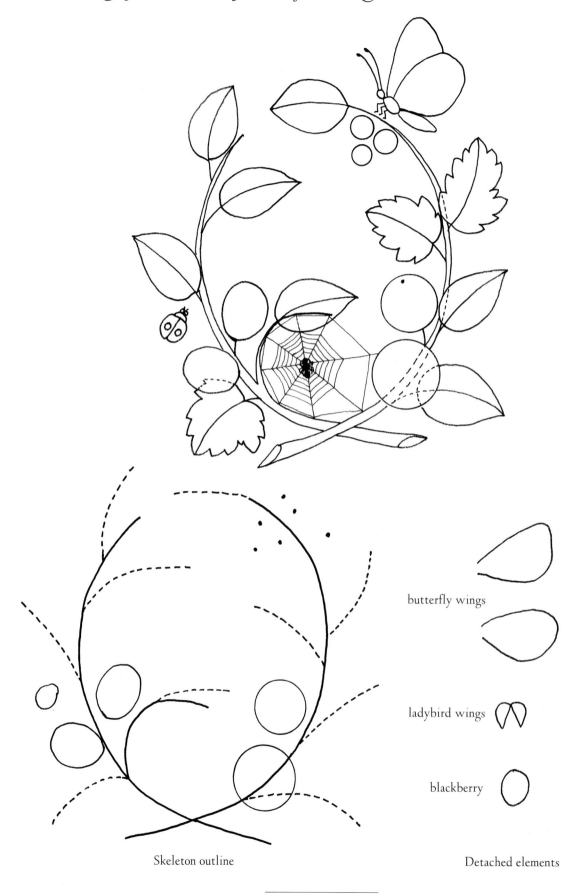

butterfly wings

ladybird wings

blackberry

Skeleton outline

Detached elements

BUTTERFLY AND BERRIES

Spikes – 3031
Sepals – Kanagawa Silk 1000 denier col. 113

· Blueberries: Au Ver à Soie Soie Perlée 636 or Kanagawa Silk 1000 denier col. 818

· Oranges: 301, 3776, 402

· Spider: Cifonda Silk black

· Red currants: 75

· Ladybird: 817 or 666 or 900, 310 (black)

· Butterfly: Choice of twisted silk threads for wings – Au Ver à Soie Soie Perlée or Kanagawa Silk 1000 denier, Kreinik Cord 215c
Body – 3709, Tapestry Cotton 2609, chenille thread

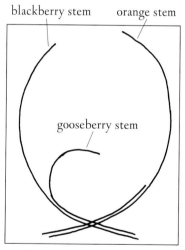

blackberry stem   orange stem

gooseberry stem

Placement of padding threads

ORDER OF WORK

1. Mount the main fabric and backing fabric (both 30 cm x 30 cm, or 12" x 12") into a 23 cm (9") hoop.

2. Trace the skeleton outline onto thin tracing paper and transfer to the main fabric with tacking (p. 41).

3. The stems are worked in raised stem band, using one strand of brown thread and soft cotton thread for padding:

Blackberry With stitches 2–3 mm (1/8") apart, couch one strand of soft cotton from the tip of the blackberry stem and one strand of soft cotton from the tip of the gooseberry stem, couching both strands together from where they join, to the base. Cover the couched threads with rows of raised stem band, working a few extra 'short' rows to make the lower stem thicker.

Orange Couch one strand of soft cotton from the tip of the orange stem to the orange, add a second strand, then couch

both strands together over the blackberry stem to the base.
Cover the couched threads with rows of raised stem band in
two shades of thread, the lighter shade in the centre, working
a few extra 'short' rows to make the lower stem thicker.
Finish the base of both stems with a detached chain stitch.

4. Embroider the leaves on the main fabric:

Orange Outline in slanted stem stitch (to give a serrated
edge) and embroider with stem stitch filling (method 3, p. 36).
   Red currant Outline in split backstitch, and embroider in
long and short stitch (method 2, p. 35).
   Gooseberry Outline in split backstitch and embroider in
padded satin stitch (method 1, p. 35).
   Blackberry Outline in single feather stitch (to give a spiked
edge) and embroider in long and short stitch (method 2, p. 35).

5. Gooseberries (p. 93).

6. Embroider the blackberries (p. 60), working the spikes in
straight stitches with stranded thread.

7. Blueberries (p. 63).

8. Oranges (p. 104).

9. Spider and spider web (pp. 130, 131).

10. Red currants (p. 80).

11. Ladybird (p. 101).

12. Needlelace butterfly (p. 69).

13. Embroider the detached leaves:

Orange Work in long and short stitch (method 2, p. 34).
Blueberry Work in long and short stitch (method 2, p. 34).
Gooseberry Work in padded satin stitch (method 1, p. 34).
Blackberry Work in stem stitch filling (method 3, p. 35).

Christmas Rose and Dragonfly
Plate 33, p. 296

SUGGESTED THREADS

- Stems: 829

- Leaves: Holly – 895
  Blackberry – 3346, 3345

- Blackberries: 902, 815, 304, 347, 3328
  Sepals – Kanagawa Silk 1000 denier col. 113

- Christmas rose: Petals – white (cotton or Madeira Silk)
  Centre – 3348, 744

- Dragonfly: Wings – 830 or Madeira Silk 2114, Madeira
  No. 40 astro-1 or astro-3
  Body – Tapestry Cotton 2830, bronze chenille thread,
  Kreinik Cord 205c

ORDER OF WORK

1. Mount the main fabric and backing fabric (both 20 cm x 20 cm, or 8" x 8") into a 10 cm (4") hoop.

2. Trace the skeleton outline onto the main fabric.

3. Work the stems in whipped chain stitch using two strands of brown thread.

4. For the holly leaves on the main fabric, work the central vein in chain stitch and embroider the leaves in buttonhole stitch (method 4, p. 36).

5. Work the blackberries (p. 60). Using one strand of green thread, work the sepals with detached chain stitches.

Skeleton outline

Detached leaves

CHRISTMAS ROSE AND DRAGONFLY

6. Christmas rose (p. 74).

7. Dragonfly (p. 82).

8. Embroider the detached leaves:

  Holly Work in padded satin stitch (method 1, p. 34).
  Blackberry Work in stem stitch filling (method 3, p. 35).

9. To complete, apply three 3 mm red pearls or beads for holly berries. Stitch 3 mm gold 'laser' sequins to the background, using nylon clear thread.

Pomegranate and Gooseberries
Plate 25. p. 289

SUGGESTED THREADS

- Stems: 300

- Leaves: 732, 733

- Gooseberries: 3013 or 3047, 801, Cifonda Silk 44 or Madeira Metallic No. 40 gold 7

- Pomegranate: 350, 351, 352

- Small snail: 3024, 3820, Tapestry Cotton 2921, Kreinik Cord 215c

- Ladybird: 900, 310 (black)

Skeleton outline

Ladybird wings

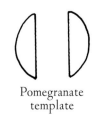

Pomegranate template

ORDER OF WORK

1. Mount the main fabric and backing fabric (both 20 cm x
20 cm, or 8" x 8") into a 10 cm (4") hoop.

2. Trace the skeleton outline onto the main fabric.

3. Work the stems in whipped chain stitch, using three
strands of thread for the lower stem and two strands for all the
smaller stems.

4. For the big leaf on the main fabric, work the central vein
in chain stitch, then embroider the leaf in buttonhole stitch
(method 4, p. 36). Work the small leaves in detached chain
stitches with two strands of thread (one of each green).

5. Gooseberries (p. 93).

6. Pomegranate (p. 116).

7. Small snail (p. 128).

8. Ladybird (p. 101).

9. Work the detached leaf in padded satin stitch (method 1,
p. 34).

10. Mount the finished embroidery inside or on top of the lid
of a small box (p. 42).

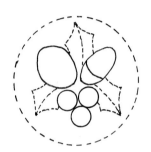

Skeleton outline

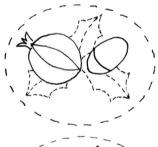

Pomegranate template

Christmas Acorn and Berries
Plate 27, p. 291

AND

Christmas Acorn and Pomegranate
Plate 28, p. 291

These tiny Christmas projects can be mounted into purchased boxes or brooch forms and make charming gifts.

SUGGESTED THREADS

- Holly leaves: 895

- Acorn: Kernel – 3045
  Base – Madeira Metallic No. 5 (Art. 9805) gold 5014

- Blackberry: 902, 815, 304, 347

- Split pomegranate: 350, 351, 352

- Red currants: 75

ORDER OF WORK

1. Mount the main fabric and backing fabric (both 20 cm x 20 cm, or 8" x 8") into a 10 cm (4") hoop.

2. Trace the skeleton outline onto the main fabric.

3. Work the central vein of the holly leaves in split backstitch. Embroider the leaves in buttonhole stitch (method 4, p. 36).

4. Embroider the acorn (p. 47), replacing the silk buttonhole twist with metallic thread.

Skeleton outline

5.   Embroider the blackberry (p. 60) or the split pomegranate
(p. 117).

6.   Embroider the red currants (p. 80). Finish the top of each
with a Mill Hill Petite Glass Bead 42028.

7.   To complete, stitch 3 mm gold 'laser' sequins to the
background, using nylon clear thread.

Dragonfly and Berries, Plate 30. p. 293

SUGGESTED THREADS

*   Stems: Blackberry – 801
    Pomegranate – 610, 611

*   Leaves: Pomegranate – 469, 937
    Blackcurrant – 469, 3051
    Gooseberry – 3052, 3362
    Blackberry – 3052, 3051

*   Gooseberries: 3013 or 472 or 3047, 801, Cifonda Silk 44
    or Madeira Metallic No. 40 gold 7

*   Blackberries: 902, 815, 304, 347, 3328, 3712, 760, 754,
    3013
    Sepals – Kanagawa Silk 1000 denier col. 113

*   Pomegranates: 350, 351, 352

*   Spider web – Madeira Metallic No. 40 silver

*   Spider: Cifonda Silk black

*   Black currants: Au Ver à Soie Soie d'Alger 3326

*   Ladybird: 817 or 666 or 900, 310 (black)

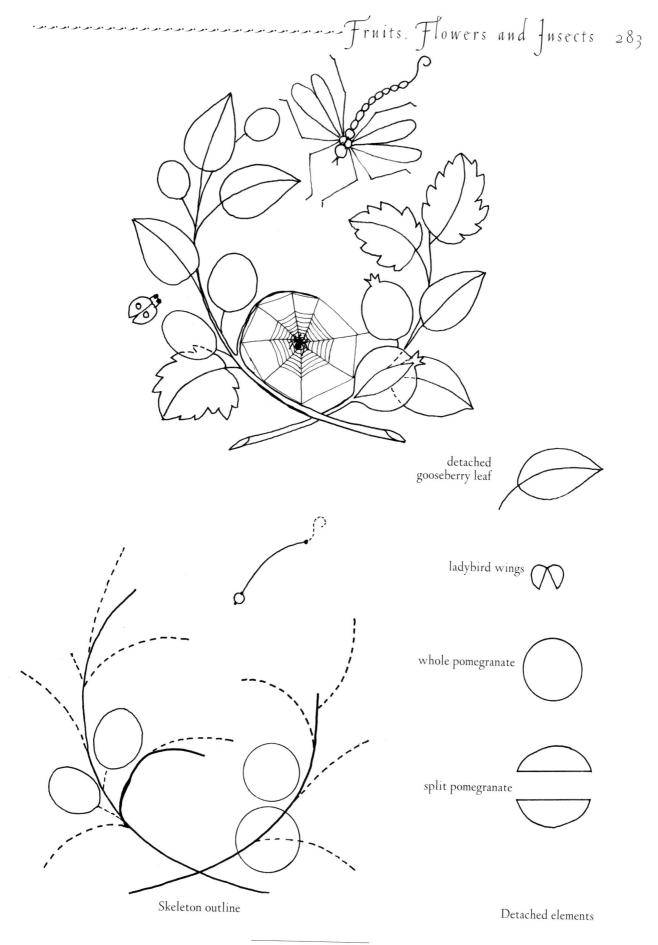

detached
gooseberry leaf

ladybird wings

whole pomegranate

split pomegranate

Skeleton outline

Detached elements

DRAGONFLY AND BERRIES

· Dragonfly: Wings – 3808, Madeira Rayon No. 40 col.
1045
Body – Tapestry Cotton 2131, teal chenille thread,
Kreinik Cord 205c

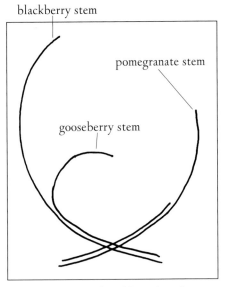

Placement of padding threads

ORDER OF WORK

1. Mount the main fabric and backing fabric (both 30 cm x
30 cm, or 12" x 12") into a 23 cm (9") hoop.

2. Trace the skeleton outline onto thin tracing paper and
transfer to the main fabric with tacking (p. 41),

3. The stems are worked in raised stem band, using one strand
of brown thread and soft cotton thread for padding.

Blackberry With stitches 2–3 mm (1/8") apart, couch one
strand of soft cotton from the tip of the blackberry stem and
one strand of soft cotton from the tip of the gooseberry stem,
couching both strands together from where they join, to the
base. Cover the couched threads with rows of raised stem
band, working a few extra 'short' rows to make the lower
stem thicker.
Pomegranate Couch one strand of soft cotton from the tip of
the pomegranate stem to the pomegranate, add a second strand,
then couch both strands together, over the blackberry stem, to
the base. Cover with rows of raised stem band in two shades
of thread, the lighter shade in the centre, working a few extra
'short' rows to make the lower stem thicker.
Finish the base of both stems with a detached chain stitch.

4. Embroider the leaves on the main fabric:

Pomegranate Outline in slanted stem stitch (to give a
serrated edge) and embroider the leaf in stem stitch filling
(method 3, p. 36),
Black currant Outline in split backstitch and embroider the
leaf in long and short stitch (method 2, p. 35),

Plate 21

ACORN, THISTLE AND BEE

Plate 22
ROSE AND BEE

Plate 23

ACORN, THISTLE AND BUTTERFLY

Plate 24

ROSE, POMEGRANATE AND STRAWBERRIES

Plate 25

POMEGRANATE AND GOOSEBERRIES

Plate 26

CHRISTMAS ROSE, BERRIES AND DRAGONFLY

Plate 27

CHRISTMAS ACORN AND BERRIES

Plate 28

CHRISTMAS ACORN AND POMEGRANATE

Plate 29

MEDIEVAL MIRROR FRAME 2

Plate 30

DRAGONFLY AND BERRIES

Plate 31

BUTTERFLY AND BERRIES

Plate 32

HELLEBORE, BERRIES AND DRAGONFLY

Plate 33

CHRISTMAS ROSE AND DRAGONFLY

Gooseberry Outline in split backstitch and embroider the leaf in padded satin stitch (method 1, p.35).

Blackberry Outline in single feather stitch (to give a spiked edge) and embroider the leaf in long and short stitch (method 2, p. 35).

5. Gooseberries (p. 93).

6. Blackberries (p. 60).

7. Pomegranate (p. 116).

8. Spider and spider web (pp. 130, 131).

9. Black currants (p. 80).

10. Ladybird (p. 101).

11. Dragonfly (p. 82).

12. Embroider the detached leaves:

Pomegranate Work in long and short stitch (method 2, p. 34).
Gooseberry Work in padded satin stitch (method 1, p. 34).
Blackberry Work in stem stitch filling (method 3, p. 35).

Hellebore, Berries and Dragonfly
Plate 32. p. 295

SUGGESTED THREADS

- Stems: Ivy – 730
  Blackberry – 829

- Fruiting ivy: Berries – 315, 3740
  Cups – Au Ver à Soie Soie Perlée 274

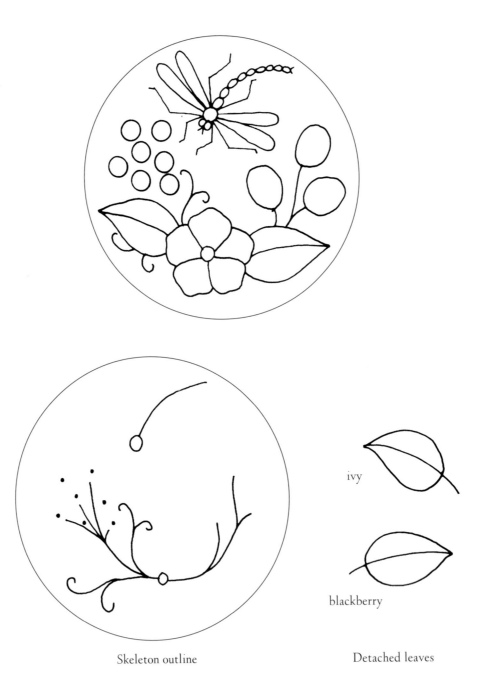

ivy

blackberry

Skeleton outline   Detached leaves

HELLEBORE, BERRIES AND DRAGONFLY

- Blackberries: 902, 815, 304, 347, 3328, 3712, 760, 754, 3013
  Sepals – Au Ver à Soie Soie Perlée 274

- Hellebore: white, 316, 472, 743, 744

- Dragonfly: Wings – 3808, Madeira Rayon No. 40 col. 1045
  Body – Tapestry Cotton 2131, teal chenille thread, Kreinik Cord 205c

- Leaves: 580, 581

ORDER OF WORK

1. Mount the main fabric and backing fabric (both 20 cm x 20 cm, or 8" x 8") into a 10 cm (4") hoop.

2. Trace the skeleton outline onto the main fabric.

3. Embroider the stems:

   Ivy Work in chain stitch with one strand of thread.
   Blackberry Work in whipped chain stitch with two strands of thread.

4. Fruiting ivy (p. 91).

5. Blackberries (p. 60).

6. Hellebore (p. 98).

7. Dragonfly (p. 82).

8. Embroider the detached leaves:

   Ivy Work in stem stitch filling (method 3, p. 35).
   Blackberry Work in padded satin stitch (method 1, p. 34).

Christmas Rose, Berries and Dragonfly
(in white) Plate 26, p. 290

This piece was the result of a 'challenge' issued to a class who were working the same project in colours. They were asked 'to interpret the design in whites, creams or a mixture of both', and the results were fascinating – one student even worked the whole piece in goldwork. Imagine the bodice of a wedding gown embroidered in an assortment of ivory threads and beads!

SUGGESTED THREADS

- Stems: 739

- Fruiting ivy: Berries – Au Ver à Soie Soie Ovale (flat silk) creme
  Cups – Kanagawa Silk 1000 denier col. 97 or Au Ver à Soie Soie Perlée 080

- Blackberries: ecru, 712, 739, Au Ver à Soie Soie Ovale creme, Madeira Decora 1471, Madeira Silk white
  Sepals – Kanagawa Silk 1000 denier col. 97 or Au Ver à Soie Soie Perlée 080

- Christmas rose: Outside buttonhole stitch – Raj Mahal Art Silk 96 (white)
  Petals – Madeira Silk white, Madeira Decora 1471

- Dragonfly: Wings – Raj Mahal Art Silk 96
  Abdomen – Madeira Decora 1471, Tapestry Cotton white
  Thorax – white/cream chenille thread
  Veins and legs – Madeira Metallic No. 40 gold 7

- Leaves: Ivy – 712 (leaf), Raj Mahal Art Silk ecru (veins)
  Blackberry – ecru (leaf), Raj Mahal Art Silk 96 (veins)

ORDER OF WORK

1. Mount the main fabric and backing fabric (both 20 cm x 20 cm, or 8" x 8") into a 10 cm (4") hoop.

2. Trace the skeleton outline of the Hellebore, Berries and Dragonfly (p.298) onto the main fabric.

3. Embroider the stems:

   Ivy   Work in chain stitch with one strand of thread.
   Blackberry   Work in whipped chain stitch with two strands.

4. Fruiting ivy (p. 91). Substitute Mill Hill Pebble Beads 5147 (pearl) for the base and Mill Hill Petite Glass Beads 42027 for the top of the ivy berries.

5. Blackberries (p. 60). Use Mill Hill Glass Seed Beads 123 (cream) with the assortment of cream threads.

6. Christmas rose (p. 74). Use Mill Hill Petite Glass Beads 42030 for the centre of the flower.

7. Dragonfly (p. 82). Use the threads suggested above, and pearl metal organdie for the wings. The head is a 4 mm pearl bead, while the eyes are Mill Hill Antique Glass Beads 3037 (abalone).

8. Embroider the detached leaves:

   Ivy   Work in stem stitch filling (method 3, p. 35).
   Blackberry   Work in padded satin stitch (method 1, p. 34).

9. Mount into the top of a frosted glass bowl.

Berries Brooch, Plate 17. p. 266

SUGGESTED THREADS

- Stems: 801

- Leaves: 470, 937

- Soldier-fly: Body – 3765
  Wings and legs – Madeira No. 40 astro-1 or astro-3,
  Kreinik Cord 205c

- Blackberries: 902, 815, 304, 347, 3328, 3712, 760, 754,
  3013
  Sepals – Kanagawa Silk 1000 denier col. 113

- Black currants: Au Ver à Soie Soie d'Alger 3326

ORDER OF WORK

1. Mount the main fabric and backing fabric (both 20 cm x
20 cm, or 8" x 8") into a 10 cm (4") hoop.

2. Trace the skeleton outline onto the main fabric using
dressmaker's carbon paper.

3. Work the stems in stem stitch with two strands of thread.
Do three rows of stem stitch for the main stem, each row
leading to a leaf or blackberry.

4. Outline the leaves on the main fabric in single feather
stitch to give a spiked edge. Embroider the leaves in padded
satin stitch (method 1, p. 35).

5. Soldier-fly (p. 129).

6. Blackberries (p. 60).

Skeleton outline

7. Black currants (p. 80).

8. Work the detached leaf in padded satin stitch (method 1, p. 34).

9. Make the brooch following the directions in Finishing Techniques (p. 44). Use two 5 cm (2") circles of 5 mm (¹/₄") thick cardboard and Mill Hill Antique Glass Beads 3024.

Medieval Mirror Frame 1, Plate 18, p. 267

These mirror frames were inspired by medieval illuminated manuscripts, their margins adorned with all manner of flowers and insects amid twining foliage. Most elements can be quite easily replaced, and the frame can be embroidered as a 'garland' with the addition of extra leaves and insects. Try whipping the vine with gold thread for an exotic effect.

SUGGESTED THREADS

- Vine: 936

- Fronds: 469

- Grapes and vine leaf: 937, 470, Au Ver à Soie Soie d'Alger 4636

- Fennel: 470, Cifonda Silk 522, 3047, Madeira Decora 1426

- Carnation: Flower – Madeira Silk 2307
  Base – 470, Tapestry Cotton 2470

- Hoverfly: Au Ver à Soie Metallic 050, Madeira Rayon No. 40 col. 1078, Kreinik Cord 205c

- Spider web: Madeira Metallic No. 40 silver

MEDIEVAL MIRROR FRAME 1

MEDIEVAL MIRROR FRAME 1

Skeleton outline

- Spider: 310 (black) or Cifonda Silk black

- Snail: Body – 3023, 3022, 310 (black), Tapestry Cotton 2647
  Shell – Needle Necessities Overdyed 130, Tapestry Cotton 2610

- Bud – 469, 472, Pearl (8) cotton DMC 472

- Ladybird: 900 or 666 or 817, 310 (black)

- Peas: Pods – 936, 469, 470, 471, 472
  Flower – white

- Aubergine: Fruit – Au Ver à Soie Soie d'Alger 4636, 4635, 4634
  Calyx and bud – 731, 732, Pearl (5) cotton thread 731

- Tulip: 948, 754, 352, 351, 3031
  Stem: 936

- Butterfly: Wings – 924, 3768, Kreinik Cord 215c, 900, ecru
  Body – 3790, Tapestry Cotton 2609, tan chenille thread

- Red currants: 75, 898
  Stalks – 937

- Central lower bud: 580, 470, 3047, Madeira Decora 1426

- Poppy: 742, 743, 744, Pearl (8) cotton DMC 469

- Anemone: 349, 350, 351, 310 (black)
  Sepals – 936

- Cricket – 829, 831, 832, Tapestry Cotton 2831

- Leaves – 580, 470, 469, 937, 472, 471, 581, Au Ver à Soie Soie d'Alger 4635

tulip petals

hoverfly wings

ladybird wings

pea flower petal

butterfly wings

central lower bud   detached cricket wing

gold snakeskin

Detached elements

ORDER OF WORK

1. Mount the main fabric and backing fabric (both 45 cm x 50 cm, or 18" x 20") into a 25 cm x 30 cm (10" x 12") or 30 cm x 35 cm (12" x 14") wooden stretcher frame. (See the method for attaching fabric to square frames on p. 21).

2. Trace the skeleton outline onto thin tracing paper and transfer to the main fabric with tacking (p. 41).

3. The vine outline is embroidered in whipped chain stitch. With three strands of thread, stitch the vine outline (the solid lines on the skeleton outline) in chain stitch, working from the base to the top, then whip the chain stitches back to the base. Work the second row of the vine outline (from the base to the lower flowers) in the same way. Repeat for the other side of the vine.

   The stems of individual elements (the dotted lines) are worked later in whipped chain stitch, using two strands of the specified thread, unless otherwise indicated.

   All the fronds are worked in vertical fly stitch with one strand of thread.

Work the individual elements in the following order, applying the detached pieces at the end.

4. Grapes and vine leaf (p. 95).

5. Fennel (p. 85).

6. Carnation (p. 71).

7. Hoverfly (p. 100).

8. Spider and spider web (pp. 130, 131).

9. Snail (p. 125).

10. Poppy seed pod (p. 121).

11. Ladybird (p. 101).

12. Peas (p. 112).

13. Aubergine (p. 52).

14. Tulip (p. 137). Embroider the leaves on the main fabric in rows of stem stitch in 470, working a row of 471 for the veins.

15. Butterfly (p. 64).

16. Red currants (p. 80). Embroider the leaves on the main fabric in padded buttonhole stitch using 937, and work the veins in 470.

17. Central lower bud. Using one strand of thread:

(a) Couch then buttonhole the covered wire around the edge in 580, starting in the centre of the bud. Leave the tail free to apply the bud.

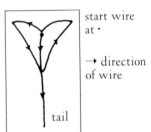

start wire at •

→ direction of wire

tail

(b) Work the bud in rows of stem stitch in alternating colours (580 and 470).

(c) Carefully cut out the bud. Using 58, wrap the tail of wire to form a stalk and insert through to the back of the work. Secure the bud with invisible stitches at the base and points.

(d) Fill the bud with a mixture of beads (Mill Hill Petite Glass Beads 40123) and French knots (3047 and Madeira Decora 1426 – 2 strands, 2 wraps).

18. Poppy (p. 118).

19. Anemone (p. 50).

20. Cricket (p. 78).

21. Work the detached leaves on calico and apply when all the elements are completed. Secure at the back of the work, then trim the wires.

Central lower leaves   Overcast (or buttonhole) the outside wire using 580, embroider in stem stitch filling (method 3, p. 35), working rows in alternating colours (580 and 470). Cut out the leaves and wrap the stems before applying.

Fennel and carnation leaves   Buttonhole the outside wire, then embroider in stem stitch filling (method 3, p. 35). Use 469 for the veins, 937 for the leaves.

Pea leaf   Overcast the outside wire, then embroider in padded satin stitch (method 1, p. 34). Use 472 for the veins, 470 for the leaf.

Aubergine leaf   Buttonhole the outside wire, then embroider in long and short stitch (method 2, p. 34). Use Au Ver à Soie Soie d'Alger 4635 for the veins, 937 for the leaf.

Tulip leaf   Overcast the outside wire, then embroider in stem stitch filling (see 'Leaf without a wired central vein', p. 35). Use 471 for the veins, 470 for the leaf.

Red currant leaf   Buttonhole the outside wire, then embroider in padded satin stitch (method 1, p. 34). Use 470 for the veins, 937 for the leaf.

Upper leaves   Buttonhole the outside wire, then embroider in long and short stitch (method 2, p. 34). Use 470 for the veins, 580 for the leaves.

Poppy and anemone leaves   Buttonhole the outside wire, then embroider in long and short stitch (method 2, p. 34). Use 470 for the veins, 937 for the leaves.

Medieval Mirror Frame 2, Plate 29, p. 292

Instead of a mirror, a photograph, monogram or personal treasure can be mounted inside the embroidered border.

SUGGESTED THREADS

- Vine: 3345

- Fronds: 3346

- Cottage pink: Petals – 3712, 3051, 3052
  Base – 3347, Tapestry Cotton 2347

- Miniature globe thistle: 3041, 3740, 3051, 3052, Au Ver
  à Soie Soie d'Alger 3326

- Owl: 3045, 869, 3787, 3032, 3033, 310 (black)

- Leaves: 3345, 3346, 3347

- Soldier-fly: Body – 3765 or 3820
  Wings and legs – Madeira No. 40 astro-1 or astro-3,
  Kreinik Cord 205c

- Foxgloves: 927, 926, 3768
  Sepals – 3346, 3347

- Blackberries: 347, 3328, 3712, 760, 754, 3013, 3346,
  3345
  Sepals – Kanagawa Silk 1000 denier col. 113

- Thistle: Base – 3053, 3051, 356
  Top – (3607, 718, 917) or (3727, 316, 3726) or (3042,
  3041, 3740) or (340, 3746, 333)

- Leaves – 3051, 3052

Medieval Mirror Frame 2

MEDIEVAL MIRROR FRAME 2

Skeleton outline

- Bee: Body – 310 (black), 783
  Wings and legs – Madeira Rayon No. 40 col. 1001,
  Kreinik Cord 205c

- Cotoneaster: 922, 3346, 3345

- Fig: 3371, 936, 433, Au Ver à Soie Soie d'Alger 4636, 3326

- Strawberry: 321, 937, Kanagawa Silk 1000 denier col. 4

- Strawberry flower: white, 3347, 743, 3346

- Beehive: 729, 680, 3371

- Tiny bees: 310 (black), 783, Kreinik Cord 105c

- Hedgehog: 612, 611, 610, Cifonda Silk 497, 498, 222

- Spider web: Madeira Metallic No. 40 silver

- Spider: 310 (black) or Cifonda Silk black

- Central lower bud: 3346, 3347

- Dragonfly: Wings – 3808, Madeira Rayon No. 40 col.
  1045
  Body – Tapestry Cotton 2131, teal chenille thread,
  Kreinik Cord 205c

- Pansies and buds: 3830, 742, Au Ver à Soie Soie d'Alger
  4636, 2926, 1316, Minnamurra Stranded Cotton 110,
  Cifonda Silk 174
  Sepals – 3345
  Leaves – 3345, 3346

hedgehog
padding

central lower
bud

pansy petals

Detached elements

ORDER OF WORK

1. Mount the main fabric and backing fabric (both 45 cm x 50 cm, or 18" x 20") into a 25 cm x 30 cm (10" x 12") or 30 cm x 35 cm (12" x 14") wooden stretcher frame. (See the method for attaching fabric to square frames on p. 22).

2. Trace the skeleton outline onto thin tracing paper and transfer to the main fabric with tacking (p. 41).

3. The vine outline is embroidered in whipped chain stitch. With three strands of thread, stitch the vine outline (the solid lines on the skeleton outline) in chain stitch, working from the base to the top, tapering to two strands at the top branches (above the owl and foxgloves), then whip the chain stitches back to the base. Work the second row of vine outline (from the base to the pansies) in the same way. Repeat for the other side of the vine.

    The stems of individual elements (dotted lines) are worked later in whipped chain stitch (using two strands) unless otherwise indicated.

    All the fronds are worked in vertical fly stitch with one strand of thread.

Work the individual elements in the following order, applying the detached pieces at the end.

4. Cottage pink (p. 76).

5. Miniature globe thistle (p. 92).

6. Owl (p. 106). Embroider the small leaves near the owl. The central veins are in chain stitch (3347) and the leaves are in padded satin stitch (3346). Using the same greens, work the small detached leaf as for the 'Leaf without a wired central vein' (p. 35).

7. Soldier-fly (p. 129).

8. Foxgloves (p. 89).

9. Blackberries (p. 60). Work the 'almost ripe' and 'unripe' berries.

10. Thistle (p. 134). Embroider the thistle leaf on the main fabric. Work the central vein in chain stitch (3052), the leaf in padded buttonhole stitch (3051), then the side veins in straight stitches.

11. Bee (p. 55).

12. Cotoneaster (p. 75).

13. Fig (p. 86).

14. Strawberries (p. 132), and strawberry flower (p. 134).

15. Beehive and tiny bees (pp. 58, 60).

16. Hedgehog (p. 97)

17. Spider and spider web (pp. 130, 131).

18. Work the central lower bud as for Mirror Frame 1, substituting colours 3346 for the edge and 3346, 3347 for alternating colours. Fill the bud with a mixture of beads (Mill Hill Petite Glass Beads 42028) and French knots (using 3830, 922 and Soie d'Alger 2926 – 2 strands, 2 wraps).

19. Dragonfly (p. 82).

20. Pansies and pansy bud (p. 110).

21. Work the detached leaves on quilter's muslin and apply when all the elements are completed. Secure at the back of the work, then trim the wires.

Central lower leaves   Overcast (or buttonhole) the outside wire (3346), embroider in stem stitch filling (method 3, p. 35). working rows in alternating colours (3346, 3347). Cut out the leaves and wrap the stem before applying.

Pansy leaves   Buttonhole the outside wire, then embroider in padded satin stitch (method 1, p. 34). Use 3346 for the veins, 3345 for the leaves.

Cottage pink and miniature globe thistle leaves   Overcast the outside wire, then embroider in stem still filling (see 'Leaf without a wired central vein', p. 35), Use 3052 for the veins, 3051 for the leaves.

Foxglove and 'above owl' leaves   Buttonhole the outside wire, then embroider in padded satin stitch (method 1, p. 34). Use 3347 for the veins, 3346 for the leaves.

Blackberry and cotoneaster leaves   Buttonhole the outside wire, then embroider in padded satin stitch (method 1, p. 34). Use 3346 for the central veins, 3345 for the leaves.

Strawberry leaf   Buttonhole the outside wire, then embroider in long and short stitch (method 2, p. 34). Use 3347 for the veins, 3346 for the leaf.

Thistle leaf   Buttonhole the outside wire, then embroider in padded satin stitch (method 1, p. 34). Use 3052 for the veins, 3051 for the leaf.

Chapter 9 Needlework Accessories and Gifts

Needlework Accessories

This group of needlework accessories consists of a small silk pouch containing a pin wheel, thimble pipkin, scissors scabbard and needlebook all embellished with raised embroidery and beads.

GENERAL REQUIREMENTS

- Bronze silk (or fabric of choice) — 50 cm x 115 cm (20'' x 45'')
- Good quality calico (or quilter's muslin) — 50 cm x 115 cm (20'' x 45'')
- Pellon (thin wadding) — 50 cm (½ yard)
- 10 cm (4'') and 20 cm (8'') embroidery hoops
- Thin cardboard — 1 mm (¹⁄₁₆'') or template plastic
- Tracing paper (GLAD Bake)
- Paper-backed fusible web (e.g. Vliesofix) — 50 cm (½ yard)
- Paper glue (e.g. UHU glue stick)
- Craft knife and cutting board (or scissors)
- Emery board (or fine sandpaper)
- Fine HB lead pencil
- Fine ball-point pen (can be empty) for tracing
- Ruler and set square
- Silk pouch (see p. 349)
- Needlebook (see p. 344)
- Pin wheel (see p. 325)
- Scissors scabbard (see p. 340)
- Thimble pipkin (see p. 328)
- Needles: Crewel/embroidery 3-10
  Straw/milliners 3-9
  Tapestry 26
  Sharps (or beading) 12
  Chenille 18
- Threads: Fine machine thread (in a contrasting colour) for tacking/basting (preferably Silk 50 or Rayon 40)
  Bronze (or colour to match silk) machine thread
  Bronze (or colour to match silk) stranded thread to join the cardboard shapes (DMC 610, 611)

GENERAL PREPARATION

Silk

Cut the silk into pieces as indicated on the diagram. If the fabric is 112 cm (44") wide, reduce the width of all pieces except the pouch. If the fabric is less than 112 cm (44") wide you will need an extra 25 cm (10").

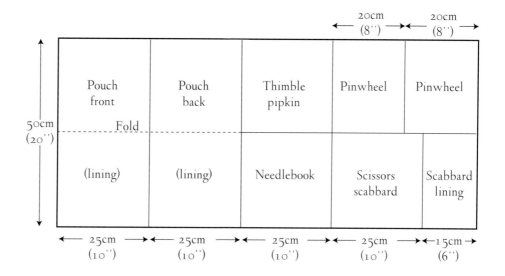

		20cm (8")	20cm (8")
50cm (20")	Pouch front	Pouch back	Thimble pipkin	Pinwheel	Pinwheel
Fold	(lining)	(lining)	Needlebook	Scissors scabbard	Scabbard lining
	25cm (10")	25cm (10")	25cm (10")	25cm (10")	15cm (6")

Calico/Muslin

Cut the calico into pieces as indicated on the diagram. It is used as a backing and for the embroidered applied elements (owl and foxgloves).

50cm (20")	Pouch	Thimble pipkin	Scissors scabbard	Foxgloves (pinwheel)	Owl (scabbard)
	Pouch	Needlebook		Pinwheel	Pinwheel
	25cm (10")	25cm (10")	25cm (10")	20cm (8")	20cm (8")

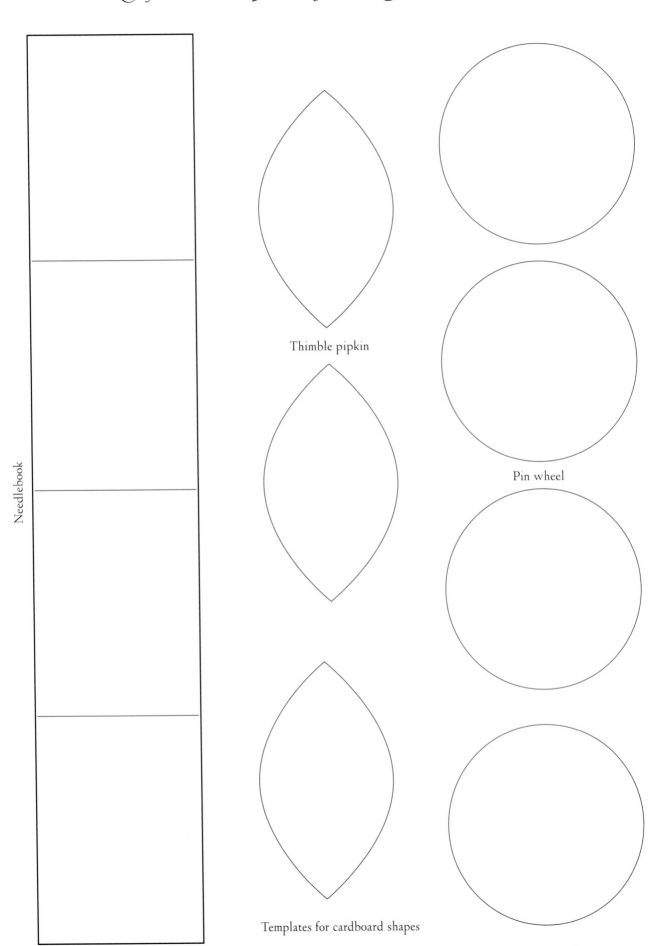

Needlebook

Thimble pipkin

Pin wheel

Templates for cardboard shapes

Cardboard Shapes

(Template plastic may be substituted for cardboard.)

1.   Trace or photocopy template outlines onto paper then glue to cardboard.

Note: When working with glue and cardboard, dry the shapes under heavy books to prevent buckling.

2.   Cut out the shapes with a craft knife or scissors. Glue two circles together (see Note) for each pin wheel shape, and two rectangles together for each needlecase shape, as a thicker cardboard is better for these items. Smooth the edges of all pieces with an emery board. You should now have the following cardboard shapes:

Pin wheel	— 2 circles
Thimble pipkin	— 3 segments
Needlebook	— 2 rectangles
Scissors scabbard	— 1 front and 1 back
	— 1 front lining and 1 back lining

3.   Attach a layer of pellon to one side of each cardboard shape using paper-backed fusible web and an iron (or glue). When using the fusible web, use a pressing cloth and minimum pressure with the iron so as not to flatten the pellon too much.

4.   Iron a piece of paper-backed fusible web to the other side of each cardboard shape except those required for the needlecase. Do not remove the paper until assembling the article. (Step 4 is optional).

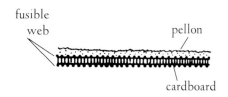

fusible web   pellon

cardboard

Templates for cardboard shapes

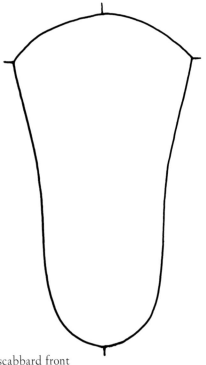

Scissors scabbard front

Front lining

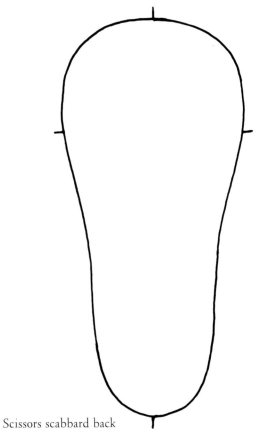

Scissors scabbard back

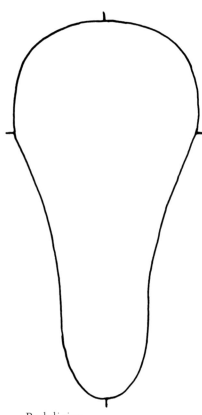

Back lining

GENERAL INSTRUCTIONS

TRANSFERRING A DESIGN TO THE BACK OF MAIN FABRIC

Note: The following method is useful when it is preferable to have the design on the back of the main fabric e.g. when the fabric is coloured or patterned.

To ensure that your design is the right way up on the main fabric, transfer the *skeleton outline* to the calico backing fabric as follows:

1.   Transfer the template shape onto the calico backing with marking pen or pencil. Tack/baste around this shape with rayon machine thread.

2.   Trace the template shape and the skeleton outline of the design on to tracing paper (I use GLAD Bake) with lead pencil.

3.   Place the tracing *right (pencil) side down* on to the calico backing, within the tacked template shape.

4.   Draw over the skeleton outline with an empty ballpoint pen (or pencil), thus transferring the pencil outline onto the calico backing.

TO EMBROIDER FROM A DESIGN ON THE BACK OF THE MAIN FABRIC

Embroider the design on the main fabric using one of the following methods:

1.   *Thread trace* the design through to the main fabric by working a row of small running stitches along the skeleton outline with silk or rayon machine thread. Remove the tracing threads as you embroider.

2.   Another option is to outline the design on the main fabric in backstitch, using the traced outline on the calico backing as a guide. The backstitches will be covered by embroidery.

3.   You can also embroider the design without a thread tracing or backstitches, by referring to the back of the work as you stitch.

JOINING CARDBOARD SHAPES

You will need:

— Fabric covered cardboard shapes

— Bronze stranded thread (two strands of 611 and one strand of 610)

— Straw/milliners needle size 7

With the wrong sides facing, join both edges of cardboard together with Palestrina knot stitch, working the stitches quite firmly and fairly close together. It is a good idea to work a sample first to ascertain the tension required.

Pin Wheel. Plate 36. p. 331

Foxgloves, worked separately then applied within a wreath of leaves decorate one side of the pin wheel; a dragonfly with metallic wings and beaded body, the other. The circles are joined together with Palestrina knot stitch. Pins can then be inserted around the outside edge.

REQUIREMENTS

- Bronze silk — 2 squares 20 cm x 20 cm (8'' x 8'')

- Calico/muslin — 2 squares 20 cm x 20 cm (8'' x 8'')

- 10 cm (4'') embroidery hoop

- Prepared cardboard shapes (see p. 321)

- Cream woollen doctor flannel or felt — 4 cm (1⅝'') circle

- Dragonfly (see p. 367)

- Foxgloves (see p. 369)

- Threads: Dark green stranded (DMC 937 or Au Ver à Soie d'Alger 2126)
  Bronze stranded (DMC 610, 611)

Skeleton outline

ORDER OF WORK

1.   Mount a square of silk and a calico backing into a 10 cm (4'') hoop. Using the cardboard shape as a template, mark the pin wheel outline on the calico backing. Tack/baste around the outline with rayon machine thread.

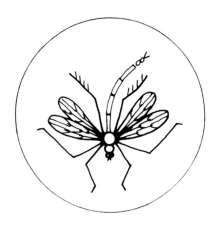
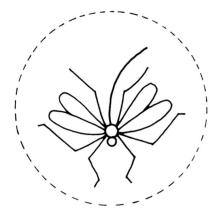

Skeleton outline

2. Trace the skeleton outline of the design onto the calico backing, inside the tacked circle (see p. 323).

Repeat Steps 1 and 2 for the other side of the pin wheel.

3. *Foxglove stems and leaves*
Thread trace the stems from the skeleton outline, then embroider in whipped chain stitch with dark green thread (937 or 2126), removing the tracing threads as you work. Starting at the base of the stem, work the chain stitch with three strands of thread to the first single leaf, two strands to the flower stems then 1 strand to the foxgloves. Whip all stems with one strand of thread, finishing the base with a detached chain stitch.

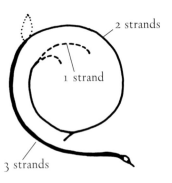

2 strands

1 strand

3 strands

Using one strand of dark green thread, outline each leaf in backstitch, using the traced outline on the calico backing as a guide, then embroider in padded satin stitch.

4. Foxgloves (see p. 369).

5. Dragonfly (see p. 367).

TO COMPLETE THE PIN WHEEL

You will need:

— two prepared cardboard circles

— strong thread for gathering

— iron and pressing cloth (and/or GLAD Bake)

— circle of woollen flannel or felt

— bronze thread in a size 7 straw needle (two strands of 611 and one strand of 610).

1.   Remove the paper backing (from the fusible web) from the other side of the prepared cardboard circles (see Step 4, p. 321).

2.   Cut out the embroidered pin wheel shape, leaving a 2 cm (1") turning allowance outside the tacked/basted outline on both the silk and the calico backing. Run a row of gathering stitches within this allowance, using strong thread.

3.   Gather the embroidery around one cardboard shape (pellon side against the calico backing), having the cardboard aligned with the tacked outline. Secure the gathering thread and work a few lacing stitches. Remove the tacking/basting. Press the gathered turning allowance to flatten (and fuse to the cardboard if using fusible web).

4.   Repeat for the other side of the pin wheel. Insert the circle of flannel (or felt) between the two shapes (to protect the pins).

5.   Join the cardboard circles together with Palestrina knot stitch. Pins can then be inserted around outside edge, between the knots.

Thimble Pipkin, Plate 35. p. 330

The three segments which make up the pipkin are embroidered with a padded hedgehog with silken spines; a spider web and spider (for luck); and a tiny vine enclosing your initials (for the base). The shapes are joined with Palestrina knot stitch to form a case for your thimble.

REQUIREMENTS

- Bronze silk — 25 cm x 25 cm (10'' x 10'')

- Calico/muslin — 25 cm x 25 cm (10'' x 10'')

- 20 cm (8'') embroidery hoop

- Prepared cardboard shapes (see p. 321)

- Plum/wine felt — 10 cm x 20 cm (4'' x 8'')

- Paper-backed fusible web

- Mill Hill Petite Beads — 42012 (royal plum)

- Mill Hill Petite Beads — 40161 (crystal)

- Hedgehog (see p. 97)

- Spider and web (see pp. 130, 131)

- Tiny bee (see p. 200)

- Threads: Dark green stranded (DMC 937 or Au Ver à Soie d'Alger 2126)
  Dark plum stranded (DMC 3802)
  Brown stranded cotton in three shades (DMC 610, 611, 612)

Plate 34

NEEDLEWORK ACCESSORIES

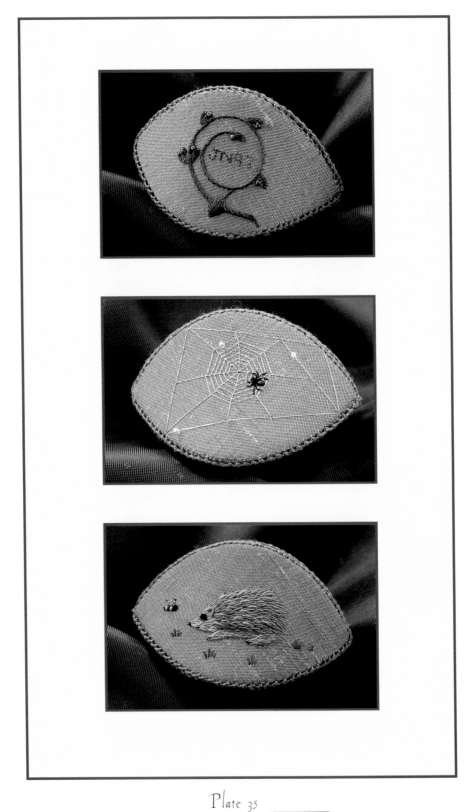

Plate 35

THIMBLE PIPKIN (SIDES AND BASE)

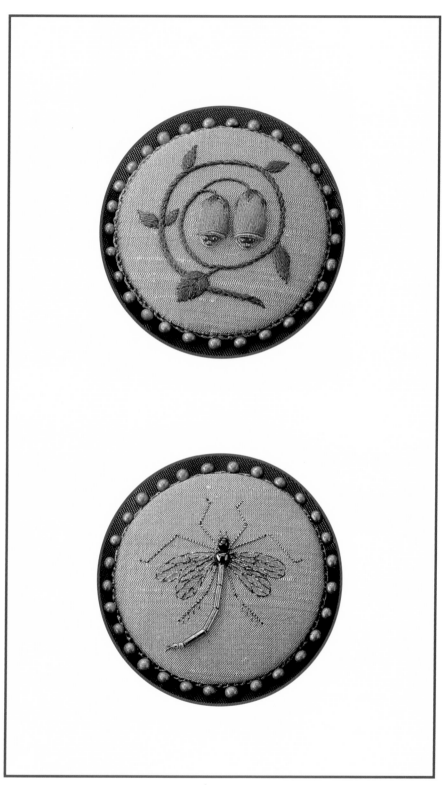

Plate 36
PIN WHEEL

Plate 37

SCISSORS SCABBARD

Plate 38

NEEDLEBOOK (FRONT)

Plate 39

NEEDLEBOOK (BACK)

Plate 40

ACCESSORIES POUCH (BACK)

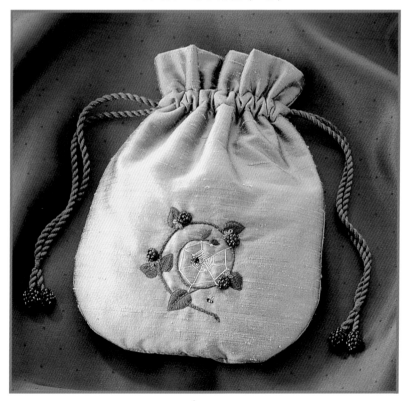

Plate 41

ACCESSORIES POUCH (FRONT)

Plate 42

Stumpwork Name Brooch

Plate 43

WALNUT PINCUSHION

Plate 44

BOYSENBERRY PENDANT

Brown silk thread in three shades (Cifonda 497, 498, 222)

Silver metallic (Madeira Metallic No. 40 — silver)

Bronze stranded (DMC 610, 611)

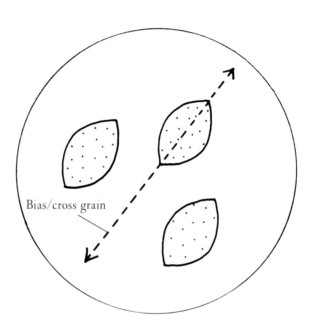

Bias/cross grain

ORDER OF WORK

1.   Mount the silk and calico backing into the embroidery hoop. Using the cardboard shapes as templates, mark three pipkin outlines on the calico backing, placing the segments on the bias (cross) grain of the fabric with a space between each for a turning allowance. Tack/baste around the outlines with rayon machine thread.

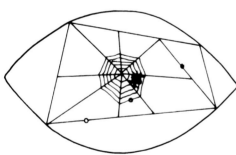

2.   *Spider web segment* Trace the skeleton outline of the web onto the calico backing, inside the tacked segment. Work a spider web and spider within the segment outlines, using the tracing as a guide. Add crystal petite beads for dewdrops if desired.

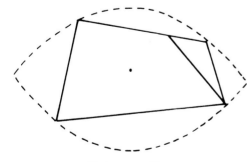

Skeleton outline

3.   *Hedgehog segment* Trace the skeleton outline of the design onto the calico backing, inside the tacked segment. Embroider the hedgehog, using the tracing as a guide to placement.

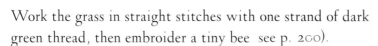

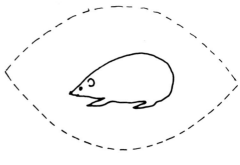

Skeleton outline

Work the grass in straight stitches with one strand of dark green thread, then embroider a tiny bee see p. 200).

Hedgehog padding

4.   *Base segment* Trace the skeleton outline of the design onto the calico backing, inside the tacked segment. Thread trace the vine from the skeleton outline, then embroider in whipped chain stitch with dark green thread (937 or 2126), removing the tracing threads as you work. Starting at the base of the vine, work the chain stitch with two strands of thread to the first single leaf, then with one strand to the tip. Whip back down the vine with one strand of thread, then finish the base with a detached chain stitch. Work the small leaves with detached chain stitches, and the large leaf in padded satin stitch.

Using one strand of dark plum thread, apply the petite beads then backstitch the initials and the date.

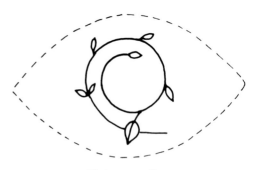

Skeleton outline

TO COMPLETE THE THIMBLE PIPKIN

You will need:

— three prepared cardboard segments

— strong thread for gathering

— iron and pressing cloth (and/or GLAD Bake)

— plum/wine felt

— paper-backed fusible web

— bronze thread in a size 7 straw needle (two strands of 611 and one strand of 610).

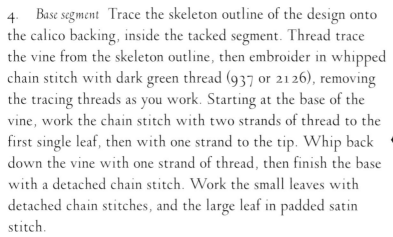

1.   Remove the paper backing (from the fusible web) from the other side of the prepared cardboard segments (see Step 4, p. 321).

2.   Cut out the embroidered pipkin shape, leave a 7mm ($^1/_4$'') turning allowance outside the tacked/basted outline on the silk only — cut the calico backing close to the tacking. Run a row of gathering stitches within the silk allowance, using strong thread.

3.   Gather the embroidery around one cardboard shape (pellon side against the calico backing), having the cardboard aligned with the tacked outline. Secure the gathering thread. Remove the tacking/basting. Trim and neaten the corners, then press the gathered turning allowance to flatten, (and fuse to the cardboard if using fusible web).

4.   Repeat for the other two sides of the pipkin.

5.   The pipkin is lined with the wine-coloured felt. Trace three segment shapes onto the paper side of the fusible web, then iron it on to the felt. Cut out the felt shapes, check for size and trim if necessary (they should be a shade smaller than the fabric covered cardboard), then remove the paper and fuse one to the back of each pipkin segment.

6.   Work a row of Palestrina knot stitch across the top edge of both pipkin sides, catching in the edge of the felt. These edges will be the opening of the pipkin. Join the lower edge of the sides to the pipkin base with Palestrina knot stitch.

Note: To open your thimble case, gently squeeze the corners towards each other.

Scissors Scabbard, Plate 37. p. 332

The front of the scabbard is decorated with a padded owl perched in a vine of beaded boysenberries; the back with a tiny soldier-fly. The scabbard pieces are joined with Palestrina knot stitch.

REQUIREMENTS

- Bronze silk:— 25 cm x 25 cm (10'' x 10'')
  — 25 cm x 15 cm (10'' x 6'') for lining

- Calico/muslin — 25 cm x 25 cm (10'' x 10'')

- 20 cm (8'') embroidery hoop

- Prepared cardboard shapes (see p. 321)

- Boysenberries (see p. 363)

- Owl (see p. 197)

- Soldier-fly (see p. 371)

- Thread: Dark green stranded (DMC 937 or Au Ver à Soie d'Alger 2126)
  Medium green stranded (DMC 469 or Au Ver à Soie d'Alger 2125)
  Bronze stranded (DMC 610, 611)

ORDER OF WORK

1.   Mount the square of silk and calico backing into the embroidery hoop. Using the cardboard shapes as templates, mark one front and one back scabbard shape on to the calico backing, leaving at least 3 cm (1 ¼'') between the shapes to allow for turnings. Tack/baste around the shape lines with rayon machine thread.

Front skeleton outline

Scabbard front

2.   Trace the skeleton outline of the design on to the calico backing then thread-trace the vine outline (p. 323). Work the vine in whipped chain stitch in dark green thread, using two strands for the vine and one strand for the berry stems. Remove the tracing threads as you work.

3.   The leaves are worked with one strand of dark green thread. Outline with small backstitches, using the traced outline on the calico backing as a guide, then embroider in padded satin stitch.

4.   Embroider the owl then apply to scabbard front, using the traced outline on the calico backing as a guide.

5.   Work three boysenberries, one at the end of each stem. Embroider three detached chain stitches at the base of each berry to form the sepals, using one strand of medium green thread.

Scabbard back

6.   Transfer the soldier-fly outline to the calico backing.

Work the soldier-fly(see p. 371).using the outline on the calico as a guide.

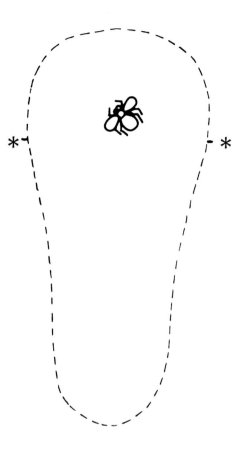

TO COMPLETE THE SCISSORS SCABBARD

You will need:

— prepared cardboard scabbard pieces (front, front lining, back and back lining)

— strong thread for gathering

— iron and pressing cloth (and/or GLAD Bake)

— PVA glue

— bronze thread in a size 7 straw needle (two strands of 611 and one strand of 610).

1.   Remove the paper backing (from the fusible web) from the other side of the prepared cardboard scabbard shapes (see Step 4, p. 321).

2.   Cut out the embroidered front scabbard shape, leave a 1 cm ($^1/_2$'') turning allowance outside the tacked/basted outline on the silk only — cut the calico backing close to the tacking. Run a row of gathering stitches within the silk allowance, using strong thread.

3.   Gather the embroidery around the front scabbard cardboard shape (place the pellon side against the calico backing), having the cardboard aligned with the tacked outline. Secure the gathering thread. Remove the tacking/basting. Trim and neaten the corners, then press the gathered turning allowance to flatten (and fuse to the cardboard if using fusible web).

4.   Repeat for the scabbard back.

5.   Mark both scabbard lining shapes onto the back of the lining silk, leaving at least 3 cm (1 and $^1/_4$'') between shapes

to allow for turnings. Cut out the shapes leaving a 1 cm ($^1/_2$'') seam allowance. Gather the lining around the prepared cardboard lining shapes, placing the pellon side against the silk. Secure the gathering thread. Trim and neaten the corners, then press the gathered turning allowance to flatten (and fuse to the cardboard if using fusible web).

6.   Glue the front and front lining, and back and back lining together, making sure that the top edges between * and * are even, and using a minimal amount of glue. Place the glued shapes on a soft towelling pad (embroidered side down), and press under books until dry.

7.   Work a row of Palestrina knot stitch across the top edge of each scabbard piece between * and * (catching the scabbard piece and its lining together). These edges will be the opening of the scabbard. Join the scabbard shapes together around the lower edge between * and * with Palestrina knot stitch, securing the stitches well at *.

Needlebook, Plates 38 and 39, p. 332

A padded squirrel with a velvety tail is embroidered on the front of the needlebook; a beehive with tiny bees on the back. The needlebook has leaves of wool flannel or felt.

REQUIREMENTS

* Bronze silk — 25 cm x 25 cm (10'' x 10'')

* Calico/muslin — 25 cm x 25 cm (10'' x 10'')

* 20 cm (8'') embroidery hoop

* Prepared cardboard shapes (see p. 321)

* Cream woollen doctor flannel or felt

* Beehive (see p. 199)

* Squirrel (see p. 372)

* Tiny bees (see p. 200)

* Threads: Olive green chenille
  Dark green stranded (DMC 937 or Au Ver à Soie d'Alger 2126)
  Bronze stranded (DMC 610, 611)
  Bronze machine thread (to match silk)

ORDER OF WORK

1.   Mount the silk and calico backing into the embroidery hoop. Draw the needlecase outline onto the backing and tack/baste around these lines with rayon machine thread.

2.   Trace the skeleton outline of the design onto the calico backing, inside the tacked outline (see p.129).

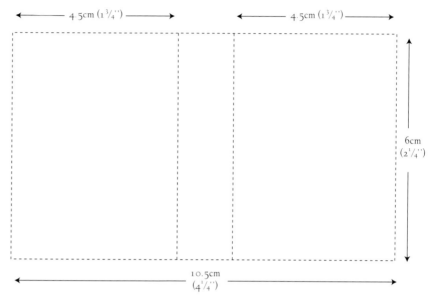

Needlebook outline

Skeleton outline

3.   *Needlebook front.* With one strand of dark green thread, outline the mound under the squirrel with backstitch (following the outline on the calico backing). Fill the mound with rows of couched chenille thread, starting at * and ending in the centre of the mound. Use one strand of dark green thread to couch the chenille and to secure the chenille thread ends at the back of the work.

Note: If chenille thread is unavailable, work the mound in Turkey knots using two strands of dark green thread.

Work the squirrel (see p. 372) over the mound, using the tracing as a guide to placement.

4.   *Needlebook back.* Referring to the tracing on the back for placement, work the beehive (see p. 199) using only one layer of felt for padding (top layer). Stitch the legs at the base of the beehive in satin stitch with one strand of dark gold thread (680). For grass, couch two rows of chenille thread at the base of the beehive. Use one strand of dark green thread to couch the chenille and to secure the chenille thread ends at the back of the work.

Note: If chenille thread is unavailable, work the grass in Turkey knots using two strands of the dark green thread.

5. Tiny bees (see p. 200). Work tiny bees on the front and the back of the needlebook.

TO COMPLETE THE NEEDLEBOOK

You will need:

— Two prepared cardboard rectangles (see p. 321)

— Iron

— Ruler and pencil (or fine marking pen)

— Machine thread to match the silk

— Cream woollen doctor flannel or felt — two pieces 6 cm x
    10 cm (2⅜'' x 4'')

— Bronze thread in a size 7 straw needle (two strands of 611
    and one strand of 610).

1.   Remove the needlebook embroidery from the hoop and iron lightly on the back to flatten the edges.

2.   Rule the following lines on to the calico backing to form the needlebook pattern:
— 2 mm (³/₁₆'') away from the upper and lower edges of the needlebook outline (these lines become the stitching lines on the upper and lower edges).
— 2 mm (³/₁₆'') away from the side edges of the needlebook outline (these lines become the fold lines on the side edges).

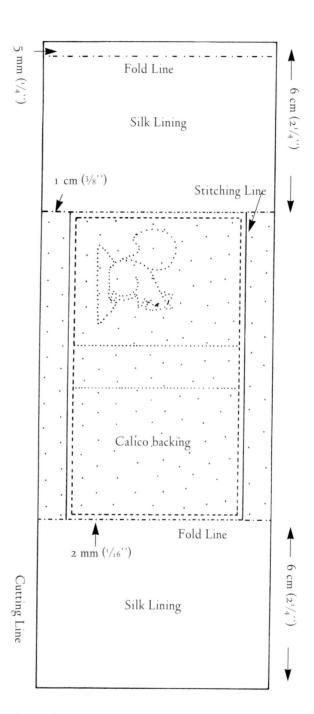

3. Rule the following lines on to the calico backing, then cut the calico (and the silk) along these lines
— 1 cm (³/₈'') away from the upper and lower stitching lines (this becomes the seam allowance).
— 6 cm (2³/₈'') away from the fold lines on each side edge (this will become the lining of the needlebook).

4.   To reduce bulk, cut the 6 cm (2 ½'') calico lining section away close to the fold lines on each side, leaving a silk lining only. On the side edge of the silk front lining (squirrel side), press a 5 mm (³/₈'') seam allowance to the wrong side.

5.   With right sides facing, fold the front lining along the fold line (over the squirrel), then fold the back lining along the fold line (the back lining will overlap the front lining). Pin the edges together, making sure that the upper and lower edges are even.

Cross-section

Front Lining   Back Lining

Front   Back

6.   With the calico side up, stitch the upper and lower edges of the needlebook along the stitching lines 1 cm (½'') from the edge. Trim seams. Cut calico close to stitching and reduce silk seam allowance to 5 mm (³/₈'').

7.   Turn the back of the needlebook to the right side through the central opening and insert one cardboard shape (pellon side towards calico). Then turn the front of the needle-book to the right side and insert the remaining cardboard shape. Ease the cardboard shapes into the corners of the needlebook, then close the opening with slip stitches. (Trim the cardboard shapes to fit if necessary).

8.   Trim the edges of the flannel pieces with pinking or scal-loping shears. Place both pieces of flannel inside the needle-book to form pages for needles and back stitch all layers together down the centre fold with machine thread. Work a row of Palestrina knot stitch (with bronze stranded thread) on the spine of the needlebook to cover these back stitches. Trim the flannel page edges with shears, if necessary.

Embroidered Pouch, Plates 40 and 41, p. 333

Each surface of this pouch, which can be used to carry your needlework accessories, is embroidered with a garland of beaded boysenberries enclosing a spider web and spider on one side, and your initials on the other. Beaded berries are worked at the ends of twisted cords to form the drawstrings. The pouch can also be used as an evening bag. Work a smaller version, perhaps in creams, for a jewellery pouch or as a beautiful wrapping for a gift.

REQUIREMENTS

Note: It is important to cut the fabrics accurately as the measurements form the pattern for the pouch.

- Bronze silk — 2 rectangles 50 cm x 25 cm (20'' x 10'')

- Calico/muslin — 2 squares 25 cm x 25 cm (10'' x 10'')

- Thin wadding (Pellon) — 2 squares 25 cm x 25 cm (10'' x 10'')

- 20 cm (8'') embroidery hoop

- Plum/wine felt — small piece

- Mill Hill Frosted Glass Beads — 62056 (boysenberry)

- Mill Hill Frosted Glass Beads — 60367 (garnet)

- Mill Hill Glass Seed Beads — 367 (garnet)

- Mill Hill Petite Beads — 40161 (crystal)

- 1 m (40'') purchased dark green twisted cord or two
  skeins of green stranded thread (DMC 937) to make your
  own.

- Boysenberries (see p. 363)

- Tiny bees (see p. 200)

- Threads: Dark green stranded (DMC 937 or Au Ver à
  Soie d'Alger 2126)
  Medium green stranded (DMC 469 or Au Ver à Soie
  d'Alger 2125)
  Deep red stranded (DMC 815 or Au Ver à Soie d'Alger
  2926)
  Silver metallic (Madeira Metallic No.40 silver) for web

ORDER OF WORK

Preparation

Cross-section of fabric sandwich

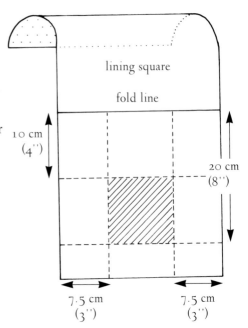

1.   Fold one piece of silk in half (wrong sides together) to
form a 25 cm (10'') square and press the fold. Unfold the silk
and place one half over a pellon and a calico square to form a
fabric sandwich. Pin then tack/baste the three layers together
around all edges of the square. The remaining half of the silk
will form the lining of the pouch.

2.   Using a ruler and lead pencil, draw the following lines
on the calico side of the fabric sandwich (edge tacking lines
are not shown).
— 10 cm (4'') from the fold line
— 20 cm (8'') from the fold line
— 7.5 cm (3'') from each side

3.   Tack around the central 10 cm (4'') square formed by these lines.

4.   Mount the fabric sandwich in a 20 cm (8'') hoop, silk side up, taking care to keep the basted square 'square'. (Fabric needs to be firm but it is not necessary to be drum tight). Trace the skeleton outline onto the calico backing — centring the design within the tacked square. Take care to place the design so that it will be the right way round on the silk upper layer.

Repeat this procedure with the remaining fabrics for the other side of the pouch.

Skeleton outline for both
sides of the pouch

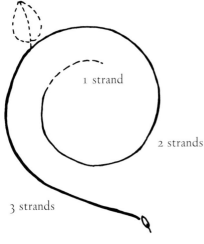

1 strand

2 strands

3 strands

5.   *Vine.* Thread trace the vine outline, then embroider in whipped chain stitch with dark green thread (937 or 2126), removing the tracing threads as you work. Starting at the base, work the chain stitch with three strands of thread to the first single leaf, two strands of thread until 1 ½ cm (³/₄'') from the end, then one strand to the end of the stem. Whip back down the stem with one strand of thread, then finish the base with a detached chain stitch.

6.   *Leaves.* The large leaves are embroidered with one strand of dark green thread as follows:
— work the central veins and stalks in chain stitch
— outline each leaf in backstitch, using the traced outline on the calico backing as a guide
— pad the leaf surface with straight stitches
— embroider each side of the leaf with close buttonhole stitches, the buttonholed edge just covering the backstitch outline.

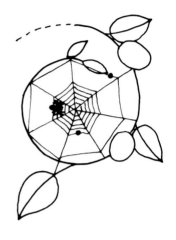

Outline the small leaves with backstitch, then embroider in padded satin stitch.

7.   *Boysenberries* (see p. 363)

Work three detached chain stitches at the base of each berry to form the sepals, using one strand of medium green thread (DMC 469 or Au Ver à Soie d'Alger 2125).

8.   Spider web and spider (see pp. 130, 131). Add crystal petite beads for dewdrops if desired.

9.   Using the alphabet provided, work initials in chain stitch using one strand of deep red thread (DMC 815 or Au Ver à Soie d'Alger 2926).

10. Tiny Bees (see p. 200) are worked where desired on each side of the pouch.

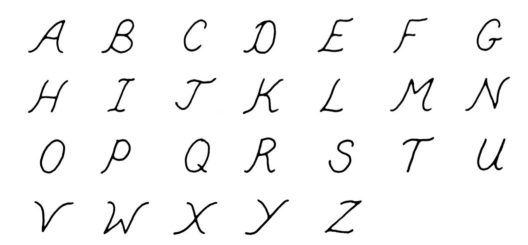

TO COMPLETE THE POUCH

PREPARE BOTH SIDES OF THE POUCH AS FOLLOWS:

1.   Remove the fabric sandwich from the hoop and draw the following lines on the calico backing (see Construction Lines diagram on page 355):

(a) 2.5 cm (1'') and 4 cm (1½'') from the fold — these are the casing lines.

(b) 3 cm (1⅛'') from the fold — tack/baste this line to keep the three layers in place when stitching the casing.

(c) 5 cm (2'') from each side — round the corners of these lines (I used a 10 cm, 4'' tin as a template). These lines (with their rounded corners) are the stitching lines for the pouch.

2.   Cut away 3.5 cm (1⅜'') from all edges of the silk (both the sandwich and the lining) to leave a 1.5cm (⅝'') seam allowance. Round all the corners as above.

MACHINE STITCH THE POUCH (WITH MATCHING THREAD) AS FOLLOWS:

3.   With right sides facing and matching the fold lines, pin both sides of the pouch and pouch lining together around the outside edge (insert the pins at right-angles to the seam line and remove as you stitch). Beginning and ending securely, machine stitch around the outside edge of the pouch, with a seam allowance of 1.5 cm (⅝'') for the padded section of the pouch, and 1.8 cm (¾'') for the pouch lining. Leave openings between the casing lines and for 5 cm (2'') at the lower edge of the lining (between the large dots • on the diagram).

4.   Trim the seam allowance then turn the pouch to the right side through the opening in the lining. Finger press the seams then slip stitch the lining opening closed. Ease the lining inside the pouch and press along the fold.

5.   To form a casing for the drawstrings, machine stitch 2.5 cm (1'') and 4 cm (1½'') from the top edge (fold). Remove the tacking/basting threads. The casing should coincide with the openings at the sides to allow for the insertion of the cords.

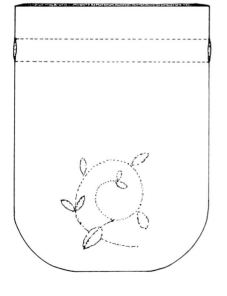

Make two twisted cords as follows:

6.   Use one skein 8 m (8 yards) of stranded thread (DMC 937) for each cord:

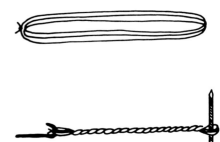

   (a) Unwind the skein of thread and fold into six equal lengths. Knot the ends.

   (b) Loop one end of threads over a pencil and the other end over a hook. Keeping the threads taut, twist the pencil round and round until the threads begin to twist on them-selves.

   (c) Holding the cord firmly, fold in half and the cords will twist together. Whip the ends together then trim off any uneven ends or previous knots.

   or Cut the bought cord into two 50 cm lengths.

7   Thread both cords through the casing, having each cord beginning and ending on opposite sides of the pouch.

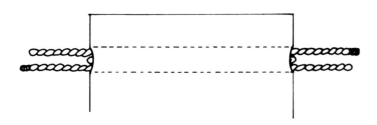

8.   Work a detached beaded boysenberry (see p. 364) at the ends of each cord.

9.   Using one strand of matching green thread, stitch then wrap the cord ends together about 1.5 cm (⅝'') above the berries.

CONSTRUCTION LINES FOR POUCH

Diagrams not to scale

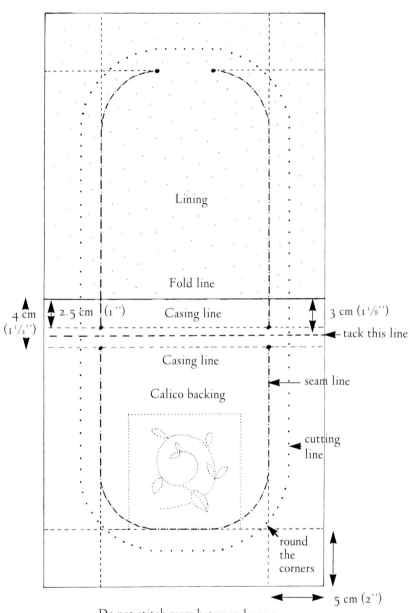

Lining

Fold line

4 cm (1½'')   2.5 cm (1'')   Casing line   3 cm (1⅛'')

← tack this line

Casing line

← seam line

Calico backing

← cutting line

→ round the corners

5 cm (2'')

Do not stitch seam between large ●

OUTLINES FOR SMALLER POUCHES

Use your own choice of threads and beads

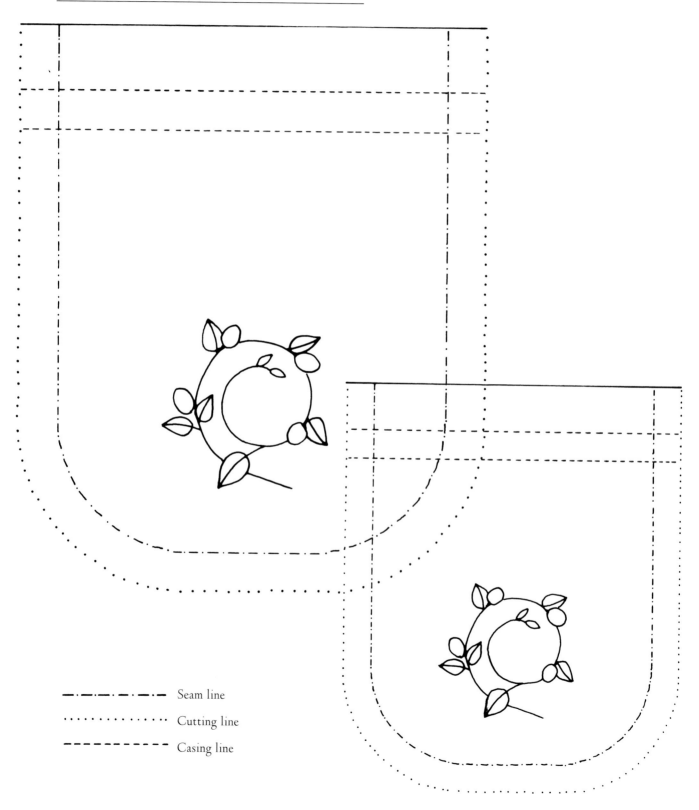

 ⎯ · ⎯ · ⎯ · ⎯ ·   Seam line

 ··················   Cutting line

 ⎯ ⎯ ⎯ ⎯ ⎯   Casing line

Walnut Pincushion, Plate 43. p. 335

A walnut pincushion makes a charming gift or attach a fine gold cord and hang it on your Christmas tree. This tiny project can also be mounted into a small oval frame or pendant.

REQUIREMENTS

- Ivory or bronze silk — 15 cm x 15 cm (6'' x 6'')
- Calico (or quilter's muslin) — 15 cm x 15 cm (6'' x 6'')
- Red homespun — 15 cm x 15 cm (6'' x 6'')
- 10 cm (4'') embroidery hoops
- Walnut shell (halved)
- Wire — fine flower wire in 12 cm (5'') length
- Red marking pen to colour wire if desired
- Stuffing (wool or polyester)
- Mill Hill Frosted Glass Beads — 62056 (boysenberry)
- Mill Hill Frosted Glass Beads — 60367 (garnet)
- Mill Hill Glass Seed Beads — 367 (garnet)
- Mill Hill Petite Beads — 42014 (black)
- Needles: Crewel/embroidery 10
  Sharps/Appliqué 12
  Large yarn darner or chenille 18
- Thread: Dark green stranded (DMC 937)
  Medium green stranded (DMC 469)
  Dark purple/plum stranded (Au Ver à Soie d'Alger 3326 or DMC 902)
  Red stranded (DMC 349)
  Black stranded (DMC 310)

ORDER OF WORK

1. Mount the silk and calico backing into the embroidery hoop and mark the cutting line. Trace the skeleton outline, inside the marked oval, indicating the centre of the boysenberries with a short line (3mm or $1/8''$).

2. *Stems.* Using one strand of dark green thread, embroider the stems in stem stitch. Work one row to each berry (two rows side by side at the base) and to each leaf.

3. *Leaves.* Embroider the leaves in fishbone stitch with one strand of dark green thread.

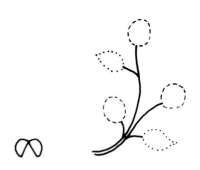

4. *Boysenberries* (see p. 363). Work three detached chain stitches at the base of each berry for sepals, using one strand of medium green thread.

5. *Tiny ladybird* (see p.169). Using the wing size shown on the design outline.

6. Remove the embroidery from the hoop and cut along the marked oval. Trim calico backing layer to an oval shape along the calico cutting line. Run a gathering thread around the outside edge, insert a tight wad of stuffing (it takes more than imagined!), then pull up the gathering thread and secure. Force the shape into the walnut shell, easing the gathers around the edges. A little PVA glue can be used in the base of the walnut shell if desired. This embroidery can also be mounted in a small oval frame or pendant.

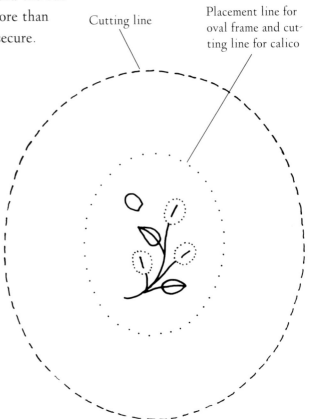

Cutting line

Placement line for oval frame and cutting line for calico

Skeleton outline

Stumpwork Name Brooch, Plate 42. p. 334

Other fruits and insects could be substituted to produce your own version of this stumpwork name brooch.

MATERIALS REQUIRED

- Ivory/gold satin — 2 squares, 20 cm x 20 cm (8'' x 8'')

- Calico (or quilter's muslin) — 20 cm x 20 cm (8'' x 8'')

- 10 cm (4'') embroidery hoop

- Dark green stranded thread (DMC 937 or Au Ver à Soie d'Alger 2126)

- Acorn (see p. 47)

- Grapes (see p. 95)

- Pomegranate (see p. 116)

- Red currants (see p. 80)

- Small snail (see p. 128)

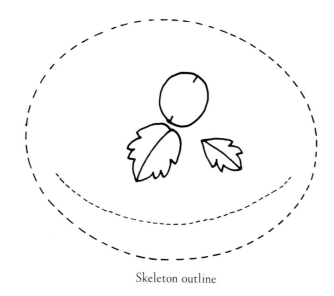

Skeleton outline

Pomegranate template

ORDER OF WORK

1. Mount the satin and calico backing into the embroidery
hoop. Using the cardboard shape as a template, mark the
brooch outline on to the calico backing. Tack/baste around the
outline with rayon machine thread.

2. Trace the skeleton outline of the design onto the calico
backing, inside the tacked oval (see p. 323).

3. The leaves are embroidered with one strand of dark green
thread as follows:
— work the central veins in chain stitch
— outline each leaf in backstitch, using the traced outline on
the calico backing as a guide
— pad the leaf surface with straight stitches
— embroider each side of the leaf with satin stitch (covering
the outline).

4. Pomegranate.

5. Grapes.

6. Acorn.

7. Red currants.

8. Small snail.

9. *Initials.* Using the alphabet provided, work the initials in back stitch with one strand of dark green thread, then whip with a fine gold thread.

ALPHABET FOR NAME BROOCH

A B C D E F G H I J
K L M N O P Q R S
T U V W X Y Z

TO COMPLETE THE NAME BROOCH

You will need:
— two ovals of 1mm cardboard (the size of the brooch)
— pellon and fusible web
— strong thread
— brooch pin
— glass seed beads for edging

1. Prepare two oval cardboard shapes (see p. 321, steps 3 and 4). Remove the paper backing (from the fusible web) from the other side of the prepared cardboard ovals.

2. Cut out the embroidered oval with a 1.5 cm ($^3/_4$'') turning allowance. Run a row of gathering stitches within this allowance, using strong thread.

3. Gather the embroidery around one cardboard oval (pellon side against the calico backing), having the cardboard aligned with the tacked outline. Secure the gathering thread and work a few lacing stitches. Remove the tacking. Press the gathered turning allowance to flatten (and fuse to the cardboard if using fusible web).

4. Cut an oval of satin and gather over the remaining cardboard, as above, for the brooch back. Attach a brooch pin to the back by stitching through the fabric and the cardboard.

5.　Stitch the front oval to the back oval with invisible slip stitches (ladder stitch), making sure that the brooch pin is in the correct position.

6.　To make a bead edging, thread on to one strand of strong thread enough seed beads to fit snugly around the circumfer- ence of the brooch. Tie the thread into a circle around the edge of the brooch, allowing the beads to rest in the groove formed between the two ovals of cardboard. Slip stitch the strong thread in place between every three or four beads.

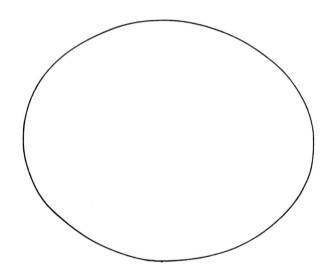

Template for cardboard oval

Boysenberries, Plate 44. p. 336

MATERIALS REQUIRED

- Beads: Mill Hill Frosted Glass Beads 62056 (boysenberry)
  Mill Hill Frosted Glass Beads 60367 (garnet)
  Mill Hill Glass Seed Beads 367 (garnet)
- Plum/purple felt — small piece
- Needles: Crewel/embroidery 10
- Thread: Dark purple/plum stranded (Au Ver à Soie d'Alger 3326 or DMC 902)

BOYSENBERRIES ON FABRIC

1.   Mark the centre of the berries with a short line, 3mm (¹/₈''). The berries are formed by stitching beads to the main fabric, in two layers as shown, using one strand of purple/plum thread. Apply the beads one at a time and mix the colours as desired.

Lower layer

a.   Stitch two beads on the centre line.

b.   Backstitch nine beads around the centre then run three rounds of thread through these beads to draw them into a tight oval (as if threading a necklace).

Upper layer

c.   Stitch one bead in the centre (take the needle between the beads in the lower layer through to the back).

d.   Back stitch seven beads around the centre then run three rounds of thread through these beads to draw them into a tight oval. Secure the thread at the back.

2.   *Sepals* — see individual instructions, e.g. point 7, page 352.

Detatched Beaded Boysenberries

The boysenberry, a variety of trailing blackberry, belongs to the rose family, Rosaceae. This dark, shiny reddish-black berry is rather soft and has a tart flavour.

These boysenberries can be worked as cord ends for a draw-string bag, or, when worked over padding, can be applied as detached berries to an embroidery.

MATERIALS REQUIRED

- Beads: Mill Hill Frosted Glass Beads 62056 (boysenberry)
  Mill Hill Frosted Glass Beads 60367 (garnet)
  Mill Hill Glass Seed Beads 367 (garnet)

- 3 mm (¹/₈'') twisted cord (made or purchased) for draw-strings

- Plum/purple felt — 8 mm (¹/₃'') strip to wind around the ends of the cords.

- Needles: Crewel/embroidery 10
  Darning 18

- Thread: Dark purple/plum stranded (DMC 902 or Au Ver à Soie d'Alger 3326)
  Dark green stranded (DMC 937 or Au Ver à Soie d'Alger 2126)
  Dark green soft cotton (DMC Tapestry Cotton 2936)

Preparation for cord (drawstring) ends

1.   Cut the cord to the required length and wrap the cut ends with green stranded cotton to prevent unravelling.

Note: Insert the cords through the casing before working the berries.

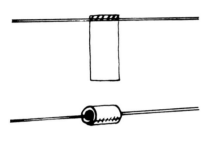

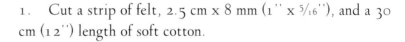

2.   Wind one layer of felt around each end of the cords and secure with a few stitches.

Preparation for detached berries to apply

to embroidery

1.   Cut a strip of felt, 2.5 cm x 8 mm (1'' x 5/16''), and a 30 cm (12'') length of soft cotton.

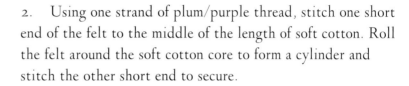

2.   Using one strand of plum/purple thread, stitch one short end of the felt to the middle of the length of soft cotton. Roll the felt around the soft cotton core to form a cylinder and stitch the other short end to secure.

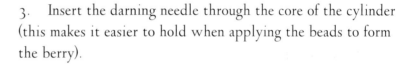

3.   Insert the darning needle through the core of the cylinder (this makes it easier to hold when applying the beads to form the berry).

To work the berries

Use one strand of plum/purple thread to stitch the beads to the felt base, selecting the colours at random. Each bead is applied with a backstitch, which goes through the previous bead as follows:

(a)   Bring the needle up at 1, back through the bead, then down at 2.

(b)   Bring the needle up at 3, back through two beads, then down at 2.

(c)   Bring the needle up at 4, back through two beads, then down at 1.

(d)   Bring the needle up at 5, back through two beads, then down at 3 and so on.

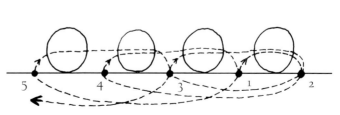

Each berry has six rows of beads:

Rows 1 and 2: Backstitch two rows of beads around the centre of the felt (12 beads in each row). Run a thread through each row of beads to form a smooth circle.

Rows 3 and 4: Rows 3 and 4 are stitched at the same time (to avoid a gap occurring). Using backstitch as above to apply each bead, stitch bead 1 in Row 3, then slip the needle through the felt to stitch bead 1 in Row 4. Slip the needle through the felt to stitch bead 2 in Row 3, then slip the needle through the felt to stitch bead 2 in Row 4, and so on until all beads are applied (10 beads in each row). Run a thread through each row of beads to draw together smoothly into a circle.

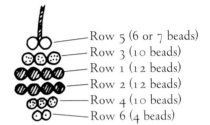

Row 5 (6 or 7 beads)
Row 3 (10 beads)
Row 1 (12 beads)
Row 2 (12 beads)
Row 4 (10 beads)
Row 6 (4 beads)

Rows 5 and 6: Rows 5 and 6 are stitched at the same time, slipping the needle through the felt between each row as above. Stitch 7 beads (Row 5) around the cord at the top of the berry (use 6 beads if using soft cotton) and at the same time stitch 4 beads to form the base of the berry (Row 6). Run a thread through Row 5 to draw the beads into a circle. Secure the thread.

Note: If working detached berries to apply to embroidery, thread the soft cotton from the lower end of the berry into the darning needle, and pull through to the top of the berry before stitching Rows 5 and 6. Trim this thread close to the felt (the remaining thread will be wrapped to form a stalk). When the berry is complete, wrap the soft cotton thread with one strand of dark green thread to the desired length to form a stalk. Secure.

Dragonfly. Plate 36. p. 331

MATERIALS REQUIRED:

- Bronze organza — 10 cm x 10 cm (4'' x 4'')

- Gold metal organdie — 10 cm x 10 cm (4'' x 4'')

- Paper-backed fusible web — 10 cm x 10 cm (4'' x 4''), and another small piece

- Beads: Eyes — Mill Hill Petite Beads 40374 (teal)
  Head — 4 mm teal bead (Hotspotz SBXL – 449)
  Thorax — 6 mm teal bead (Hotspotz SBX6 – 449)
  Abdomen — Mill Hill Small Bugle Beads 72053 (nutmeg)
  — Mill Hill Petite Beads 42024 (nutmeg)

- Needles: Straw/milliners 9
  Sharps/Appliqué 12

- Threads: Bronze/black metallic (Kreinik Cord 215c)
  Peacock-green metallic filament (Kreinik Blending Filament colour 085)
  Nylon clear thread

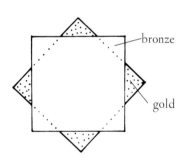

bronze

gold

Note: Thread trace the dragonfly head, thorax and abdomen from the skeleton outline, using rayon machine thread.

Dragonfly wings

1.   Prepare the wing sandwich by fusing the bronze organza and the gold organdie together using paper-backed fusible web. A pretty effect is gained by applying one layer of fabric on the cross-grain.

2.   Trace the wing outlines (from the skeleton outline) onto the paper side of the remaining piece of fusible web and iron to the gold side of the wing sandwich (the bronze side is the right side of the wing sandwich). Carefully cut out the wing shapes. Remove the paper backing and fuse the wing shapes in position on the silk, using a piece of GLAD Bake to protect the wings and the iron. (Use pins inserted from the back along

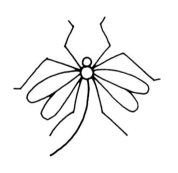

skeleton outline

the traced lines to indicate the wing positions — remove
before you iron).

3.   With the blending filament in the straw needle and the
nylon thread in the sharps needle, couch a line of blending filament around the outside edge of each wing, using the nylon
thread to work the couching stitches (stitch *from* the silk *towards*
the wing to prevent the wing edge lifting). Using the blending
filament, work the veins of the wings in feather stitch.

diagram not to scale

Dragonfly body

Note: The beads for body of the dragonfly are applied with
one strand of bronze/black metallic thread in the sharps needle. Remove the tracing threads as you work.

1.   *Thorax.* Bring the needle up at A and stitch the 6mm bead
in place with two vertical straight stitches over the thorax
(where all the wings join).

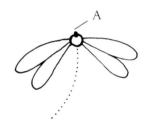

2.   *Abdomen.* Bring the needle up at A (and through the thorax bead), then thread on 4 bugle beads and 2 petite beads
(nutmeg) and insert the needle at B (make sure the length of
the stitch is longer than the combined length of the beads so
that the beads will sit smoothly). Bring the needle up at C,
then couch between each bead back to B, removing the tracing
thread as you go. Work a fly stitch for the tail and bring the
tie-down thread back through all the beads to A (you may
need tweezers to pull the short needle through).

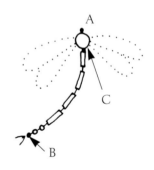

3.   *Head.* Bring the needle up at A and apply the 4mm bead
for the head. To work the eyes, apply two petite beads
together (with a straight stitch from side to side), close to the
head. Finish with one stitch between the beads towards the
head — this makes the beads sit together.

4.   *Legs.* With two strands of the bronze/black metallic
thread in the straw needle, work three back stitches for each
leg, using the traced outline on the calico backing as a guide.
With one strand of thread, work straight stitches for the
hairs on the back legs and a fly stitch for the feelers.

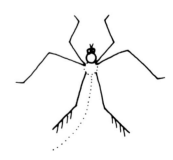

Foxgloves, Plate 36. p. 331

MATERIALS REQUIRED

- Calico (or quilter's muslin) — 20 cm x 20 cm (8'' x 8'')

- 10 cm (4'') embroidery hoop

- Wire: Fine flower wire, cut in 12 cm (5'') lengths

- Small amount of stuffing and a saté stick (optional)

- Mill Hill Petite Beads 42012 (royal plum)

- Needles: Crewel/embroidery 10
  Chenille 18
  Sharps 12 (or beading needle)

- Threads: Dark green stranded (DMC 937 or Au Ver à Soie d'Alger 2126)
  Dark pink stranded (DMC 309 or Au Ver à Soie d'Alger 2934)
  Medium pink stranded (DMC 335 or Au Ver à Soie d'Alger 2933)

To embroider the upper foxglove shapes

1.   Mount the calico into the hoop and trace the upper fox-glove outlines, enlarging them slightly at the sides and top edge to allow for the raised shape.

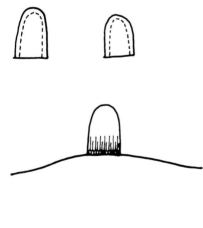

2.   Couch, then buttonhole stitch the wire to the calico along the lower edge with the medium pink thread (leaving the tails of wire free), then work a row of long and short but-tonhole stitch close to the wire. Using one strand of dark pink thread, embroider the remainder of the shape in long and short stitch.

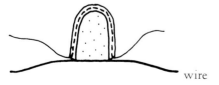
wire

3.   Make a row of running stitches 1 mm away from the sides and top of the embroidered shape, leaving thread tails at each side. Carefully cut out the flower shape, leaving a small turning around the outside edge and cutting close to the wire at the lower edge (do not cut off the wire or thread tails).

To apply upper foxglove shape to main fabric

1.   With one strand of medium pink thread, outline the fox-glove shapes (on the main fabric) in backstitch, using the traced outline on the calico backing as a guide. Work the lower edge of the foxglove shapes in long and short button-hole stitch, covering the lower third of the shape.

2.   To apply the embroidered shape, gently pull the thread tails to ease the turning to the inside. Position the top of the shape at the end of the stem with a stab stitch, then, using a chenille needle, insert the wires at the lower points • and secure at the back of the work. Stab stitch the outside edge in place along the outline, gently pulling the thread tails to ease the shape to size. Cut the thread tails. Cover the stab stitches with straight stitches in blending colours, if required. A little stuffing can be inserted into each foxglove to maintain the shape when the pin wheel is used.

3.   Using two strands of dark green thread, embroider four detached chain stitches at the top of each flower to form the sepals. Use a saté stick to gently raise and shape the upper layer of the foxglove.

4.   Complete by stitching three petite beads in the throat of each foxglove.

Soldier-Fly, see Plate 17. p. 266

MATERIALS REQUIRED

- Gold organza ribbon (or scrap of wing sandwich from dragonfly wings)

- Paper-backed fusible web

- Mill Hill Petite Glass Beads 40374 (blue/black)

- Thread: Dark orange stranded (DMC 919 or Au Ver à Soie d'Alger 616)
  Peacock-green metallic filament (Kreinik Blending Filament colour 085)
  Bronze/black metallic thread (Kreinik Cord 215c)
  Bronze chenille thread

- Needles: Straw 9
  Crewel 10
  Sharps/Appliqué 12
  Chenille 18

Wings

1.   Trace the wing outline on to the paper side of the paper-backed fusible web and iron to the back of the wing fabric. Carefully cut out the wing shape, remove the paper backing, then fuse the wing to the main fabric (protect with GLAD Bake). Couch a line of peacock blending filament around the wings, using another length of blending filament (in a straw needle) to work the couching stitches, then work a fly stitch in each wing for the veins.

Body

2.   Work one or two stitches with chenille thread between the wings to form the thorax. Using one strand of dark orange thread, outline the abdomen with small backstitches, pad stitch, then satin stitch across the abdomen, covering the backstitches. Apply two petite beads for eyes. Embroider the legs in straight stitches with two strands of bronze metallic thread in a straw needle.

Squirrel, Plate 38. p. 332

The European red squirrel has a large bushy tail and tufted ears that lighten before each moult. The summer coat of rich chestnut red fades to dull brown in winter. The last strongholds of this endangered species are pine forests, where they feed on conifer shoots and cones, chewing off the cone scales to remove the seeds.

MATERIALS REQUIRED

- Cream felt, paper-backed fusible web and silk organza —
  8 cm x 5 cm (3'' x 2'')

- Eyebrow brush/comb

- Mill Hill Glass Seed Bead — 221 (bronze)

- Mill Hill Petite Bead — 42014 (black)

- Needles: Crewel/embroidery 5-10
  Sharps 12 (or beading needle)

- Threads: Dark brown stranded (DMC 3371)
  Shades of medium to light tan (DMC 434, 435, 436,
  738, 739)
  Brown/grey stranded (DMC 3022)

1. Iron the fusible web to the organza (protect the iron and ironing board with GLAD Bake). On the organza side, trace the squirrel body and all internal lines (not the tail or the back ear), and two successively smaller shapes for padding. Remove the paper and fuse the organza to the felt. Cut the shapes out carefully.

2.   With one strand of light tan thread, stab stitch the three layers of felt in place, starting with the smallest shape and keeping the organza side uppermost (using the mound and the back tracing as a guide to placement). Outline the squirrel shape with buttonhole stitch around the top layer of felt.

3.   Stitch along the internal lines with small stab stitches to sculpt the squirrel body, then, using the internal lines as a guide, embroider the squirrel in long and short stitch. Work in the following order with one strand of the suggested colours, to achieve the desired shading.

> Belly — 738, 739
> Back leg and back ear — 434, 435
> Lower half of body — 434, 435, 436, 738
> Upper half of body — 3022, 434, 435, 436, 738

4.   The tail is worked in Turkey knots using two strands of thread. Start at the upper edge of the tail and following the outline as shown, work rows of knots gradually shading from dark to light (434, 435, 436, 738). Using very sharp scissors and the eyebrow comb, cut and sculpt the squirrel's tail.

5.   To complete the squirrel, work the nose and claws in straight stitches with one strand of dark brown thread (3371). Stitch a black petite bead in place for the eye, and a bronze bead at the end of the paws for the nut.

There are countless numbers of embroidery stitches, often with variations in name and methods of working. This glossary contains all the stitches used in this book and describes how the stitches have been worked for these projects. For ease of explanation, some of the stitches have been illustrated with the needle entering and leaving the fabric in the same movement. When working in a hoop this is difficult (or should be if your fabric is tight enough!), so the stitches have to be worked with a stabbing motion, in several stages.

The stitches are listed alphabetically for ease of reference.

Stitch Glossary

BACKSTITCH

This is a useful stitch for outlining a shape, e.g. the bee body. Bring the needle out at 1, insert at 2 (in the hole made by the preceding stitch) and out again at 3. Keep the stitches small and even.

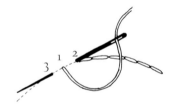

BACKSTITCH — SPLIT

This is an easier version of split stitch, especially when using one strand of thread. Commence with a backstitch. Bring the needle out at 1, insert at 2 (splitting the preceding stitch) and out again at 3. This results in a fine, smooth line, ideal for stitching intricate curves.

BULLION KNOTS

These require some practice to work in a hoop. Use a straw needle of the appropriate size, with the number of wraps depending on the length of the knot required, e.g. the hedge-

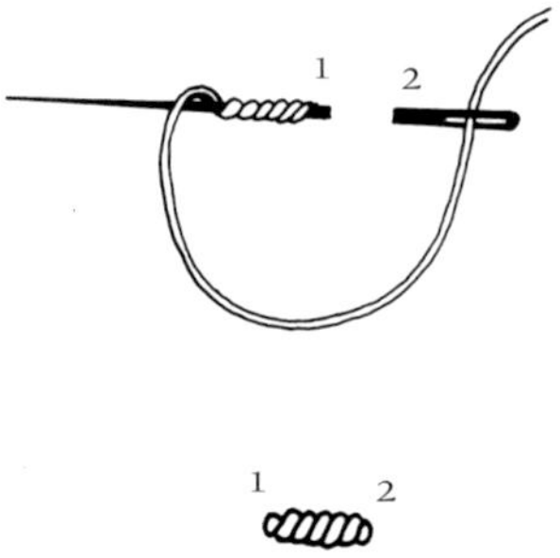

hog's spines. Bring the needle out at 1, insert at 2 leaving a long loop. Emerge at 1 again (not pulling the needle through yet) and wrap the thread around the needle the required number of times. Hold the wraps gently between the thumb and index finger of the left hand while pulling the needle through with the right hand. Pull quite firmly and insert again at 2, stroking the wraps into place.

Buttonhole couching (see p. 390)

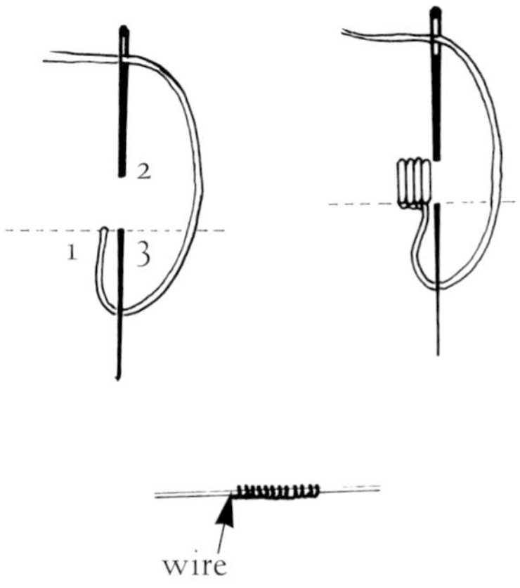

Buttonhole Stitch

These stitches can be worked close together or slightly apart. Working from left to right, bring the needle out on the line to be worked at 1 and insert at 2, holding the loop of thread with the left thumb. Bring the needle up on the line to be worked at 3 (directly below 2), over the thread loop and pull through to form a looped edge. If the stitch is shortened and worked close together over wire, it forms a secure edge for cut shapes, e.g. a detached leaf.

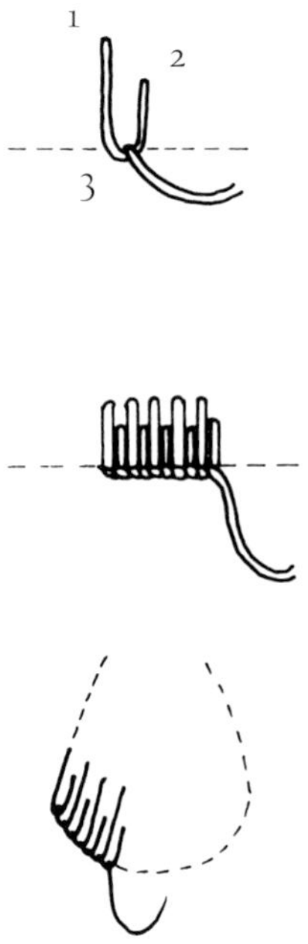

Buttonhole Stitch — Long and Short

In long and short buttonhole stitch, each alternate stitch is shorter. If using the stitch to give a ruffled edge to flower petals, a better shape is achieved if the stitch is commenced above the edge. Bring the needle out at 1, insert at 2 and up again at 3 (like an open detached chain stitch). When embroidering a petal, angle the stitches towards the centre of the flower.

Buttonhole wheel and wedge

This is buttonhole stitch worked in a circle, each stitch entering the material through the same central hole (e.g. owl's eyes). If only part of the circle is worked, it forms a wedge shape which can be useful for working small petals (e.g. the strawberry flower). For both of these stitches it is easier to start with a chain stitch through the central hole.

Wheel

Wedge

Detached Buttonhole Stitch

Buttonhole stitch can be worked as a detached filling, attached only to the background material at the edges of the shape. First work a row of backstitches around the shape to be filled. Change to a fine tapestry needle. Bring the needle out at 1, work buttonhole stitches in to the top row of backstitches then insert the needle at 2. Come up again at 3 and work a buttonhole stitch into each loop of the preceding row. Insert the needle at 4. Quite different effects can be achieved when these stitches are worked close together or spaced apart.

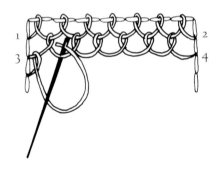

Detached buttonhole stitch can also be worked in circular form as a spiral, starting either from the outside edge or the centre.

This stitch can be used as a filling for a detached wired shape. Cover the wire with a foundation of buttonhole stitches to form the edge into which the detached filling is worked.

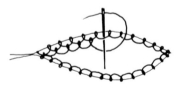

CORDED DETACHED BUTTONHOLE STITCH

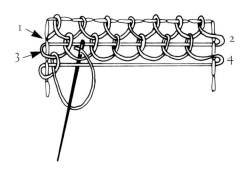

Detached buttonhole stitch can be worked over a laid thread. Outline the shape to be filled with backstitches. Using a tapestry needle, come up at 1 and work the first row of buttonhole stitches into the top row of backstitches. Slip the needle under the backstitch at 2. Take the needle straight back to the left side and slip under the backstitch at 3. Work another row of buttonhole stitches, this time taking the needle into the previous loops and under the straight thread at the same time. Slip the needle under the backstitch at 4 and continue as above.

To obtain a neater edge, the needle can be taken through to the back of the work at the end of each row (instead of under the backstitches), if preferred, e.g. the cornflower base. A contrasting thread (or gold thread), worked in another needle, can replace the straight thread, with interesting results.

Corded detached buttonhole stitch can also be used as a filling for a detached wired shape, e.g. the beetle wings.

CHAIN STITCH

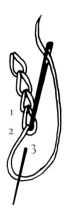

Can be used as an outline or filling stitch. Bring the needle through at 1 and insert it again through the same hole, holding the loop of thread with the left thumb. Bring the needle up a short distance along at 2, through the loop, and pull the thread through. Insert the needle into the same hole at 2 (inside the loop) and make a second loop, hold, and come up at 3. Repeat to work a row of chain stitch, securing the final loop with a small straight stitch.

CHAIN STITCH — DETACHED

Detached chain stitch, also known as Lazy Daisy Stitch, is worked in the same way as chain stitch except that each loop is secured individually with a small straight stitch. The securing stitch can be made longer if desired, to form sepals or thorns for roses. Different effects can be achieved by working several detached chain stitches inside each other.

CHAIN STITCH — INTERLACED

This stitch, when interlaced with gold thread, forms a very pretty braid.

Work a row of chain stitch as a foundation, with two or three strands of thread. Interlace each side of this chain stitch with gold thread in a tapestry needle, as follows:

(1) Come out at 1, slide the needle under the second chain at 2.

(2) Slide the needle under both the first chain and interlacing thread at 3.

(3) Slide the needle under the next chain at 4.

(4) Slide the needle under both the chain and interlacing thread at 5.

(5) Repeat the last two steps to the end of the row. Take the thread to the back of the work at the end of the last chain and secure.

Interlace the other side of the row of chain stitch. Bring the needle out at 1 and work as above, reversing the direction of the needle.

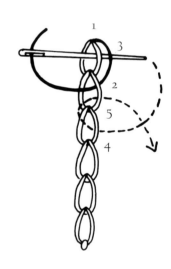

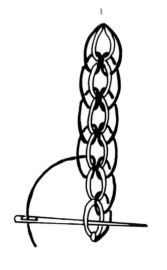

CHAIN STITCH — WHIPPED

This is a useful method for working slightly raised outlines. Work a row of chain stitch, then bring the needle out slightly to one side of the final securing stitch. Using either the eye of the needle or a tapestry needle, whip the chain stitches by passing the needle under each chain loop from right to left, back to the beginning of the row. A contrasting (or gold) thread can be used for the whipping. When whipped chain stitch is used for stems, the thickness of the outline can be varied by the number of threads used.

COUCHING

Couching, with tiny upright stitches worked at regular intervals, is a way of attaching a thread, or group of threads, to a background fabric. The laid thread is often thicker or more fragile (e.g. gold or chenille) than the one used for stitching, and other types of stitches can be used to couch the threads e.g. buttonhole stitch. Couching stitches are also used for attaching wire to the base fabric before embroidering detached shapes.

COUCHING – LATTICE

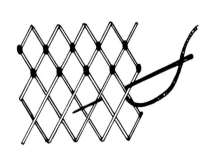

Lattice couching is one of the endless variations of couched fillings. The design area is filled with a network of laid, parallel, evenly spaced threads. Where two threads cross, they are secured to the background with a small straight stitch. Lattice couching can also be worked over a satin-stitched shape, such as the thistle base.

FEATHER STITCH

This stitch is made up of a series of loops, stitched alternately to the right and to the left, each one holding the previous loop in place. Come up on the line to be followed at 1. Insert the needle to the right at 2 and come up on the line again at 3, holding the thread under the needle with the left thumb. Repeat on the left side of the line, reversing the needle direction, e.g. veins for the gooseberry.

FEATHER STITCH—SINGLE: Work the feather stitch loops in one direction only to give a feathered outline to a shape, e.g. a rose leaf.

FISHBONE STITCH

This stitch is useful for filling small leaf shapes. Bring the thread out at the tip of the leaf 1, and make a small straight stitch along the centre line (vein). Bring the needle out at 2, make a slanted stitch and go down on the right of the centre line. Bring the needle out at 3, make a slanted stitch and go down on the left of the centre line, overlapping the base of the previous stitch. Continue working slanted stitches alternately from the left and the right, close together, until the shape is filled.

FLY STITCH

Fly stitch is actually an open detached chain stitch. Bring the needle out at 1 and insert at 2, holding the working thread with the left thumb. Bring up again at 3 and pull through over the loop. Secure the loop with an anchoring stitch which can vary in length to produce different effects, e.g. a short tie-down stitch is used for antennae. When working a row of vertical fly stitches, a longer tie-down stitch is required.

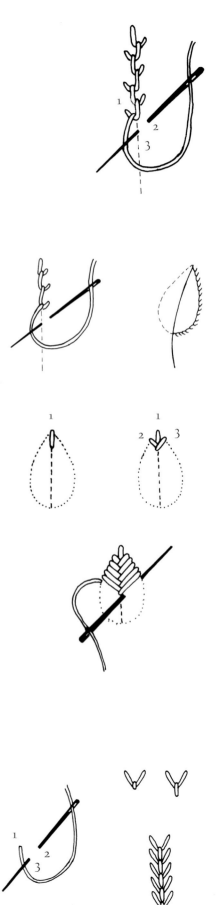

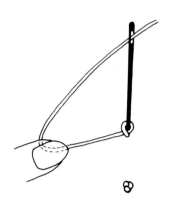

FRENCH KNOTS

Using a straw needle, bring the thread through at the desired place, wrap the thread once around the point of the needle and re-insert the needle. Tighten the thread and *hold taut* while pulling the needle through. To increase the size of the knot use more strands of thread, although more wraps can be made if desired.

LONG AND SHORT STITCH

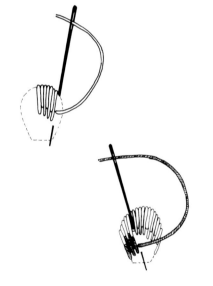

This stitch can be used to fill areas too large or irregular for satin stitch, or where shading is required. The first row, worked around the outline, consists of alternating long and short satin stitches. In the subsequent rows, the stitches are all of similar length, and fit into the spaces left by the preceding row. For a more realistic result when working petals, direct the stitches towards the centre of the flower. The surface will look smoother if the needle either pierces the stitches of the preceding row or enters at an angle between the stitches.

NEEDLEWEAVING

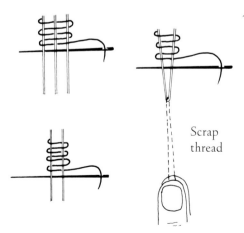

Scrap thread

Needleweaving is a form of embroidery where thread in a tapestry needle is woven in and out over two or more threads attached to the background fabric. Work needleweaving over a loop to form sepals e.g. dandelions. Use a length of scrap thread to keep the loop taut while weaving.

OVERCAST STITCH

This stitch is made up of tiny, upright satin stitches, worked very close together over a laid thread or wire, resulting in a firm raised line. When worked over wire it gives a smooth, secure edge for cut shapes, e.g. bees wings. Place the wire along the line to be covered. Working from left to right with a stabbing motion, cover the wire with small straight stitches, pulling the thread firmly so that there are no loose stitches which may be snipped when the shape is cut out. As cut shapes are fragile, ensure that the maximum amount of fabric is caught by the stitch, by holding the needle at right angles to the wire when piercing the fabric.

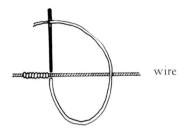

wire

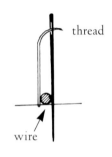

thread

wire

PAD STITCH

Pad stitch is used as a foundation under satin stitch when a smooth, slightly raised surface is required. Padding stitches can be either straight stitches or chain stitches, worked in the opposite direction to the satin stitches. Felt can replace pad stitch for a more raised effect.

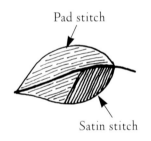

Pad stitch

Satin stitch

PALESTRINA KNOT STITCH

This stitch is also known as Double Knot Stitch. It makes a beautiful textured line or can be used to join two edges together decoratively, as in the stumpwork chatelaine.

Working from left to right, bring the needle out on the line to be covered, or edges to be joined. Make a small slanting stitch to the right (inserting the needle at right angles to the line), going down at 2 and coming up at 3. Pull the thread

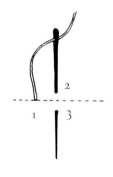

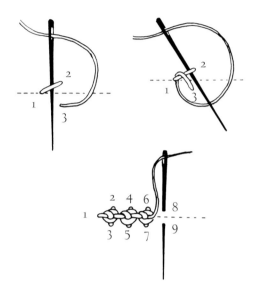

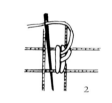

through then slide the needle, from above, under the stitch just made. Pull through then hold the thread below the stitch with the thumb. Coming from above, slip the needle under the first stitch again, to the right of the previous thread, bringing the needle through *over* the held thread (as in button-hole stitch).

Make the next slanting stitch to the right and continue as above, working the knots fairly close together. Experiment with threads, tension and spacing for different effects.

RAISED CUP STITCH (see p. 391)

ROCOCO STITCH

Rococo stitch is a counted thread stitch very popular in the seventeenth century. It consists of diamond shaped bundles of stitches drawn together with holes between each bundle — the tighter the stitches are pulled the lacier the result. Rococo stitch is used on single canvas or wide-meshed double canvas, and is most easily worked in diagonal rows from the top right to bottom left of the area to be embroidered. Each bundle consists of four vertical stitches, worked over two canvas

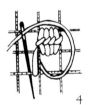

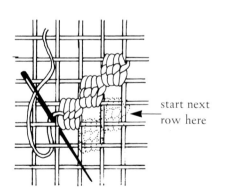

start next row here

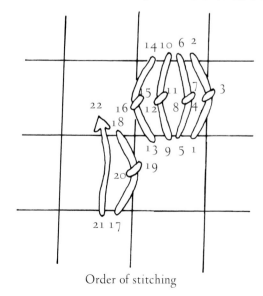

Order of stitching

threads, sharing the same holes at the top and bottom. Each of these vertical stitches is tied with a small horizontal stitch worked from right to left. The two outside vertical stitches are tied to the canvas with these horizontal stitches. Experiment with thread, canvas and tension with this stitch as a variety of effects can be achieved. When properly worked, no canvas background should remain showing. The diagrams show the order of stitching and the starting point for the next bundle.

Roumanian Couching

This form of couching is useful for filling in large spaces.

Bring the needle out on the left, take a long stitch across the space to be filled then insert the needle on the right. This laid thread is then caught down with loose, slanting, couching stitches going from right to left. Traditionally the couching was worked with the same thread, however, a contrasting thread in another needle is very effective

Satin Stitch

Satin stitch is used to fill shapes such as petals or leaves. It consists of horizontal, vertical or slanted straight stitches, worked close enough together so that no fabric shows through, yet not overlapping each other. Satin stitch can be worked over a padding of felt or pad stitches and a smooth edge is easier to obtain if the shape is first outlined with split backstitch. When working a shaped area such as the poppy seed pod, work the centre stitch first then fill the shape with long stitches angled towards the stem for a realistic, rounded effect.

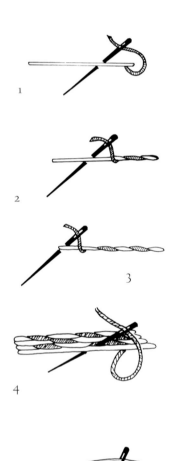

Satin Stitch — Encroaching

Encroaching satin stitch is a useful method of shading, as in the second and all subsequent rows, the head of each stitch is taken between the base of two stitches in the row above so that the rows blend softly into each other, e.g. the wings of the Blue butterfly.

Slip Stitch

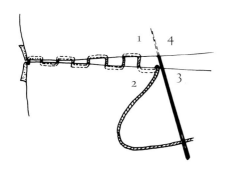

Slip stitch is a dressmaking stitch, used to join two folds of fabric together, invisibly, with small running stitches. The stitches are of equal length and enter and leave each fold of fabric directly opposite each other. Come out at 1, enter at 2, slide the needle through the fold and come out at 3, enter at 4 and so on, pulling the thread to bring the folds of fabric together. This stitch is used to join the front and back together in the Stumpwork Name Brooch.

Stab Stitch

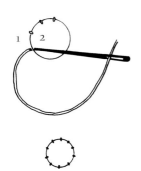

Stab stitch is used to apply a detached fabric shape, or felt, to the main fabric. It consists of small straight stitches made from the main fabric into the applied fabric, e.g. the owl or layers of felt for padding. Bring the needle out at 1, and insert at 2, catching in the edge of the applied piece.

Stem Stitch

Worked from left to right, the stitches in stem stitch overlap each other to form a fine line suitable for outlines and stems. To start, bring the needle out at 1 on the line to be worked. Go down at 2, come up at 3 and pull the thread through. Insert the needle at 4, holding the thread underneath the line with the left thumb, and come up again at 2 (in the same hole made by the previous stitch) then pull the thread through. Go down at 5, hold the loop and come up again at 4, then pull the thread through. Repeat to work a narrow line. If the stem stitches are worked at a slight angle a broader outline is formed, e.g. the leaves of the cornflowers.

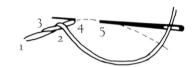

Stem Stitch — Filling

Rows of stem stitch can be worked close together, following an outline, to form a very effective filling stitch. It is an ideal method for embroidering detached leaves, the rows of stem stitch being worked inside the wire outline, e.g. the leaves of the Oriental poppy.

Stem Stitch Band — Raised

Stem stitch can be worked over a foundation of straight stitches to form a detached filling. When this foundation of stitches is applied over lengths of padding thread, a raised, smooth, stem stitch band can be worked, ideal for branches and insect bodies. Lay a preliminary foundation of padding stitches worked with soft cotton thread. Across this padding,

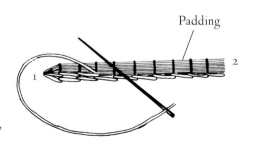

Padding

at fairly regular intervals, work straight stitches at right angles to the padding thread (do not make these stitches too tight). Then proceed to cover the padding by working rows of stem stitch over these straight stitches, using a tapestry needle so as not to pierce the padding thread. All the rows of stem stitch are worked in the same direction, close together and ending either at the same point, e.g. 1, or spaced as in satin stitch, e.g. 2.

STRAIGHT STITCH

Individual straight stitches, of equal or varying length, can be stitched with a variety of threads to achieve interesting effects, e.g. the rays on pansy petals in variegated thread.

TACKING (BASTING)

Tacking, a dressmaking term, is a row of running stitches, longer on the top of the fabric, used to temporarily mark an outline or to hold two pieces of fabric together.

TENT STITCH (see p. 392)

TRELLIS STITCH

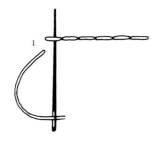

Trellis stitch, popular in the seventeenth century, is a needlelace filling stitch, attached only at the edges, and is most easily worked with a twisted silk thread. The first row of trellis stitch is worked into a foundation of backstitches, the size depending on the effect desired — close together and the trellis stitches resemble tent stitches in canvas work, further apart and an open trellis is the result.

Bring the needle out at 1, slip it under the first backstitch (forming a t — a good way to remember this stitch), pull the thread through holding the resulting loop with the left thumb. Slip the needle through this loop (2) then pull the thread down, forming a firm knot. Repeat, to work a row of firm knots with loops in between. Insert the needle into the fabric at the end of the row.

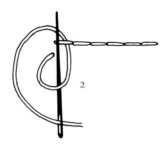

To work a second row, bring the needle out at 3 and slip the needle through the loop between two knots, pull the thread through holding the resulting loop with the left thumb. Slip the needle through this loop (4) then pull the thread down, forming a firm knot. Repeat to the end of the row, insert the needle and continue as above.

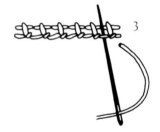

The knots formed in trellis stitch are slanted in the direction the row is worked. When rows are worked in alternate directions the knots form a zig zag pattern, ideal for strawberries. When worked only in one direction the result is parallel slanting lines, e.g. the base of the acorn.

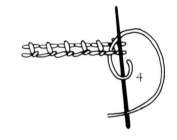

Turkey Knots

Turkey knots are worked then cut to produce a soft velvety pile, e.g. for cornflower heads. Although there are several ways to work Turkey knots, the following method works well for small areas such as the bee's body. Use two strands of thread in a Number 9 crewel or straw needle.

Insert the needle into the fabric at 1 and pull through, holding a 5 cm (2'') tail with the left thumb. Come out at 2 and go down at 3 to make a small securing stitch. Bring the needle out again at 1 (can pierce the securing stitch), pull the thread down to form the second tail and hold with the left thumb.

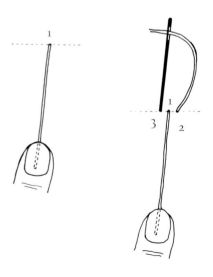

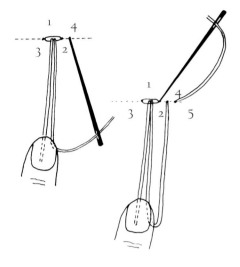

For the second Turkey knot, insert the needle at 4, still holding the tail. Come out at 5 and go down at 2 to make a small securing stitch. Bring the needle out again at 4, pull the thread down and hold with the left thumb as before. Repeat to work a row.

Work each successive row directly above the previous row, holding all the resulting tails with the left thumb. To complete, cut all the loops, comb with an eyebrow comb, and cut the pile to the desired length. The more the pile is combed the fluffier it becomes. The rows can be worked in alternate directions or all in one direction, and the density of the resulting pile depends on the number of stitches and rows worked in the area.

cut

Whipped Spider Web Stitch

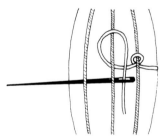

Whipped spider stitch is a form of needleweaving worked over a grid of foundation threads, which can be used to fill many different shapes, e.g. the carnation. First lay the foundation stitches, usually in a heavier thread, over the shape to be worked (this can be padded if required). Working from right to left, whip each of these laid threads with a backstitch, using a tapestry needle so as not to pierce the threads or the background fabric. Bring the needle out at the edge of the shape and slide under thread 1. Work a backstitch over 1 then slide the needle under thread 2. Work a backstitch over 2 then slide the needle under thread 3. Work a backstitch over 3 then insert the needle at the edge of the shape. Repeat, always working in the same direction, until the shape is filled, resulting in whipped ribs on the surface.

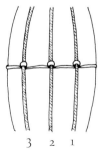

3   2   1

To work a circular, raised, whipped spider web lay four long foundation stitches, as shown, securing the thread at the back of the work. Gather and tie all these threads together in the centre with a temporary length of thread. Using a tapestry needle, bring the working thread up between these threads and start whipping the spokes, working in a clockwise direction and pulling on the temporary thread at the same time, causing the web to be raised in the middle. Continue, working back over one strand and forward under two until the spokes are filled to the required amount, then remove the spare thread, e.g. the centre of the Oriental poppy.

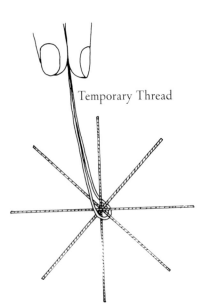

Temporary Thread

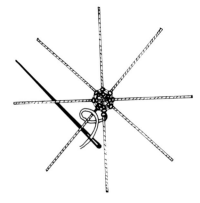

Temporary thread not
shown for clarity

Buttonhole couching

Buttonhole stitches worked with a space between can be used to couch laid surface threads. Rows of buttonhole couching worked in metallic thread over laid silk is a pretty way to embroider butterfly wings.

A  B

Bring the surface threads up at A and insert at B. Work a row of buttonhole stitches over these laid threads (piercing the ground material).

RAISED CUP STITCH

Although raised cup stitch is most easily worked with a
twisted thread such as silk buttonhole twist, by using a
variety of threads and altering the size of the foundation
triangle, you can achieve many different effects.

1. Make a foundation for raised cup stitch by stitching three
backstitches into a triangle of the required size (about 4 mm,
or 3/16").

2. Using a tapestry needle, come up at A and work three
buttonhole stitches into each 'leg' of the triangle, working in a
clockwise direction.

3. Continue in rounds of buttonhole stitch, inserting the
needle into the loops between each knot and increasing when
necessary by working two knots into a loop. The resulting
'cup' can be left as it is, or it can have a covered bead inserted
as in the fruiting ivy.

To form 'blueberries', continue working rounds of
buttonhole stitch, decreasing where necessary by missing a
loop, until the bead is covered. Insert the thread down the
centre of the bead, pulling firmly, and secure at the back of the
work.

TENT STITCH

Tent stitch is a canvaswork stitch worked over single-thread canvas or silk mesh (see the oranges). The stitch, which resembles a half cross-stitch, when correctly worked is longer on the reverse side than on the front. This has a padding effect and gives better coverage than half cross-stitch. The stitch is worked from left to right.

1. Bring the needle out at A, insert at B, out again at C, down at D and so on, making a horizontal row of slanting stitches.

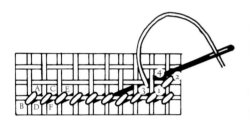

2. At the end of the line, turn the canvas and work a row of identical stitches, coming up at 1, down at 2, up at 3 and so on.
    By turning the canvas around at the end of each line, the rows may always be worked from left to right, which ensures that the stitches are alike on both sides of the canvas.

Bibliography and Further Reading

Alford, Lady Marian. *Needlework as Art*, Sampson, Low, Marston, Searle & Rivington, London, 1886

Bahouth, Candace. *Medieval Needlepoint*. Conran Octopus, London, 1993.

Baker, Muriel. *Stumpwork: The Art of Raised Embroidery*, Charles Scribner's Sons, New York, 1978.

Beck, Thomasina. *Embroidered Gardens*, Angus and Robertson, Sydney, 1979.

Beck, Thomasina. *The Embroiderer's Garden*, David and Charles, London, 1988.

Beck, Thomasina. *The Embroiderer's Flowers*, David and Charles, London, 1992.

Beck, Thomasina. *The Embroiderer's Story*, David and Charles, London, 1995.

Best, Muriel. *Stumpwork: Historical and Contemporary Raised Embroidery*, Batsford, London, 1987.

Brooke, Xanthe. *Catalogue of Embroideries*, Alan Sutton, UK, 1992.

Brown, Walter R. *The Stuart Legacy: English Art 1603-1714*, Birmingham Museum of Art, USA, 1991.

Castelvetro, Giacomo. *The Fruit, Herbs and Vegetables of Italy*, Penguin, London, 1989.

Caulfield, S. & Saward, B, *Encyclopedia of Victorian Needlework*, Dover, New York, 1972.

Christie, Grace. *Embroidery and Tapestry Weaving*, Pitman, London, 1906.

Christie, Grace. *Samplers and Stitches*, Batsford, London, 1920.

Clabburn, Pamela. *The Needleworker's Dictionary*, Macmillan, UK, 1976.

Clabburn, Pamela. *The National Trust Book of Furnishing Textiles*, Penguin, London, 1988.

Cole, Herbert. *Heraldry Decoration and Floral Forms*, Crescent Books, New York, 1988.

Coombes, Alana. 'Studies in Stumpwork', *Embroidery*, Autumn 1989.

Davis, Mildred J. *The Art of Crewel Embroidery*, Vista Books, London, 1962.

Don, Sarah. *Traditional Embroidered Animals*, David and Charles, UK, 1990.

Embroiderers' Guild Practical Study Group. *Needlework School*, Quarto Publishing, Sydney, 1982.

Enthoven, Jacqueline. *The Stitches of Creative Embroidery*, Schiffer, USA, 1987.

Fassett, Kaffe. *Glorious Inspiration*, Random House, Sydney, 1991.

Fraser, Antonia. *Charles II: His Life and Times*, Weidenfeld & Nicolson, London, 1979.

Garzoni, Giovanna. *Florentines, A Tuscan Feast*, Pavilion Books, London, 1992.

Gostelow, Mary. *Art of Embroidery*, Weidenfeld & Nicolson, London, 1979.

Gostelow, Mary. *The Complete Guide to Needlework Techniques and Materials*, Chartwell Books, London, 1982.

Hand, Sydney (ed.). *Old English Needlework of the Sixteenth and Seventeenth Centuries*, Sydney Hand Ltd, London, n.d.

Hillier, Malcolm. *Flowers*, Dorling Kindersley, London, 1988.

Hirst, Barbara and Roy. *Raised Embroidery*, Merehurst, London, 1993.

Hirst, Barbara and Roy. *New Designs in Raised Embroidery*, Merehurst, London, 1997.

Hirst, Barbara. 'Modern Figurative Stumpwork', *Embroidery*, Autumn, 1988.

Hodges, Felice. *Period Pastimes*, Weidenfeld & Nicolson, London, 1989.

Hughes, Therle. 'English Furniture Needlework', *Country Life Annual*, date unknown.

Hughes, Therle. 'English Pictorial Needlework', *Country Life Annual*, date unknown.

Hughes, Therle. 'The English Embroiderer at Lesiure', *Country Life Annual*, 1963.

Hughes, Therle. *English Domestic Needlework 1660 - 1860*, Abbey Fine Arts, London.

Huish, Marcus. *Samplers and Tapestry Embroideries*, Longmans Green, London, 1913.

Isaacs, Jennifer. *The Secret Meaning of Flowers*, Simon and Schuster, Australia, 1993.

Kendrick, A.F., *English Needlework*, A. & C. Black Ltd, London, 1933.

King, Donald, and Levey, Santina. *Embroidery in Britain from 1200 to 1750*, Victoria and Albert Museum, London, 1993.

Lilley, E. and Midgley, W. *Studies in Plant Form and Design*, Chapman and Hall, London, 1916.

Milda, Sara. *In and Out of the Garden*, Sidgwick & Jackson. London, 1981.

Morse, Richard. *The Book of Wildflowers*, Collins. London.

Nahmad, Claire. *Garden Spells*, Pavilion Books, London, 1994.

Parker, Rozika, *The Subversive Stitch*, The Women's Press, London, 1984.

Pickles, Sheila. *The Language of Wild Flowers*, Pavilion Books, London, 1995.

Saint-Aubin, Charles Germain de. *Art of the Embroiderer*, David Godine, Boston, 1983.

Snook, Barbara. *English Embroidery*, Batsford, London, 1960.

Speirs, Gill, and Quemby, Sigrid. *A Treasury of Embroidery Designs*, Bell and Hyman, London, 1985.

Swain, Margaret. *Historical Needlework*, Barrie and Jenkins, UK, 1970.

Swain, Margaret. *Embroidered Stuart Pictures*, Shire Album, UK, 1990.

Swain, Margaret. 'John Nelham's Panel' *Embroidery*, Autumn 1984.

Swain, Margaret. 'The Embroidered Box' *Embroidery*, Autumn 1987.

Swain, Margaret. 'The Embroidered Cabinet' *Embroidery*, Winter 1987.

Synge, Lanto. *Antique Needlework*, Blandford, London, 1982.

Synge, Lanto. *Book of Needlework and Embroidery*, Collins, London, 1986.

Thomas, Mary. *Dictionary of Embroidery Stitches*, Hodder and Stoughton, London, 1934.

Thomas, Mary. *Embroidery Book*, Hodder and Stoughton, London, 1936.

Warelde, Patricia, *Guide to English Embroidery*, Victoria and Albert Museum, London, 1970.

Ware, Dora, and Stafford, Maureen. *An Illustrated Dictionary of Ornament*, Allen & Unwin, London, 1974.

Wilson, Erica. *Embroidery Book*, Charles Scribner's Sons, New York, 1973.

Index

Thread Conversion Information

I have used DMC stranded cotton to embroider these designs unless otherwise specified. Other threads have been used for their qualities of lustre, colour or variegation when required. As some of these threads may not be readily available in other countries, a description and the nearest DMC equivalent or substitute is provided.

Au Ver à Soie d'Alger: 100% pure silk, spun — 7 strands, moderate lustre, floss weight, made in France.

Soie d'Alger	DMC
611	741
612	740
616	919
645	721
646	720/900
1316	327
1336 (bright purple)	No match
1343	340
1344	3746
1345	333
2125	469
2126	937
2131	772
2132	3012
2134	3011
2926	814
2933	335
3024	3350
3322	3743
3323	3042
3326 (midnight purple)	No match / 939
3336	550
4634	3726
4635	315
4636	902
4643	778
4644	3726
4645	3802

Madeira Silk: 100% pure silk, spun — 4 strands, moderate lustre, floss weight, made in Germany.

Madeira Silk	DMC
113	743
114	742
210	666/349
903	333
1714	317
2307	3825
Black	310
White	blanc

Cifonda Art Silk: fine, spun — 6 strands, high lustre, made in India. (Similar to Rajmahal).

Cifonda	DMC
102	402
123	522
125	550
174	741
181	794
212	415
214	414
215	930
222	435
496	3033
497	612
498	610
1115	726
1116	725
Black	310

Minnamurra Cotton: hand-dyed, spun — 6 strands, floss weight, made in Australia. Each skein combines two or more colours which overlap and blend.

Minnamurra	DMC
110 (mauve blended to yellow) 552 ›‹ 3820	

Acknowledgements

I would like to extend my sincere thanks to all the people who have shared their passion for stumpwork with me. Whether by letter or in class, your enthusiasm has been an inspiration.

My adventures with stumpwork would not have been possible without the love and support of my family – John, Joanna, Katie and David. I am indebted to my husband, John, for his patience, versatility and sense of humour!

Special thanks to my dear 'sewing friends', for their encouragement, and the opportunity to share ideas and cherished stitching time.

Finally, to all those involved in the production of the book at Sally Milner Publishing – your expertise, and belief in my work, is greatly appreciated.

JANE NICHOLAS, 2005

About the Author

From Australia, Jane Nicholas is an experienced embroiderer in
goldwork, crewel and ethnic embroidery but specialises in
stumpwork. She has been researching this technique for nearly
twenty years, has authored four books on raised embroidery,
and was awarded a Churchill Fellowship to further her studies
in the UK in 1999. In 2005, Jane was awarded a Medal of the
Order of Australia (OAM) for 'service to the craft of hand
embroidery as an artist, author and teacher'. She teaches regu-
larly in Australia and New Zealand, and has taught for the
Embroiderers' Guilds of the USA and Canada. Jane has a
passion for books and is an avid collector of old textiles, needlework tools and insect specimens—to embroider in stumpwork.
She is married, has three grown children and lives in Bowral,
New South Wales, Australia.

Stumpwork Supplies and Kit Information

The threads, beads and needlework products referred to in this book (Au Ver à Soie, Cifonda, DMC, Framecraft, Kreinik, Madeira, Mill Hill) are available from specialist needlework shops.

A mail order service for embroidery and stumpwork supplies is available from Jane Nicholas Embroidery. All materials required for the projects may be obtained either in kit form or individually. Please write, telephone or fax for a catalogue and price list.

Jane Nicholas Embroidery
Chelsea Haberdashery
P.O. Box 300
BOWRAL   NSW   2576
AUSTRALIA
Tel./fax: 61 2 4861 1175